The Tyndale New Testament Commentaries

General Editor: Professor R. V. G. Tasker, M.A., D.D.

THE GOSPEL ACCORDING TO ST. JOHN

THE GOSPEL ACCORDING TO

ST. JOHN

AN INTRODUCTION AND COMMENTARY

by

R. V. G. TASKER, M.A., D.D.

Professor Emeritus of New Testament Exegesis
in the University of London

LONDON
THE TYNDALE PRESS
Thirty-nine · Bedford Square · W.C.1

First Edition — February 1960
Reprinted — January 1962
Reprinted — February 1964
Reprinted — April 1966
Reprinted — November 1968
Reprinted — February 1970

STANDARD BOOK NUMBERS:
Tyndale Press Edition 85111 608 6
International Edition 85111 801 1

Made and printed in England by
STAPLES PRINTERS LIMITED
at their Rochester, Kent, establishment

GENERAL PREFACE

ALL who are interested in the teaching and study of the New Testament today cannot fail to be concerned with the lack of commentaries which avoid the extremes of being unduly technical or unhelpfully brief. It is the hope of the editor and publishers that this present series will do something towards the supply of this deficiency. Their aim is to place in the hands of students and serious readers of the New Testament, at a moderate cost, commentaries by a number of scholars who, while they are free to make their own individual contributions, are united in a common desire to promote a truly biblical theology.

The commentaries are primarily exegetical and only secondarily homiletic, though it is hoped that both student and preacher will find them informative and suggestive. Critical questions are fully considered in introductory sections, and also, at the author's discretion, in additional notes.

The commentaries are based on the Authorized (King James) Version, partly because this is the version which most Bible readers possess, and partly because it is easier for commentators, working on this foundation, to show why, on textual and linguistic grounds, the later versions are so often to be preferred. No one translation is regarded as infallible, and no single Greek manuscript or group of manuscripts is regarded as always right! Greek words are transliterated to help those unfamiliar with the language, and to save those who do know Greek the trouble of discovering what word is being discussed.

There are many signs today of a renewed interest in what the Bible has to say and of a more general desire to understand its meaning as fully and clearly as possible. It is the hope of all those concerned with this series that God will graciously use what they have written to further this end.

R. V. G. TASKER.

'The authority of Scripture appears to me the more venerable and worthy of religious acceptance, in that, while it is easily read by all, yet it reserves in a deeper meaning its secret greatness; offering itself to all in most plain words and in lowliest style, yet demanding the closest study of those who have the power of applying themselves to it; that it may receive all in its open bosom, and through its narrow chinks transmit a few to Thee—a few, yet many more than if it stood not on such a height of authority, nor drew multitudes within the folds of its holy lowliness.'

From THE CONFESSIONS OF ST. AUGUSTINE

'The Gospels are the first fruits of all writings, and the Gospel of John is the first fruits of the Gospels, and no one can receive its meaning who has not himself lain back on Jesus' breast.'

From Origen,
COMMENTARY ON THE GOSPEL OF JOHN

'He expressed a wish that I should read to him: and when I asked "from what book?" he said, "Need you ask? There is but one." So I chose the fourteenth chapter of St. John. And after listening with devotion he said, "Well, that is a great comfort." '

From J. G. Lockhart,
LIFE OF SIR WALTER SCOTT

AUTHOR'S PREFACE

IN preparing this volume on the Gospel of John it has obviously been impossible to comment on the text verse by verse, as I did in the volumes on James and 2 Corinthians which I have already contributed to this series. Instead, I have divided the Gospel into sections, commented on each section as a whole, and added further notes on points of exegetical interest and importance not already considered.

In the necessarily brief Introduction I have confined myself strictly to a survey of the evidence, external and internal, for the authorship, date and purpose of the Gospel. I have refrained from attempting to review numerous alternative critical opinions, and have said little or nothing about the religious background of the Gospel or the possible source or sources for the religious ideas contained in it. A comprehensive summary of the former can be found in the Introduction to Hoskyns' Commentary; and the latter was adequately discussed by Stanton and Bernard, and has recently been treated at great length in the large work on the Fourth Gospel by C. H. Dodd.

My long experience as a teacher of the New Testament has convinced me that there are many students and teachers, who find the massive commentaries on the Fourth Gospel, often running into two large volumes, more than they can assimilate. Small books on great subjects are notoriously difficult to write, and no-one is more conscious of their limitations and shortcomings than myself. Nevertheless, the writing of such books must be attempted; and the kindly reception given to my previous volumes leads me to hope that this further brief and circumscribed contribution may enable some, who have neither the leisure nor the aptitude for studying the larger commentaries, to gain a fuller understanding of the meaning of the text, and a deeper appreciation of the abiding truths contained in what is the simplest and yet the most profound of the Christian Gospels.

R. V. G. Tasker.

INTRODUCTION

I. THE APOSTOLIC 'AUTHORSHIP' OF THE GOSPEL

THE Fourth Gospel has been designated since the second century 'according to John'; and this has been taken to imply in Christian tradition that the authority of the apostle John, the son of Zebedee, lies behind it, and that it embodies his testimony to the life and teaching of Jesus. The present commentator is in full agreement with the dictum of the late Archbishop William Temple, who wrote: 'I regard as self-condemned any theory about the origin of the Gospel which fails to find a very close connection between it and John the son of Zebedee. The combination of internal and external evidence is overwhelming on this point.' He does not however feel any more sure than Temple, and many other conservative scholars, that 'the combination of internal and external evidence' proves conclusively that John the son of Zebedee was the actual *writer* of the book. But it cannot be too strongly asserted that, even though an objective study of the evidence may lead us to regard it as probable that a friend or disciple of the son of Zebedee was the amanuensis of the Gospel, nothing of primary importance is lost. Just as the value of the Gospel of Mark for the early Church, and for ourselves today, lies in the fact that it embodies the witness of Simon Peter, so what we need to be assured about is that the Fourth Gospel contains not the imaginative reflections of some second-century mystic, but the testimony of one of the original apostles to the life and teaching of Jesus. Christianity claims to be an historical religion, and the apostles are the sole link between believers of a later age and Jesus as He was known in the days of His flesh. The apostles knew Him as no-one else did, and a 'Gospel', claiming to record His words and deeds, which is neither directly nor indirectly apostolic, may be a very interesting specimen of religious literature, but it cannot be a sure foundation for faith. As F. C. Burkitt, who was far from being a conservative scholar, well remarked, 'the important thing for us is not whether the Fourth Gospel was *written* by John the son of Zebedee, but whether it truly reports the teaching of our Lord.'[1]

Before we review the internal evidence for the authorship of the Gospel, it is necessary to decide whether every part of it, as we now have it, can be regarded as the work of a single author. Scholars are unanimous that textual evidence and difference of style combine to make it impossible to regard the section vii. 53–viii. 1 as part of the original Gospel of John (see commentary *ad loc.*). There is also general agreement that the author originally brought his work to a conclusion with the statement of his purpose in writing at the end of chapter xx, and that chapter xxi was added later. There is no evidence that the Gospel was ever in circulation without the last chapter; but that it was felt in early days to be an addition would seem clear from the remark of Tertullian that the statement in xx. 31 came in the closing section (*in clausula*). Many commentators, moreover, would maintain that while chapter xxi. 1–23 may well be a later addition, made either by the author of chapters i–xx or by someone else, verses 24 and 25 are in the nature of a *testamur* added by the authorities of the church at Ephesus when the Gospel was first published. Westcott, who held this view, maintained that what is being testified in verse 24 is that the disciple whom Jesus loved wrote the *whole* Gospel. Stanton, who also regarded verse 24 as in fact the earliest 'external' evidence with regard to the authorship of the Gospel, concluded that 'while the framer of this statement . . . was betrayed into exaggeration when he attributed the composition of the Gospel to an immediate disciple of Christ, there was a foundation for this belief in the fact of the dependence of the writer of the Gospel on the testimony of such an immediate disciple.' Similarly, Bernard admitted that, while the words 'and who wrote these things' indicate *prima facie*

[1] *Two Lectures on the Gospels* (Macmillan, 1901), pp. 60, 61; the present author's italics.

'that the Beloved Disciple actually wrote the Gospel with his own hands, and not only that his reminiscences are behind it', nevertheless the word 'wrote' is to be understood in a causal sense. 'The elders of the Church certified that the Beloved Disciple *caused these things to be written.*'

The present commentator feels that on grounds of style the whole of chapter xxi, with the possible exception of verse 25 (on which see the commentary), is the work of the author of the rest of the book. It is in keeping with the evangelist's practice both to testify, as he does in verse 24, to the reliability of his witnesses (see xix. 35), and also to use the first person plural when he wishes to include himself among a particular group of people (see i. 14). In xxi. 24 he is saying in effect 'I and my fellow-Christians know that the witness of the beloved disciple is true'; and in i. 14 'I am among the number of those who saw the incarnate Christ'. It would seem unnatural to exclude the author from the company implied in the use of 'we' in xxi. 24, when he cannot be excluded from the company implied in the use of 'we' in i. 14. One would also have expected the elders of the Ephesian church, if it is they who are speaking in xxi. 24, to have revealed their identity in a clearer manner than by the use of the indefinite first person plural. It is natural for an author to slip into 'we' when he wishes to include others beside himself, but not so natural for a separate body of people to introduce themselves solely as 'we'. If, then, it is the author of the Gospel who is testifying in verse 24 to the truth of his main witness, it follows that this witness, the beloved disciple, was not the actual writer. Nor does the expression 'and wrote these things' militate against this conclusion, for 'these things', not '*all* these things', nor 'the words of this book' (cf. Rev. xxii. 19), is most naturally understood as a reference to the contents of chapter xxi. C. H. Dodd has recently pointed out that there is no real justification for separating verse 24 from verse 23, and he paraphrases them as follows: 'There has been a report circulating in the church . . . to the effect that the Lord promised the disciple whom He loved that he should survive until His second advent. This report is a garbled version of something which the Lord did say about the disciple in question. The true account is that given above, which rests on the authority of the beloved disciple himself; in fact he put it in writing, and his evidence is to be accepted.'[1]

It may well have been that, when this rumour became current that the disciple whom Jesus loved, who was now approaching extreme old age, was not destined to die in view of the prophecy that Jesus was said to have made about him, the evangelist who had already completed his Gospel asked that disciple to put in writing a record of what Jesus had in fact said on the subject, and that this written testimony is embodied in the closing chapter. Few chapters in the Gospel have more signs of being based on a graphic account of an eyewitness. We note in particular the colloquial nature of the conversation in verses 5 and 7; the record of the size and the exact number of the fish caught, and the recollection that the net did not give way under the strain, in verses 8 and 11. All this is evidence that a fisherman who was present is telling the story. Moreover, the statement in verse 20 that Peter looked as it were over his shoulder and saw the disciple whom Jesus loved following him, must surely have been made by that disciple himself. Our conclusion therefore is that xxi. 24 is an assurance given by the author of the rest of the Gospel that the beloved disciple is still alive and bearing his testimony to what Jesus said and did, much of which is recorded in the Gospel, and that that disciple put in writing, so that the evangelist might append it to the Gospel, an account of what happened on the occasion when Jesus was alleged to have said that he would survive until his Lord returned. If throughout the last chapter we substitute 'we' for 'the disciples'; 'my brother James and I' for 'the sons of Zebedee'; 'us' for 'them'; and 'I' or 'me' for 'the disciple whom Jesus loved', we seem to be listening to an account given in *oratio recta* by the beloved disciple himself.

The indirect evidence for identifying this disciple with John, the son of Zebedee, as Christian tradition has done, would seem to be incontrovertible. He must have been recog-

[1] 'A Note on John xxi. 24' (*Journal of Theological Studies*, 1953).

nizable under this title to the first readers of the Gospel; and he is unlikely to have been one of the disciples mentioned by name elsewhere in the narrative. James, the son of Zebedee, is excluded, for, as Bernard rightly points out, the rumour mentioned in verse 23 could not have arisen in regard to him (see Acts xii. 2). That he was one of the original twelve, however, is evident from his presence at the last supper. He was clearly associated very closely with Peter, for it was in company with Peter that he ran to the tomb on the first Easter morning, and it was Peter who showed interest and concern about his future in the incident recorded in the last chapter; and we know from the Synoptic Gospels that Peter and the two sons of Zebedee were together on several occasions to the exclusion of the other apostles.

He must also have been on intimate terms with the holy family, for it was to him that Jesus committed His mother before He died. If he was not John the son of Zebedee, there is no reference to John in the Gospel except in the expression 'the sons of Zebedee' in xxi. 2—a strange phenomenon in a Gospel which individualizes so many of the apostles, e.g. Peter, Andrew, Philip, Thomas, Nathanael, Judas son of Simon Iscariot, and the other Judas. Moreover, John the Baptist is invariably designated simply as John, presumably because there was no danger of his being confused with the apostle of the same name. The difficulty felt by some critics, that it is improbable that John a Galilaean would have been on such familiar terms with the high priest as is implied in the reference in xviii. 15, is irrelevant, if the view adopted in this commentary is correct that the unnamed disciple there mentioned was in fact a different person.

It has often been held that 'the disciple whom Jesus loved' is a description of a purely ideal disciple; but this view is only plausible on the wholly unwarranted assumption that the incidents in which he plays such a specific and important part are imaginary; and even then it would be odd that he should not have been introduced into the narrative more frequently. 'Above all', says Stanton, 'the words attributed to Simon Peter at vi. 68, "Lord to whom shall we go? thou hast the words of eternal life," should have been put into the mouth of the disciple with special insight.'

Some scholars do not regard it as unnatural that John should have made reference to himself in this indirect manner, on the ground that the use of this exalted title is an expression not of pride but of gratitude for special privileges. On this point, the present author would say with Stanton, 'This is, perhaps, a possible explanation, but I do not find it an easy one to accept.' It would seem far more natural that a disciple and friend should have described John in this manner, because he regarded his master as possessing unique insight into the mind of Christ. The description, moreover, was specially apposite when the author was recording incidents which illustrated John's remarkable spiritual understanding. In describing him as 'the disciple whom Jesus loved', R. H. Strachan pertinently remarks,[1] 'he does not suggest that Jesus showed an affection for one particular disciple as distinct from others. The evangelist speaks of His love for them all (xiii. 1). The isolation and supremacy given to this disciple is largely the product of the evangelist's own heart. The relationship is similar to that between Mark and Peter, Luke and Paul. The evangelist does not leave us without a clear glimpse of that fulness of Christian experience which is described in the title he gives to his old friend. "He that loveth me shall be loved of my Father, and I will love him, and manifest myself to him" (xiv. 21). May not these words be taken as a description of the beloved disciple? In the experience of the evangelist, this teacher was one in whom the promise had been fulfilled, "We will come unto him, and make our abode with him." '

The name of this author is unknown to us, unless he happened to have been another John. We can gather however from the manner in which he has told his story a good deal about him. He was most certainly a Jew with a first-hand knowledge of the geography of Palestine, and, in particular, of the topography of Jerusalem before the fall of the holy city. He was well acquainted with the practices, beliefs, and schools of thought within later Judaism, though curiously he never

[1] *The Fourth Gospel* (S.C.M. Press, 1941), p. 83.

mentions the Sadducees. He was probably a native of Jerusalem, who had often seen Jesus on His visits to the capital; and he may well have been himself a witness of some of the incidents he records. Later, he moved to Ephesus where he became a close friend of John the son of Zebedee. When the latter in the closing years of his life was persuaded to record for posterity his own irreplaceable testimony to Jesus, this faithful disciple undertook to commit it to writing, being himself a man of greater literary ability than we would naturally suppose the son of Zebedee to have been (see Acts iv. 13).

When we consider the much-discussed and very differently evaluated external evidence for the authorship of this Gospel, two conclusions seem to the present writer inescapable. First, John the son of Zebedee lived to a great age and was buried at Ephesus. Secondly, he was regarded in early Christian tradition as the ultimate authority behind the Gospel, which was issued with his approval though he may not have been the actual writer of it.

Irenaeus, who became bishop of Lyons in AD 177, speaks of 'John the disciple of the Lord (i.e. the well-known disciple) who reclined on His breast and himself issued (*exedōke*, 'gave out' or 'published') the Gospel at Ephesus'. This statement of Irenaeus was founded on reliable information, for he tells us that he had often heard Polycarp the saintly bishop of Smyrna, who was martyred at the age of eighty-five in AD 155, relate what he had heard from the lips of John and other disciples about Jesus. It is significant that Irenaeus does not say that John *wrote* the Gospel, but his language clearly implies that it was published with his authority.

Polycrates, bishop of Ephesus, in a letter to Victor, bishop of Rome, which is usually dated about AD 190, states that 'John who reclined on the breast of the Lord' was 'a witness (*martus*) and a teacher'. The word *martus* does not imply that John suffered death by martyrdom. The only evidence for his alleged martyrdom is late, and is probably an inference from Mark x. 39 that both the sons of Zebedee must have drunk in the same way the cup their Master drank (see Bernard for the details). The word 'witness', preceding as it does the word 'teacher' in Polycrates' statement, must indicate, it would seem, that John testified in his teaching, probably up to the time of his death, to what Jesus has said and done. This is entirely in keeping with the statement of the Gospel in xxi. 24, 'This is the disciple which testifieth of these things', the present participle implying 'at the time when the evangelist is writing'. The nature of the apostle's testimony given in his extreme old age is reflected in a moving and well-known passage in Jerome's *Commentary on the Epistle to the Galatians*, here quoted in Westcott's translation: 'When he tarried at Ephesus to extreme old age, and could only with difficulty be carried to the church in the arms of his disciples, and was unable to give utterance to many words, he used to say no more at their several meetings than this, "Little children, love one another". At length the disciples and fathers who were there, wearied with hearing always the same words, said, "Master, why dost thou always say this?" "It is the Lord's command", was his worthy reply, "and if this alone be done, it is enough." '

It has sometimes been suggested that this evidence from the last part of the second century, to the effect that the authority for the Gospel is the aged apostle John, is in fact based on a confusion between the son of Zebedee and another John, called 'the presbyter' by Papias bishop of Hierapolis, who was born in AD 70 and died about AD 146. Papias, however, carefully distinguishes this presbyter John, whom he couples with his contemporary Aristion, from his namesake whom he groups with the apostles Andrew, Peter, Philip, Thomas, James and Matthew. Moreover, though this presbyter John may have been sufficiently influential to refer to himself in the Second and Third Epistles of John simply as 'the presbyter', it would seem highly improbable that a Gospel written by him could in a comparatively short space of time, and in different parts of Christendom, have come to be regarded as the work of John the son of Zebedee.

From Rome about the year AD 170 comes the evidence of what is known as the Muratorian Fragment, which gives a list of Christian books which should be accepted as Scripture with a brief account of the origin of some of them. It clearly regards John as the virtual author of the Fourth Gospel, but the language used suggests that others besides him were concerned with its production. The fragment states that when the apostle was urged by his fellow-disciples to write, he bade them fast with him for three days, and afterwards each was to tell the others about any revelation he might have received. It was then revealed to Andrew *ut recognoscentibus cunctis Iohannes suo nomine cuncta describeret.* This is not an easy sentence. It might perhaps be paraphrased 'that John (who was now too old to write a Gospel himself) should delineate, or sketch out what he wished to be said (*describeret cuncta*), so that the information would have the stamp of his authority upon it (*suo nomine*); and that all present should certify (*cunctis recognoscentibus*) that what was eventually written down tallied with what he had said.' Some of the details in the statement in the Muratorian Fragment may be fanciful, e.g. the mention of the fast, and of the revelation to Andrew, who may have been named because he happens to be the first apostle mentioned in the Gospel. But it is significant that a tradition by no means inconsistent with it, to the effect that the Gospel was composed in John's name and with his approval by one who based his work on the evidence of the apostle, lingered on, particularly in the churches of the West, long after the Gospel had come to be known as the Gospel according to John.

The second prologue to the Gospel found in a tenth-century MS of the Latin Vulgate at Madrid, known as the *Codex Toletanus*, states that the Gospel 'was given to the churches in Asia by John while he was yet in the body, as one Papias by name, bishop of Hierapolis, a disciple of John and dear to him . . . related, he who wrote this Gospel at John's dictation (*Iohanne subdictante*)'. F. C. Burkitt suggested that some word had fallen out from the Greek underlying the Latin of this prologue, and that the original statement was not 'as Papias related, who wrote at John's dictation', but 'as Papias related *from the man* who wrote at John's dictation'.[1] Be this as it may, the prologue avoids attributing the writing of the Gospel to

[1] *Two Lectures on the Gospels*, pp. 70, 71.

John; and its evidence is much older than the MS in which it is found, for it is repeated in almost identical language in chapter ix of Jerome's *De Viris Illustribus*. The tradition that the Gospel was not written by John's own hand but dictated or suggested by him to Papias is also found in an anonymous statement in a late Greek compendium of patristic quotations, 'John suggested (*hupēgoreuse*) the Gospel to his own disciple Papias'. The assignation of the Gospel to Papias may well have been guess-work, but with this exception, the tradition seems plausible.

II. THE DATE OF THE GOSPEL

That we are right in regarding the Gospel of John as the fourth and last of the Gospels is clear not only from the fact that in the majority of MSS it is found in this position, but also from patristic references. Clement of Alexandria, for example, who died in AD 212, states on the authority of the elders of an earlier age that John wrote his Gospel last of the evangelists. If the work was published during the last days of the life of John the son of Zebedee, as the evidence we have so far considered suggests, it can be confidently dated in the last decade of the first century, probably at its close, for Irenaeus states that John survived till the reign of Trajan, which began in AD 98. Those who date the Gospel in the second century do so because they are unable on critical grounds to regard John the son of Zebedee as either its actual or virtual author, and because they assume that if the Gospel had been published before the close of the first century, with the authority of the apostle John, more traces of its use would have been found in the literature of the sub-apostolic age.

It is true that definite quotations from the Gospel in the somewhat scanty extant literature of the first half of the second century are hard to find, though several writers use what can be reasonably described as Johannine phraseology. Thus, the earliest second-century writer of whose work sufficient has survived for us to form a fair estimate, Ignatius, who suffered martyrdom in the second decade of the century, remarks that the Spirit knows *whence it cometh, and whither it goeth* (cf. Jn.

iii. 8); and, when speaking of himself, he asserts that there is no longer any fire of material longing in him but only *living water* (cf. Jn. vii. 38).

The lack of definite evidence that Polycarp made use of the Gospel is felt by many to be very surprising in view of what Irenaeus says about the vivid memories that Polycarp had of his intercourse with the apostle; but it must be remembered that we only possess Polycarp's comparatively brief letter to the Philippians and the prayer which he is said to have prayed at his martyrdom. It is generally agreed that his statement that 'everyone who does not confess that Jesus Christ has come in the flesh is Antichrist' is directly influenced by 1 John iv. 2, 3. It is not however certain whether the First Epistle of John was written before or after the Gospel; and, though many would maintain that the tradition is right which assigns both the Gospel and the First Epistle to the same author, there are some who are unwilling to admit that both documents come from the same pen. The evidence therefore that Polycarp made use of the Fourth Gospel must be regarded as indeterminate.

The date of the important early Christian work known as *The Teaching of the Twelve Apostles* is uncertain, though many would place it as early as the first or second decade of the second century. It is interesting to notice that in the prayer appointed in this document to be said at the consecration of the eucharistic cup, thanksgiving is to be made for *the holy Vine* of David, God's Son; and when the bread is consecrated thanksgiving is to be made for the *life* and *knowledge* made known to us through Jesus. But though the remarkable reference to Christ as 'the Vine' would seem to echo John xv. 1, and though 'life' and 'knowledge' are characteristically Johannine ideas, it cannot be maintained that their presence in *The Teaching* implies the literary use of the Fourth Gospel.

It must be frankly admitted that a definite literary dependence on the Gospel cannot be conclusively proved before Justin Martyr, whose two *Apologies* and *Dialogue with Trypho the Jew* were written between AD 145 and 150. Justin regards the apostle John as the author of *the Revelation*, but does not mention that he is the author of the Fourth Gospel. But not only is his theology dependent on this Gospel, particularly on the prologue, but a knowledge of its text is clearly reflected in his work. When he writes 'Christ said Except ye be regenerated ye shall not enter the kingdom of heaven', and adds, 'It is plain that it is impossible for those who were born once for all to enter into their mother's womb', he seems clearly to be quoting, though without verbal exactitude, John iii. 3–5.

But, while it must be recognized that evidence for the use of this Gospel in the first half of the second century is indirect and indeterminate, it would be wrong to conclude from this that the Gospel was unknown to the writers in question because it was not yet written, and that the apparent allusions to it in their works are only echoes of Christian language bearing some resemblance to it. Recent discoveries of MSS have done much to substantiate the traditional view that the Gospel was written at the close of the first century. It has long been known that the Harmony of the Four Gospels, known as the *Diatessaron*, written by Tatian a disciple of Justin Martyr, was composed out of our four canonical Gospels; and it is recognized that the Fourth Gospel must have been in general circulation for some considerable time before he could be justified in making such authoritative use of it. The Greek fragment of the *Diatessaron* discovered at Dura-Europus in 1920 containing the story of Joseph's request for the body of Jesus lays open the possibility that Tatian may have originally written the Harmony at Rome in Greek, and that it was composed earlier than AD 170, the date usually assigned to it. Subsequently it was translated into Syriac, and was the only form in which the Gospels were read in the Syriac-speaking church, until it was replaced by what our oldest authorities for the Syriac version call the 'separated' Gospels.

Recent discoveries in Egypt give us even more secure ground for believing that the Fourth Gospel was written early enough for it to have become known and used in that part of the world early in the second century. In 1925 three leaves of a papyrus codex acquired by the British Museum and known as 'Egerton Papyrus 2' were edited by H. I. Bell and T. C. Skeat under the title *Fragments of an Unknown Gospel and other*

Early Christian Papyri; and a little later a popular account of them was issued in a British Museum brochure entitled *The New Gospel Fragments*. This papyrus is confidently assigned by experts to the first half of the second century. The precise nature of the work of which these fragments formed a part is uncertain, but it would seem clear that their author was familiar with the Gospel of John. The most significant passage is reconstructed by the editors to read as follows:

'Turning to the rulers of the people he spake this saying: Search (*or* ye search) the Scriptures, in which ye think that ye have life; these are they which bear witness of me. Think not that I came to accuse you to my Father; there is one that accuseth you, even Moses, on whom ye have set your hope. And when they said, we know well that God spake unto Moses, but as for thee we know not whence thou art, Jesus answered and said unto them, Now is your unbelief accused. ... And the rulers laid their hands on him that they might take him and hand him over to the multitude: and they could not take him because the hour of his betrayal was not yet come. But he himself, even the Lord, going forth out of their hands departed from them.'[1]

In this passage there would seem to be unmistakable references to John v. 39, 45, ix. 29, vii. 30, and x. 39; for, as Kenyon pointed out, 'the only alternative, that the writer was using material which was afterwards incorporated in the Fourth Gospel, is highly improbable in view of the very individual style of that Gospel. There is no evidence or probability of a school of "Johannine" writers earlier than the Gospel itself.' It is unlikely that this codex was the original autograph; and a time-lag of at least thirty years must be assumed between the date of the publication of the Gospel at Ephesus and the time when it was used in Egypt in the manner reflected in this 'Gospel Fragment'. We have therefore in this codex, as Kenyon maintained, 'confirmatory evidence of the existence of the Fourth Gospel by about the end of the first century'.

[1] As quoted in F. G. Kenyon, *The Bible and Modern Scholarship* (John Murray, 1948), pp. 22, 23.

In the same year 1935, C. H. Roberts edited *An Unpublished Fragment of the Fourth Gospel*, a tiny portion of a codex acquired by B. P. Grenfell in Egypt, and presented by him to the John Rylands Library in Manchester. It contains in a very mutilated form John xviii. 31–33, 37, 38. As the codex is assigned by the papyrological experts to the second part of the first half of the second century, it is, in Roberts' words, 'the earliest known fragment of any part of the New Testament and probably the earliest witness to the existence of the Gospel according to St. John'. The significance of this discovery was clearly stated by Kenyon who wrote: 'Allowing even a minimum time for the circulation of the Gospel from its place of origin, this would throw back the date of composition so near to the traditional date in the last decade of the first century that there is no longer any reason to question the validity of the tradition.'[1]

Although the Rylands fragment is too tiny for it to throw light upon the nature of the text of the Gospel, we have every reason for believing that the textual tradition of the New Testament as a whole, and of the Gospel of John in particular, is essentially reliable. Further witness to this has been provided in recent years by the third-century Chester Beatty Papyrus of the Gospels and Acts, made known in 1931, which contains a substantial portion of John x, xi; and, on a much larger scale, by the Bodmer Papyrus, dated about AD 200, a transcription of which was recently issued by Professor J. Martin of Geneva. This contains the whole Gospel with occasional gaps. The variations of the text found in both these papyri have been made available to scholars in this country in Professor G. D. Kilpatrick's admirable critical apparatus to the second edition of the Greek Testament published in 1958 by the British and Foreign Bible Society.

III. THE PURPOSE OF THE GOSPEL

'Last of all', wrote Clement of Alexandria, 'John, perceiving that the external facts (*ta sōmatika*) had been made plain in the Gospels, being urged by his friends and inspired by the

[1] *Op. cit.*, p. 21.

Spirit, composed a spiritual (*pneumatikon*) Gospel.' Whatever else this much-discussed passage may mean, it would seem clear that Clement is not saying that the Fourth Gospel is 'spiritual' because its author was inspired, while the other evangelists were not. All the Gospels were written by those who received the necessary gift of the Spirit for the accomplishment of their work. Nor would he seem to be contrasting the literal character of the narratives of the Synoptic Gospels with the allegorical implications of the narratives of the Fourth. It is true that the adverb *pneumatikōs* can have the sense 'allegorically', as in Rev. xi. 8, where RSV translates 'and their dead bodies will lie in the street of the great city which is allegorically called Sodom and Egypt, where their Lord was crucified'. And many scholars have given a similar meaning to the adjective *pneumatikos* in the passage from Clement. On this interpretation, he is supposed to be saying that, while the other three Gospels record the bare facts, the fourth evangelist is writing an allegorical story more akin to such a work as Bunyan's *Pilgrim's Progress*. There is no doubt that Origen, Clement's successor in the catechetical school at Alexandria, believed that the primary message of this Gospel lay not in the facts that were recorded but in the allegorical interpretation that could be given to them. And this approach to the Gospel has appealed to many ever since.

The following are two recent examples of such allegorical exegesis. In commenting on 'Woman, what have I to do with thee?' (ii. 4), R. G. Bury writes,[1] 'This reply sounds unfilial; but since "woman" symbolizes "sensation", her suggestion to the Logos is otiose and impertinent. Mary may also typify the Jewish Church or Prophetism (cf. xix. 26). The human scene is merely a cloak for the allegorical sense.' Similarly, in annotating vi. 19, the same author writes, 'The measure of distance, "about 25 or 30 furlongs", is peculiar to John and may have some cryptic significance, e.g. the boat may represent the ark of the church, the storm and darkness Nero's persecution, and the number of furlongs the number of intervening years.' In this type of exegesis the Gospel becomes a kind of cryptogram,

[1] *The Fourth Gospel and the Logos-Doctrine* (Heffer, Cambridge, 1940).

the most erudite solution of which is likely to be the most correct; and the historical value of the Gospel evaporates in the process.

It is most improbable that Clement, though he was acquainted with the allegorical exegesis of the Old Testament exemplified in such writers as Philo, meant to contrast the historical and the allegorical in this way in his famous remark about the fourth evangelist. In the first place, it would seem that the opposite of *pneumatikōs* meaning 'allegorically' is usually *sarkikōs* 'literally' and not *sōmatikōs*, the word used by Clement. Secondly, although some of the writers of the New Testament indulge in allegory, they invariably indicate the particular allegorical interpretation that they have in mind. This is clear in Rev. xi. 8 already quoted, and also in Gal. iv. 24–26, where RSV reads, 'Now this is an allegory: these women are two covenants. One is from Mount Sinai, bearing children for slavery; she is Hagar. Now Hagar is Mount Sinai in Arabia; she corresponds to the present Jerusalem, for she is in slavery with her children. But the Jerusalem above is free, and she is our mother.' In the same way, the writer to the Hebrews makes his meaning clear when he allegorizes the Old Testament references to Melchizedek. 'He is first, by translation of his name, king of righteousness, and then he is also king of Salem, that is, king of peace. He is without father or mother or genealogy, and has neither beginning of days nor end of life but resembling the Son of God he continues a priest for ever (Heb. vii. 2, 3, RSV). Our evangelist does not do this; and, as Stanton pertinently asks, 'Can it be believed that he would have refrained from doing so, if he had actually had allegorical meanings in mind and attached importance to them?'

Nor would it seem probable that Clement is contrasting directly the supposedly untheological or undoctrinal character of the first three Gospels with the specifically theological emphasis of the Fourth. It is true that John was known in Christian tradition as *ho theologos*, 'the divine', or 'the theologian', and the author of the theological First Epistle of John is held by very many to be the author of the Gospel of John. But it is of immense significance that the latter writing is

Gospel and not a theological treatise. In this Gospel the author undoubtedly makes explicit what is implicit in the earlier narratives. For example, all the Gospels record that Jesus performed miracles, and all are agreed that these mighty works were not portents comparable with the 'miracles' of magicians. But while the significance of Jesus' miracles as evidence that He was the Lord's Messiah is found in the first three Gospels, not so much in the actual manner in which the miracle-stories are related, as in independent statements such as those made by Jesus in the synagogue at Nazareth (see Lk. iv. 17–21) and to the messengers of John the Baptist (see Mt. xi. 2–6), in the Fourth Gospel the record and the interpretation of what happened are closely interwoven. The miracles are 'signs' revealing who Jesus was and what He had come into the world to do. This would seem to have been the kind of phenomenon that was in the mind of Clement when he contrasts 'the external facts' of the earlier narratives with 'the spiritual Gospel' of John.

Recent study of the Gospels has made it abundantly clear that to separate doctrine and history in *any* of the four Gospels is to draw a false distinction; though it is obvious that in John doctrine is much more in evidence. The words of Westcott on this subject could scarcely be bettered. 'If we compare', he wrote, 'the avowed purpose of St. John with that of St. Luke (i. 1–4), it may be said with partial truth that the inspiring impulse was in the one case doctrinal, and in the other case historical. But care must be taken not to exaggerate or misinterpret this contrast. Christian doctrine is history, and this is above all things the lesson of the Fourth Gospel. The Synoptic narratives are implicit dogmas no less truly than St. John's dogmas are concrete facts. The real difference is that the earliest Gospel contained the fundamental facts and words which experience afterwards interpreted, while the latest Gospel reviews the facts in the light of their interpretation. But in both cases the exactness of historical truth is paramount.'

In recording the history of Jesus and interpreting its significance, in showing, in other words, the eternal meaning of the historic coming of the Word of God into human life, our evangelist delights to suggest to his readers the symbolism inherent in the particular situation. For example, it was really night when Judas left the upper room (xiii. 30), but every reader feels as he reads the narrative at this point that Judas, in leaving the fellowship of Jesus, was leaving the realm of light to become the tool of the prince of darkness. It was really dark when the disciples were crossing the Sea of Galilee after the miraculous feeding of the crowds; but when the evangelist writes, 'It was now dark, and Jesus was not come to them' (vi. 17), the reader cannot fail to infer that, from a spiritual point of view, without the company of Jesus all is dark. Many other instances of this symbolic nature of the Gospel, which is something very different from allegory, will appear in the course of the commentary. It is this characteristic of our evangelist that led Scott Holland truly to remark: 'St. John lays hold of facts in their typical and suggestive character; not that he inclines in the least to throw over the facts for the sake of the parable which they suggest, but rather to dwell with loving insistence on the value of the facts themselves just because they have proved so rich in spiritual significance.'[1]

The avowed purpose of the evangelist in composing his Gospel is clearly stated in xx. 30, 31. He points out that his work is essentially selective. He has chosen to record some of the signs that Jesus did in the presence of His disciples, that his readers may be encouraged to hold fast their belief that *Jesus is the Christ*, *the Son of God*, and that in so doing they may experience the higher, eternal life that it is in His power to bestow upon them.

That Jesus is *the Christ* is a major theme of all the Gospels. Had He not claimed Messiahship, most of the controversies with the Pharisees would never have arisen, and He would never have been crucified. The fourth evangelist stresses as fully as his predecessors that many Old Testament prophecies about the work the Messiah would accomplish find their fulfilment in Jesus. And, even more clearly than they, he shows

[1] From a sermon, 'The Feast at Cana', preached in St. Paul's Cathedral on January 18th, 1891.

that the salvation Jesus came to bring was the climax of Jewish religion; that the blessings He had to bestow were prefigured in the blessings bestowed by God upon His people in the past; and that the truths enshrined in the ritual of the great Jewish festivals, particularly the Passover, were symbolic of the final truth revealed in Him. Our evangelist portrays Jesus as performing a Messianic action in 'cleansing' the temple on His first visit to Jerusalem after His ministry had begun. Moreover, long before the events which led to His final rejection by the religious leaders, Jesus is seen to be engaged in bitter controversy with them in the temple precincts about His Messianic claims to 'work' on the Sabbath involved in the healing of the paralysed man at Bethesda, and in the gift of sight to a man born blind. It is as Messiah that His disciples accept Him from the first, even though they are not fully aware of the kind of Messiah He is. It is as Messiah that He reveals Himself to the Samaritan woman, however imperfectly she may understand the title when He applies it to Himself. It is as Messiah that He feeds the hungry Galilaeans, though He escapes from them as soon as they try to enthrone Him as an earthly monarch. And it is as Messiah that He approaches Jerusalem for the last time, though as soon as He is greeted as a warrior-king He finds an ass and rides into the city as a king of peace. Two of the constantly recurring themes of this Gospel are the nature of the unbelief which led the Jews to refuse to accept Jesus as the Messiah, and the prerequisites and the constituent factors of the faith which led His disciples to acknowledge Him as the One 'of whom Moses in the law, and the prophets, did write'.

That Jesus is the unique *Son of God* is made clear in the Synoptic Gospels by the supernatural revelation given at His baptism and on the mount of transfiguration. Matthew and Luke also record a saying of Jesus in which He expresses His consciousness of the intimate relationship existing between His heavenly Father and Himself (Mt. xi. 27; Lk. x. 22). And in the parable of the wicked husbandmen Jesus clearly refers to Himself as the only Son of the Owner of the vineyard, who is destined to be thrown out of the vineyard and put to death.

In the Fourth Gospel, this self-revelation of Jesus as the unique Son of God occupies a more conspicuous and more extensive place. Not only does the evangelist record John the Baptist's testimony, 'I have seen and have borne witness that this is the Son of God' (i. 34, RSV); but throughout the Gospel it is made very evident that it was precisely in the consciousness of Jesus that He was sent by God to accomplish a unique work, and in His certainty that the will of His heavenly Father and His own will were essentially one, that the ground for the opposition to Him of the religious leaders of Jewry really lay. He was a man, they said, who made himself equal with God, a supreme blasphemer!

This self-disclosure of His inmost nature is given for the most part in the course of the somewhat protracted controversies of Jesus with the Jews. There are many critics who compare these discourses very unfavourably with the records of the teaching of Jesus found in the other Gospels. 'There is an argumentativeness', wrote Burkitt, 'a tendency to mystification, about the utterances of the Johannine Christ, which, taken as the report of actual words spoken, is positively repellent.' And, not surprisingly, Burkitt concluded, 'It is quite inconceivable that the historical Jesus of the Synoptic Gospels could have argued and quibbled with opponents, as He is represented to have done in the Fourth Gospel. The only possible explanation is that the work is not history, but something else cast in historic form.'[1] But, as the present writer has said elsewhere: 'Though at times the utterances of Jesus in this Gospel sound harsh, particularly to those who over-emphasize the gentleness of Jesus' nature, there is no valid reason for supposing that, when dealing with the Rabbis at Jerusalem, He did not debate with them in rabbinical fashion the nature of His claims; and it may well be just this side of the Lord's ministry that the Galilean disciples knew little about, but with which the fourth Evangelist was more familiar, particularly if, as has already been suggested, he was himself a Jerusalem

[1] *The Gospel History and its Transmission* (T. and T. Clark, 1911), pp. 227, 228.

disciple'[1] It is very true that the portrait of the Johannine Christ does not at all square with the portrait that has often been drawn of Him by liberal theologians. But we have to remember that Jesus was put to death not because He was inoffensive, but because He struck at the roots of the pride, the prejudices, and the self-satisfaction of mankind. Moreover, He spake as He did, not because He was a man like other men, and nothing more, but because He was the Son of God sent to be the Saviour of the world.

The *life*, usually called in this Gospel 'eternal life', which the evangelist asserts in xx. 31 will result from a persistent belief in Jesus as *the Christ, the Son of God*, is made possible not only by a knowledge of the revelation given in the teaching of Jesus, but also by the work which He came on earth to accomplish for man's salvation. An exaggerated emphasis upon the prologue has sometimes led readers of this Gospel to conclude that redemption through the death of Jesus does not occupy the primary place in the theology of this evangelist that it occupies in the theology of Paul. 'But if', in the words of James Denney, 'we turn from the prologue to the Gospel itself, in which Jesus actually figures and in which His words and deeds are before us, we receive a different impression. . . . We find that the death of Christ comes to the front in a great variety of ways as something which is of peculiar significance for the evangelist.'[2] That the Son of God 'was manifested to take away our sins' (1 Jn. iii. 5) is very evident in the Gospel. He did this by laying down His life for the sheep (x. 11). At the outset of the narrative He is marked out as 'the Lamb of God' destined to take upon Himself, and in so doing to take away, the sin of the world (i. 29). By being lifted up on a cross, and only by being lifted up on a cross, He has power to draw all men to Himself (xii. 32, 33). By giving His flesh for the life of the world, He offers men and women God's supreme gift, and unless they 'eat' His flesh, and accept His gift, they have no life in them (vi. 33–53). By dedicating Himself and offering

[1] R. V. G. Tasker, *The Nature and Purpose of the Gospels* (S.C.M. Press, Sixth Impression, 1957), pp. 96, 97.
[2] *The Death of Christ* (Revised edition, Tyndale Press, 1950), p. 140.

the sacrifice of Himself, He makes it possible for others to consecrate their lives to God (xvii. 19). The grain of wheat, He teaches, must fall into the ground and die before it can bring forth fruit; and, in keeping with this principle, which is as true in the spiritual realm as it is in the natural, He Himself must die that men may have life and have it in abundance (xii. 24, x. 10). His whole incarnate life is, in fact, meaningless apart from 'the hour' to which it is inevitably moving, and that hour is none other than the hour of His passion (see ii. 4, vii. 7, 8, 30, xii. 23, xvii. 1).

Modern scholars are not agreed as to what extent, if at all, the fourth evangelist made use of the other three Gospels in composing his own. Some have even supposed that he was unaware of their contents. After prolonged study of this question, very different results have been reached. Of those who emphasize the comparatively few verbal agreements between John and the Synoptic writers, some (e.g. Stanton) have concluded that he used only Mark, others (e.g. Bernard) Mark and Luke, and a much smaller number Matthew, Mark and Luke. On the other hand, those who emphasize the far more numerous differences, such as P. Gardner Smith,[1] have concluded that John wrote entirely independently of the others.

The Fathers of the early Church seem to have assumed that our evangelist was familiar with the Synoptic Gospels, and that one of the purposes he had in view in the composition of his own Gospel was to supplement the others where they were inadequate. Eusebius records that John, having been shown the other Gospels, testified to their truth, but admitted that they lacked a record of the events of the early days of Christ's ministry before John the Baptist was imprisoned. The historian then goes on to say, 'For these reasons the apostle John, it is said, being entreated to undertake it, wrote the account of the time not recorded by the former evangelists, and the deeds done by our Saviour, which they passed by, for these were the events that occurred before the imprisonment of John. And this is intimated by the evangelist when he says "this beginning of miracles did Jesus", and then proceeds to make mention

[1] *St. John and the Synoptic Gospels* (C.U.P., 1939).

of the Baptist, in the midst of our Lord's deeds, stating that John was at that time "baptizing at Aenon near Salim". He plainly also shows this in the words "John was not yet cast into prison".'[1] This tradition that John wrote partly to supplement the other Gospels, particularly in the first part of Christ's ministry, is also found in the Prologue to St. John in the *Codex Toletanus*, and, with some small verbal changes, in Jerome's *De Viris Illustribus*, to which reference has already been made.

Certain it is that the narrative of the Fourth Gospel helps to elucidate much that is difficult in the other Gospels read by themselves. For example, their narratives of the call of the earliest disciples become much more intelligible when it is realized that they were already acquainted with Jesus, and had been encouraged to become His disciples by John the Baptist. It was no unknown Person that Peter, Andrew and the sons of Zebedee left their nets and their families to follow. Peter had already been some time in the company of Jesus, before he became so conscious of his unworthiness that he fell down at Jesus' knees and cried, 'Depart from me; for I am a sinful man, O Lord' (Lk. v. 8). Again, the opposition to Jesus at Jerusalem is inexplicable on the assumption that Jesus had only once visited the city during His ministry, as the narrative of Mark read by itself might lead the reader to suppose. Conversely, there would seem to be echoes of those other visits to Jerusalem, recorded only by John, in the saying of Jesus, 'O Jerusalem, Jerusalem . . . how often would I have gathered thy children together' (Mt. xxiii. 37); and in the concluding words of His lament over the holy city 'thou knewest not the time of thy visitation' (Lk. xix. 44); for, as Stanton remarks, 'it is inconceivable that Jesus should not have regarded His own coming, His own preaching and working among them, as not included in "their day of visitation", and should regard that day as already over though He had never exercised any ministry there.' That the total ministry of Jesus lasted more than one year, as the Fourth Gospel makes clear that it did, is also implicit in the statement of Mark that

[1] *Ecclesiastical History*, iii. 24.

the grass was green when the five thousand were fed, for the grass is only green in Palestine for a brief period in spring (Mk. vi. 39).

There can be no doubt that, at the time the Fourth Gospel was written, there was much erroneous teaching being given in the Church, which claimed to be Christian. An early and persistent tradition states that the evangelist was consciously opposing in his Gospel the teaching of Cerinthus, who flourished in Asia near the end of the first century, and who taught that the Son of God had no existence prior to His birth from Mary. The views of Cerinthus were akin to those of a sect known as the Ebionites, whose name by derivation means 'the poor ones', and was assigned to them because they held the poverty-stricken doctrine that Jesus was a mere man upon whom the divine Spirit descended for a season and then left him. This tradition is clearly stated in the second Prologue to the Gospel of John in the *Codex Toletanus* and is found also in similar language in Jerome. 'John the Apostle', the Prologue asserts, 'wrote this Gospel against Cerinthus and the heretics, attacking in particular the dogma of the Ebionites, who in the perversity of their folly (that is why they are called Ebionites) assert that Christ did not exist before He was born of Mary and was not begotten of God the Father before all ages. This is why He was compelled to mention His divine birth from the Father.' Eusebius also relates that Irenaeus affirmed that there were still living in his day 'men who had heard Polycarp tell that John the disciple of the Lord once went into a bath at Ephesus, and seeing Cerinthus within ran out without bathing, exclaiming "Let us flee lest the bath should fall in, as long as Cerinthus that enemy of truth is within".'[1] Some scholars have suggested that in the definition in the First Epistle of John of 'the deceiver' and 'the antichrist' as he 'that confesseth not that Jesus Christ is come in the flesh' John may be glancing at Cerinthus (see 1 Jn. ii. 22, iv. 3).

In addition to the heresy of the Ebionites, which was polytheistic in character, there was also prevalent at the time of the

[1] *Ecclesiastical History*, iv. 14.

composition of the Gospel the false teaching known as Docetism, which might be described as pantheistic. Those who professed it maintained that the manhood of Jesus was only apparent, for they regarded it as axiomatic that matter was evil. They were called Docetists because the Greek word *dokei* means 'it seems'; and to them the humanity of Jesus was a phantom under which God was revealed to man. There can be no doubt that Ignatius had these people in mind when he wrote, 'Be deaf, therefore, when any one speaks to you apart from Jesus Christ, who was of the family of David, and of Mary, was *truly* born, both ate and drank, was *truly* persecuted under Pontius Pilate, was *truly* crucified and died in the sight of those in heaven and on earth and under the earth; who also was *truly* raised from the dead.'[1] It is strange to us that this kind of teaching, which makes shipwreck of the doctrines of the incarnation and atonement, should have been the earliest heresy in the Christian Church. Speaking of the apocryphal *Acts of John*, written towards the middle of the second century, Burkitt wrote, 'To the orthodox Christian Jesus of Nazareth is very God, and at the same time true Man; to the modern agnostic He is a good man deified by His followers. But to the author of the *Acts of John* He was not Man at all. He had no proper shape or body, only an appearance, and to one person He appeared in one shape, and to another in a shape totally different; even the clothes which He seemed to be wearing were visionary.'[2] At the time of the crucifixion, so the author of this strange document relates, our Lord appeared to John who had taken refuge in a cave to avoid the anger of the Jews, and said to him, 'John, unto the multitude down below in Jerusalem I am being crucified, and pierced with lances and reeds, and gall and vinegar is given Me to drink: but unto thee I am speaking, and hearken thou to what I say.'[3] In support of this utter perversion of the truth the view was sometimes put forward by those teachers that Simon of

[1] *Epistle to the Trallians*, ix.
[2] *Two Lectures on the Gospels*, p. 62.
[3] *Acts of John*, *x. i.* The text can be found in *The Apocryphal New Testament*, M. R. James.

Cyrene, who according to the earlier Gospels carried the cross to Calvary, was crucified in Jesus' place.

Westcott did not think that it was the specific aim of the fourth evangelist to refute these views. But, whether or not he was deliberately writing to combat early Gnostic tendencies, there can be no doubt that the only adequate answer to them is contained in his profound assertion 'the Word was made flesh, and dwelt among us' (i. 14). The use of the almost crude word 'flesh' here and in vi. 52–56, and not the word 'body', makes it transparently clear that the human nature of Jesus was wholly real. And it is on the true humanity of the Saviour that this evangelist throughout his Gospel lays great stress. Jesus is weary and thirsty as He sits by the well at Sychar, and His disciples who had gone away to buy food urge Him to eat on their return (iv. 6–8, 31). He spits on the ground, when He is in the process of creating sight in the man born blind (ix. 6). He weeps at the tomb of Lazarus (xi. 35). His human spirit is disturbed as He contemplates the passion (xii. 27), and when He feels compelled to break the news to His disciples that one of them is a traitor (xiii. 21). He thirsts as He hangs on the cross (xix. 28). And blood and water flow from His dead body when a spear is thrust into it (xix. 34).

Moreover, not only does Jesus speak of Himself as 'a man that hath told you the truth' (viii. 40), but the passages in which the expressions 'Son of man', or 'the Son of man' occur emphasize the reality of His manhood. 'There can be little doubt', as Westcott pointed out, 'that the idea of true humanity lies at the foundation of these terms. Jesus was not only "like a son of man" (Dn. vii. 13), but He *was* "a Son of Man". His manhood was real not apparent. But He was not as one man among many. He was the representative of the whole race, "*the* Son of Man", in whom the potential power of humanity was gathered up.' A brief survey of the relevant passages will confirm this. It was after Andrew had recognized Jesus as Messiah, and after Nathanael had acknowledged Him to be the Son of God, that Jesus told the latter that there was something else about Him that would cause amazement to those who would be brought into close association with Him. Others, such as Jacob, had received a vision of communications being conveyed from heaven to earth through supernatural intermediaries. In Jesus, *the Son of man*, a man of flesh and blood like themselves, His contemporaries would come to see that what had hitherto been seen only in a fleeting vision was now an abiding reality (i. 51). The supreme wonder of the incarnation was that He who had come down from heaven was revealing Himself not as a demigod, but as *the Son of man* without in any way ceasing to be divine; and that the climax of that revelation would be when this Son of man, despised, humiliated and rejected, would be exalted by being lifted up on a cross (see iii. 13, 14, xii. 34). Moreover, authority is given to Jesus to pass final judgment upon humanity, precisely because as *the Son of man* He has been truly man Himself, sharing the nature of those who will stand before Him when the last assize is held (see v. 27). But the ultimate reason why the Son of God became *the Son of man* was to rid men and women of all fear of that judgment. He came not to judge the world but to save it. He came to offer men the food which abides unto eternal life, and He offers that food not as a patronizing superman condescending to meet their weakness, but as *the Son of man* who shares their weakness (see vi. 27, 53). It is when the man who was born blind and has now received the gift of sight comes to know that *the Son of man* in whom he is asked to believe is none other than Jesus who spat on the ground, made clay with the spittle, placed it on his eyes and told him to go to Siloam and wash, that he not only believes in Him but worships Him (see ix. 35–38). So real, indeed, is the humanity of the Word-made-flesh that the wonder that He could ever return to His pre-incarnate state is no less than the wonder that He could ever have left it (see vi. 62 and iii. 13). In a word, although the later Gnostics made very considerable use of the Fourth Gospel, and one of their number Heracleon was the first commentator upon it of whose work we have any considerable remains, no document is in fact more anti-Gnostic, though the detailed Gnostic systems had not been formulated when it was written.

A Saviour who was Son of God without being Son of man

could never have called forth a response from the human heart, for the words put into the mouth of David by Robert Browning find an echo in every man and woman:

> 'Tis the weakness in strength that I long for!
>   my flesh that I seek
> In the Godhead! I seek and I find it. O Saul,
>   it shall be
> A Face like my face that receives thee; a Man
>   like to me,
> Thou shalt love and be loved by, for ever; a
>   Hand like this hand
> Shall throw open the gates of new life to the e
>   See the Christ stand.

Nowhere can we 'see the Christ stand' in this sense more clearly than in the Gospel of John, the Gospel of the Word-made-flesh; and to a consideration of its text we now direct our attention.

ANALYSIS

I. JESUS THE WORD OF GOD, INCARNATE AND REVEALED (i. 1–ii. 11).

a. The prologue (i. 1–18).
b. A week of witness and revelation (i. 19–ii. 11).

II. THE NEW TEMPLE: THE NEW BIRTH: THE NEW WORSHIP (ii. 12–iv. 54).

a. The cleansing of the temple (ii. 12–25).
b. The interview with Nicodemus (iii. 1–21).
c. John the Baptist's final witness to Jesus (iii. 22–36).
d. The woman of Samaria (iv. 1–42).
e. The nobleman's son (iv. 43–54).

III. THE UNBELIEF OF ISRAEL (v. 1–vi. 71).

a. Introduction.
b. The disabled man at Bethesda (v. 1–47).
c. The feeding of the five thousand (vi. 1–71).

IV. JESUS THE APOSTLE OF GOD: THE GIVER OF SIGHT: THE SHEPHERD OF THE SHEEP (vii. 1–x. 21).

a. The Feast of Tabernacles (vii. 1–13).
b. Jesus the Apostle of God (vii. 14–52).
[Jesus and the woman taken in adultery (vii. 53–viii. 11).]
c. Jesus the Light of the world (viii. 12–30).
d. Christian freedom (viii. 31–59).
e. The man born blind (ix. 1–41).
f. Jesus the Good Shepherd (x. 1–21).

V. JESUS THE GIVER OF ETERNAL LIFE (x. 22–xii. 50).

a. The Festival of Dedication (x. 22–42).
b. The raising of Lazarus (xi. 1–57).
c. The supper at Bethany (xii. 1–8).
d. The triumphal entry and the final rejection (xii. 9–50).

VI. THE UPPER ROOM (xiii. 1–xvii. 26).

a. The feet-washing (xiii. 1–17).
b. The traitor (xiii. 18–35).
c. The disciples' questions (xiii. 36–xiv. 31).
d. The allegory of the vine (xv. 1–16).
e. Persecution (xv. 17–25).
f. The work of the Advocate (xv. 26–xvi. 15).
g. The 'little while' (xvi. 16–33).
h. The prayer of the great High Priest (xvii. 1–26).

VII. THE ARREST, THE TRIALS, AND THE CRUCIFIXION OF JESUS (xviii. 1–xix. 37).

a. The arrest of Jesus (xviii. 1–11).
b. The trial before the high priest (xviii. 12–27).
c. The trial before Pilate (xviii. 28–xix. 16).
d. The crucifixion (xix. 17–37).

VIII. THE BURIAL AND RESURRECTION OF JESUS (xix. 38–xx. 31).

a. The burial (xix. 38–42).
b. The resurrection appearances (xx. 1–29).
c. The purpose of the evangelist (xx. 30, 31).

IX. THE EPILOGUE (xxi. 1–23).

X. THE CONCLUSION (xxi. 24, 25).

grace and truth which *came by Jesus Christ* can never be dissociated from Himself (17). Even to the Christian, however, the invisible God remains invisible. But to know Jesus Christ and to listen to what He has declared to us about His heavenly Father, is to know all that we in our creaturely state are capable of knowing. One day, as our evangelist tells us elsewhere, we shall see Him as He is (see 1 Jn. iii. 2).

Additional Notes

1. *In the beginning;* i.e. when creation began. *Was* (*ēn*), i.e. was already in existence. *With God,* i.e. abode with God. The Word was a separate Person within the Godhead.

Was God. In the original, there is no definite article before God. The significance of this is that the Word does not by Himself make up the entire Godhead; nevertheless the divinity that belongs to the rest of the Godhead belongs also to Him.

3. *Were made.* The Greek *egeneto* is better rendered 'came into existence'.

3, 4. *That was made.* In the first three centuries it was customary to punctuate so that these words formed the subject of the first clause in verse 4. 'All that came into existence found its life in Him.' But from the time of Chrysostom, to avoid the danger of the Holy Spirit being classed among 'things made', the sentence came to be punctuated as in the AV translation. This is almost certainly not what the author intended. Not only is the rhythm of the Greek against it; but on this exegesis the words become tautological.

5. The Greek word *katalambano*, like the Latin *comprehendo* and the English *comprehend* (RV 'apprehend'), can denote either grasping with the mind, or grasping by force and overwhelming. It is possible that the evangelist intended the word to have this double nuance here, but more probably he is stating that the light has been shining and is still shining, and never has the darkness been able to obliterate it. So RSV 'the darkness has not overcome it'. The aorist tense of the verb implies that there has never been a single instance of such a defeat. It is best translated by an English perfect. The most signal example of the failure of the darkness was its inability to destroy Jesus. He, the true Light, still shines on.

6. *There was a man.* The Greek *egeneto* means 'there appeared on the stage of history'.

7. *Through him*; i.e. through John. It was John who first pointed men to Jesus as the Light, and it was through the belief of these men that others came to believe. Therefore all believers have in a sense been first brought to faith by John.

8. It may be that the emphatic denial of this verse is prompted by a desire to combat those in the evangelist's day who were making exaggerated claims on behalf of John the Baptist.

9. The word *alēthinos*, here translated *true*, denotes 'real' as opposed to 'counterfeit', rather than 'truthful' (*alēthēs*) as opposed to 'false'. It is a key word of the Gospel. See note on xv. 1.

That cometh into the world. It is possible to take this in agreement with *every man* as AV, or as the predicate of *was.* So RSV 'The true light that enlightens every man was coming into the world', i.e. at the time John was ministering. It is rather strange however to speak of a person already adult as 'coming into the world'; and, as Knox says, 'the notion of our Lord coming into the world by (as it were) a continuous process seems foreign to New Testament thought'. The AV rendering may therefore be right. It does not imply that the enlightenment takes place at the moment of human birth, for 'every man that cometh into the world' is a rabbinic way of saying 'everyone who is born'.

The world. This is the first occurrence of a word which is found frequently in this Gospel and in the First Epistle of John. It translates the Greek *kosmos*, which means the ordered universe; in the Johannine writings however it has the distinctive sense of the disordered, fallen world.[1]

[1] There is an interesting study of 'The World' in E. C. Hoskyns, *Cambridge Sermons* (S.P.C.K., 1938), pp. 97–104.

10. The disordered world could not continue to exist for a moment apart from the life imparted to it by its Creator, but fallen man, in spite of the light that is in him, fails to recognize the world's Creator and Preserver (see Rom. i. 20).

11. The word translated *his own* on its first occurrence in this verse is in the neuter (*ta idia*), and on its second is in the masculine (*hoi idioi*). The distinction should be brought out in translation. RV renders *hoi idioi* 'they that were his own', but keeps *his own* for *ta idia*. The light given to all men by the Word was bestowed in special measure on the Israelites, chosen by God to be the recipients of a special revelation about Himself. When the Word became flesh in a Jewish child in the land of Israel, He was in a real sense coming to His home, but His own kinsmen gave Him no welcome. So RSV 'He came to his own home, and his own people received him not'. Professor E. M. Blaiklock, in a comment on the meaning of *ta idia* in Acts xxi. 6 where AV renders 'home', writes, 'This is the only rendering Greek has for the peculiarly English expression "home". It is curious that the AV was not bold enough to translate similarly another context where the same phrase occurs, Jn. i. 11.'[1]

12. *Believe on his name;* i.e. give their allegiance to Him because He is what His name (or names) imply that He is.

13. *Which were born.* One MS of the old Latin version has 'who was born'; and Tertullian assumes that this is the right reading. If the singular is read, there is a clear reference to the virgin birth of Jesus. But the MSS evidence for the plural is overwhelming, and the concept of the new birth of Christians is an important theme of the Gospel. It may be that the particular language in which this new birth is here described is influenced by a knowledge of the virgin birth, but this must remain a matter of opinion.

Not of blood. The English versions translate by the singular what in the original is in the plural. It is usually supposed that 'bloods' reflects the belief that the blood of the two parents

[1] *The Acts of the Apostles* (*Tyndale New Testament Commentaries*, 1959) p. 170.

was intermingled in the formation of the human embryo. So Knox paraphrases 'not from human stock'. Hoskyns, on the other hand, comments 'The Evangelist cannot write that the Christians were not born of blood (singular), because their birth does in fact depend upon a death which later he describes as involving the outpouring of blood (xix. 34)'.

14. *Dwelt.* The Greek word *eskēnōsen* implies 'dwelt as in a tent' or 'tabernacled'. Its use here might be to emphasize that the incarnate life of the Word was but a temporary sojourning. More probably, it means that the divine presence, which it was believed was especially 'located' in the tabernacle and later in the temple, now came to dwell in the man Jesus.

We includes the author and other Christians who saw Jesus during His earthly life.

As of does not mean 'as if it were the glory of'. It defines the character of the glory. So Knox 'glory such as belongs to the Father's only-begotten Son'.

Grace and truth. This expression is probably influenced by the association in many passages in the Psalms of 'mercy' and 'truth', the evangelist substituting *grace* (here only in this Gospel) for 'mercy'. As Hoskyns points out, *grace* emerges in the rest of this Gospel as love and is to be seen displayed particularly in the actions of Jesus; *truth*, on the other hand, is evident more especially in His words.

15. John, though he was part of the darkness of the world, and though he belonged to the people to whom the Word-made-flesh came, was the glorious exception to the rejection stated in the words 'his own received him not'. He *bare witness* to the Word-made-flesh, to His superiority to himself, and to His prior existence.

16. *All we;* i.e. all of us Christians including those who never saw Christ in the flesh.

Grace for grace. The preposition *anti* here translated *for* does not mean 'grace answering to grace' (so Knox), but 'grace upon grace' (RSV), grace to meet every need that arises (see 2 Cor. xii. 9). *And* before *grace* should be 'even'.

17. The contrasts in this verse are not only between law and grace, and between Moses and Jesus, but between *was given* and *came*. Grace and truth are as much gifts of God as the law; but, while the law can be separated from Moses the lawgiver, and is in some of its aspects of a temporary nature, grace and truth cannot be separated from Him in whom they are embodied. As Westcott comments, 'The law was "given" for a special purpose. On the other hand, the Gospel "came" (*egeneto*), as if, according to the orderly and due course of the divine plan, this was the natural issue of all that had gone before.' Knox translates 'Through Moses the law was given to us; through Jesus Christ grace came to us, and truth'.

18. *In the bosom of* is a Hebrew idiom expressing the intimate relationship of child and parent, and of friend and friend (cf. xiii. 23).

Declared him. The Greek verb is *exēgoumai*; it means to 'expound' or 'interpret' or 'reveal a mystery'. RSV renders 'has made him known'.

b. A week of witness and revelation (i. 19–ii. 11)

The evangelist now elucidates further the nature of John's witness to Jesus, which has been touched upon in the prologue, and relates the circumstances under which some of the earliest disciples of Jesus first came into contact with Him. This section of the narrative culminates in the first 'sign' at Cana-in-Galilee; and it covers events which are presented as taking place on what would appear to be successive days in a single week.

First, the evangelist wishes his readers to know that John neither did, nor could, claim to be either the Messiah, or one of the great Old Testament figures who would, it was believed, be reincarnated before Messiah came. On the contrary, when the Jews sent priests and Levites to interrogate him, on the first day of what was destined to be a memorable week, he asserted without any reservation and with deep humility that he was neither the Christ, nor Elijah *redivivus*, nor the prophet, of whom God had spoken when He said He would raise up a prophet who would be a second Moses (see Dt. xviii. 15). John's lowly estimate of himself was that he was a *voice* (23), though, to be sure, no less a voice than the voice which heralded the release of Israel from the Babylonian exile (see Is. xl. 3). It was a voice both stern and comforting. It cried out in the wilderness of the world's need and pointed men to Him who alone can satisfy it; but it also called upon them to prepare the way for His coming by removing all that was crooked in their conduct and narrow in their outlook, like men turning a winding, narrow track in the desert into a royal highway, broad and straight. It is true that John acted as well as spoke. He was a prophet in deed, as well as in word. He baptized, and was engaged in that work when the Jewish deputation found him 'in Bethany beyond Jordan' (28, RV). But his water-baptism was negative rather than positive; it cleansed but it bestowed no gift by which the cleansed could remain clean. There was, however, standing in the present company, unrecognized by all except John, One who would supply that gift; for, as John soon reveals, He would batize with the Holy Spirit. He appeared in human history later than John, but He took preference over him, for He was already in existence when John was born; and so exalted was His status that John felt himself unworthy to render Him even such menial service as unfastening the strap of His sandals.

On the second day, John sees Jesus approaching. It soon becomes apparent to the reader that John has already baptized Jesus, and that he has been led by prophetic insight to recognize Him as the One for whose coming Israel was looking, and who would baptize with Holy Spirit, because, though a man, He was the Son of God who knew the mind and will of God as only such a Son could know it. But, as this Gospel makes abundantly clear, this baptism with the Spirit is consequent upon the redemption won for mankind by Jesus' death; it could not become effective before His atoning sacrifice had been offered. No witness to Jesus therefore is adequate which does not draw attention to His work as Saviour. Accordingly, as soon as Jesus approaches him, John designates Him, in the hearing, presumably, of his disciples, though they are not mentioned at this point, *the Lamb of God, which taketh away the sin of the world* (29). As God had provided a lamb for sacrifice in the place of Isaac (Gn. xxii. 8), so Jesus is the Lamb provided by God to be sacrificed in the place of others. He also fulfils the ritual of the Passover in which the lamb was the effective symbol of salvation from destruction (see Ex. xii. 3-17). Moreover, as a Lamb led to the slaughter and bearing the sins of many He discharges the role of the suffering Servant delineated in Isaiah liii. But John penetrates still deeper into the mystery of atonement when he states that in taking upon Himself the sin of the world Jesus 'takes it away', removing both its guilt and power.

On the third day, John repeats this testimony to Jesus as the Lamb of God to two of his disciples, one of whom the evangelist tells us later was named Andrew; and they at once transfer their allegiance from himself to Jesus, as John intended that they should. In presenting the two first disciples of Jesus as giving their allegiance to Him as *the Lamb of God* (36), however inadequately they may have understood at the time all that such a title involved, our evangelist makes it clear at the outset of his Gospel that what differentiates discipleship of Jesus from discipleship of John, or discipleship of anyone else in the world, is the recognition that Jesus is what John could never be, the Saviour of men. It was in fact a long time before the disciples of Jesus understood why He had to offer His life in sacrifice; and it was not until He was raised from the dead, and the Spirit was given at Pentecost, that they were very sure, in the words of Paul, that He had been delivered up for their trespasses and raised for their justification (Rom. iv. 25).

The first recorded word of Jesus in this Gospel is of great interest and significance. It is a question put by Him to the two disciples who have been directed to Him as the Lamb of God; and the form of the question should be noted. Jesus does not ask *who* they are looking for, but *what* they are looking for (38). It is almost as if He assumes that, like the rest of mankind, they are in pursuit of the *thing* which will satisfy their needs, give reality to their dreams and substance to their hopes. They are soon to discover that the *thing* is in fact a person, the very Person who now confronts them. At the moment, to be sure, Jesus is little more to them than a Rabbi from whom they have much to learn; and instead of answering His question they reply with a counter-question, *where dwellest thou?* (38). On the surface this is a request for information about His lodging that they may visit Him for further instruction. But like so many words in this Gospel, the word *dwell* (RV 'abide') has a double significance. Jesus may have one or more temporary shelters during His earthly pilgrimage, though none of them He can call His own; but He has one home which is most surely His. Even while on earth He dwells continually in heaven in unbroken union with His Father. So when He answers the question, *where dwellest thou?*, by saying *Come and see*, He is in fact bidding these men do something more than discover where He is staying for the night; He is inviting them to come and gain from Him an insight into the mind and purpose of God Himself. The third never-to-be-forgotten day of this wonderful week ends with these two ex-disciples of John staying with Jesus, and beginning to find in Him their strength and stay, and coming to understand that discipleship means nothing less than abiding with Him for ever.

It is of the nature of Christian experience that those who enjoy it, however partially, desire to share it with others. It is not therefore surprising that, as soon as the new day dawns, the first thing that Andrew does is to find his brother Simon, break the news to him that the Christ had appeared, and bring him to Jesus. Simon responds immediately, as he will always respond immediately, for good or for evil, to every challenge presented to him. He is at once given a new name, a sign that he will become a new man in Christ Jesus. He who knows what is in a man, knows that Simon had the affection, the loyalty, and the enthusiasm which, after he has been disciplined by the salutary expenceeri of failure and disappointment, will one day make him a man of granite. *Thou art*

Simon the son of Jona: thou shalt be called Cephas, which is by interpretation, A stone (42). It is noticeable, however, that Jesus only once addresses Simon by his new name 'Peter' (the Greek equivalent for *Cephas*) during His earthly life and only then, it would seem, to remind him that he had not yet proved worthy of it (see Lk. xxii. 34).

On the fifth day, before leaving for Galilee, Jesus invites Philip, who came from the same town as Andrew and Peter, and was therefore probably already known to them, to be another of His intimate friends who would soon form what the *Te Deum* calls 'the glorious company of the apostles'. To the evangelist the chief interest of Philip at the moment is that he at once brings another future apostle to Jesus. *Nathanael* is said later in the Gospel to have come from Cana in Galilee (xxi. 2), where the divine glory of Jesus is soon to be displayed in the first miracle that He wrought. But something of that glory is revealed to Nathanael almost immediately. His first reaction to what Philip has to tell him is very different from Simon's. He welcomes the news that Philip has found the One to whom both parts of the Scriptures were pointing—the Christ predicted by Moses and the prophets. But when Philip identifies this Christ with *Jesus of Nazareth, the son of Joseph* (45), Nathanael's prejudice is at once aroused. Nazareth was in Galilee, and Galilee had only produced hot-headed fanatics and bogus-Christs. Prejudice can be overcome only by studying all the available evidence. So Philip bids Nathanael do what Jesus had invited Andrew and the other disciple to do, to *come and see* for himself (46). Jesus with divine insight sees that the scepticism of Nathanael is in some degree at least due to his not unworthy pride in being a member of God's chosen people. Nathanael indeed deserves to bear the great name originally given to Jacob after he had wrestled with God and abandoned the cunning that had so disfigured his early life (see Gn. xxxii. 28). He is a proper *Israelite*, a type of the man pronounced 'blessed' by the Psalmist, the man 'in whose spirit there is no guile' (Ps. xxxii. 2). He makes the first venture of faith by coming to see for himself, and is deeply moved by what he sees and hears. Jesus had seen and known him before Philip called him! Such knowledge was no merely human intuition, and it calls forth from Nathanael the penetrating response *Rabbi, thou art the Son of God; thou art the King of Israel* (49).

But Nathanael's confession, though true, is not the whole truth. The second half of it, in particular, is liable to be misunderstood. For Jesus is not King of Israel alone; and His kingship is not the same as other kingships. Full faith in Him must be grounded, as He now tells Nathanael, upon the conviction that in Him as He now is, i.e. in the Word-made-flesh, is to be found the meeting-place of heaven and earth. Jacob at Bethel had dreamed of a ladder set up on earth, whose top reached to heaven (Gn. xxviii. 12). Perhaps this was the passage of Scripture which Nathanael was reading, as he sat at home, under the fig tree, when Philip found him. He now learns that Jesus is the real ladder by which the gulf between earth and heaven is bridged. In Him the glory of heaven has come down to earth, made visible in One who is Himself a man; and through contact with Him earthbound man is lifted up to heaven. This may be said to be the dominant theme of the Gospel of John. The evangelist is never tired of underlining the truth that Jesus was what He was, that He did what He did, and spoke as He spoke, because He lived in perpetual communion with His heavenly Father. To know Jesus is therefore to know the Father. Nathanael is now promised that he and all who live in constant companionship with Jesus, who is both Son of God and Son of man, 'very God and very man', will be granted that knowledge. *Because I said unto thee, I saw thee under the fig tree, believest thou? thou shalt see greater things than these.* Then, turning to the others, He added, *Verily, verily, I say unto you, Hereafter ye shall see heaven open, and the angels of God ascending and descending upon the Son of man* (50, 51).

The sixth day of this initial week would seem to be passed over in silence. But on *the third day* (ii. 1), i.e. two days after Nathanael had received the assurance of the greater things that he would see, on the occasion of a wedding at Cana, Nathanael's native village, Jesus in the presence of His disciples performs a miracle, which is the first of a series of 'sign's that precede the passion. The turning of water into wine is not a purposeless exhibition of supernatural power, but a teaching miracle of deep significance. Some critics have compared this 'luxury' miracle, as they have termed it, very unfavourably with the merciful acts of healing performed by Jesus. Was it really necessary, they have asked, to supply a wedding party with such an abundance of wine? And, even though the host was helped out of an embarrassing situation can it honestly be said that the miracle bestowed any lasting benefit on those who were present? But these are the wrong questions to ask; for none of the miracles of Jesus were kind actions to alleviate human distress *and nothing more*. They were, as this Gospel invariably calls them, *signs* displaying the glory of Jesus and the wonder of His redeeming love.

This particular miracle is not followed by a discourse expounding its spiritual truth. We are compelled therefore to deduce its significance as best we can from the narrative itself considered in the context of the Gospel as a whole; and it is a reasonable surmise, when these factors are borne in mind, that Jesus wished, through the symbolism of water turned into wine, both to expose the inadequacy of Judaism as a religion of salvation, and to initiate His disciples into the necessity for His own redeeming death. The *six waterpots of stone* were set there, the evangelist states, *after the manner of the purifying of the Jews*. This would seem to be something more than an explanatory note for the benefit of non-Jewish readers. It may well provide the clue to the interpretation of the incident. The water contained in these vessels was used for the ceremonial washing of hands as well as for the cleansing of drinking utensils. It was indicative both of the nature and of the weakness of Pharisaism. It was *this* water (not necessarily all of it, but the amount drawn off by the servants and conveyed by them to the steward in charge) that Jesus turned into wine—wine which, because it gives life and strength and, as the Psalmist said, 'makes glad the heart of man', is a fitting symbol of the new spiritual power made available for mankind by the shedding of the blood of Jesus.

In performing this sign it would seem that the thoughts of Jesus were turned to the goal towards which His earthly life was inevitably moving. It may well be that by some mysterious association of ideas the brief but poignant words of His mother, *they have no wine* (3), expressing her sensitive concern for the distress of their host, suggested to Jesus the much deeper need of humanity that He had come on earth to satisfy. It was because men 'had no wine', because they had no inherent strength to save themselves from the dire predicament in which they stood as sinners, that Jesus was destined, in Isaiah's words, 'to tread the wine-press alone' (see Is. lxiii. 3), and pour out the wine of His own most precious blood. That this is something more than the whim of a fanciful imagination is seen in the reply of Jesus to His mother, which has long been a *crux interpretum.* Without in the least reproving her, He indicates that *His* concern is very different from *hers*, *so* different that neither she nor any other human being can share it. Moreover, it is impossible to interpret the words *mine hour* on the lips of Jesus without reference to other passages in the Gospel where 'the hour' invariably refers to the hour of the passion. The certainty that one day that hour would strike would seem to have conditioned, directly or indirectly, all that Jesus said or did in preparation for it and not least the signs He performed, even, we may believe, when He was present with His disciples at a village wedding, into the happiness of which He would be eager that both He and they should enter.

But this greater concern of Jesus did not prevent Him from acceding to His mother's unspoken request. He will indeed take action, as she was very sure He would when she told the servants to do whatever He told them, but He will act in His own way, for His own reasons, and at His own time. He had not come into the world *primarily* to satisfy men's physical needs, nor *primarily* to add to the sum total of their happiness; and it would not be solely for either or both of these reasons that He would exercise His supernatural power on this occasion. He would act because wine, lavishly provided and freely offered, was a fitting symbol of the full salvation to be won by the sacrifice of the Lamb of God. The real significance of Jesus' action in turning water into wine at Cana must always be hidden from those whose faith is not centred upon Christ crucified. To 'the steward of the feast' (8, RSV) the fresh supply of wine, whose source was unknown to him, was merely a cause for surprise that the bridegroom should have kept back for so long wine of such good vintage. *The disciples* alone, as the evangelist states at the conclusion of the narrative (11), saw in what had happened a revelation of the glory of Jesus, and, we may not unreasonably infer, a further ground for believing in Him as the Lamb of God destined to take away the sin of the world.

Additional Notes

i. 19. The expression *the Jews* in this Gospel designates either 'the Judaeans' or, as here, 'the Jewish religious authorities'. The frequent use of this term does not indicate that the author is not himself a Jew. Writing for non-Jewish readers he frequently does not differentiate between the different parties within Judaism but uses this comprehensive title.

21. John the Baptist, it is evident, did not himself claim to be another Elijah. Jesus however did not discourage people from thinking of John under this category. 'If you are willing to accept it', He told them, 'he is Elijah who is to come' (Mt. xi. 14, RSV).

24. The text followed by AV implies that the whole deputation consisted of Pharisees, the evangelist, as so often, supplying this information somewhat late in his narrative. A variant reading is translated by RV and RSV 'they had been sent from the Pharisees'; this also is a delayed footnote. The variant could also be rendered 'some Pharisees had also been sent', implying that it is *they*, and not the Sadducees in the deputation, who now intervene by asking 'Why baptizest thou?'.

28. The best attested reading is 'Bethany beyond Jordan' (RV and RSV), so described to distinguish it from the better-known Bethany on the mount of Olives (xi. 18). It was an obscure village, and *Bethabara* was substituted for it at an early date. There is a further reference to the locality in x. 40.

39. *The tenth hour.* For the reckoning of time in this Gospel see the Additional Note on xix. 14.

40. It is usually assumed, probably right, that the other *of the two* was John the son of Zebedee, unmentioned by name in this Gospel. It may well be that he also fetched his brother James, but it will be evident from the note on the next verse that this is by no means a certain inference from the text.

41. *First.* There are three readings here:

1. *prōtos*, a superlative adjective in the nominative singular agreeing with the subject of the sentence. Those who adopt this reading usually interpret the superlative as a comparative, giving the sense 'Andrew *before the other* of the two disciples found *his own* brother', implying that later the other disciple (probably John the son of Zebedee) found *his* brother James.

2. *prōton*, which is the best attested reading of the three. This can be construed in two ways, (a) as an adjective in the masculine accusative case agreeing with *brother*, giving the sense, 'Andrew found his own brother *first*, and later found someone else'. Those who accept this assume that it was Andrew, not Jesus, who subsequently found Philip, pointing out that it is not necessary to assume that Jesus is the subject of the verb *would go forth* and *findeth* in verse 43 but only of *saith*. So RV renders verse 43, 'On the morrow he was minded to go forth into Galilee, and he findeth Philip: and Jesus saith unto him, Follow me.' (b) As an adverb, giving the sense, 'The first thing that Andrew did was to find his brother' (there is no necessity to translate 'his own' as the Greek word *idios* does not always convey that emphasis in late Greek). This is probably the best sense that can be made of the passage. It does not necessarily imply that it was Andrew who found Philip later, but it does not rule out the possibility.

3. *prōi*, 'early' (i.e. early next morning). This reading is found only in a few MSS giving an ancient Latin version, and in the old Syriac version. It is possible, as Bernard argues, that

this is the original reading, but it would seem to be more naturally explained as an attempt to avoid the difficulties of the other readings. It makes it clear that Andrew found Simon on the day after Andrew and the other of John's disciples followed Jesus. This is implicit in verse 39, where it is stated that it was *about the tenth hour* when the two disciples arrived at Jesus' lodging, and stayed with him the rest of *that day*.

Findeth probably implies that Andrew went to look for Simon, not that he accidentally met him. (So also in verses 43 and 45.)

43. It is much more probable that the decision to move to Galilee, which is here recorded, is *Jesus*' and not Andrew's. So AV and RSV. The RV rendering leaves the matter open. The subject of *would go forth* is in fact the same as that of the last sentence in verse 42. AV would appear to be right also in assuming that it was Jesus and not Andrew who found Philip.

45. The close association of Philip with Bartholomew in the first three Gospels, and the juxtaposition of Philip and Nathanael in this passage, have led Christians from the earliest days to identify Bartholomew with Nathanael.

50. Nathanael was dwelling safely *under the fig tree* when Philip called him away to what was to prove to be the greater spiritual security of becoming a disciple of Jesus, even though it would involve leaving his earthly home. (See 1 Ki. iv. 25 and Mi. iv. 4.)

51. For the significance of *Verily, verily* see note on iii. 3.

ii. 4. *Woman* in the vocative in modern English conveys the erroneous impression that Jesus is reproving His mother. 'Lady' will not do as a substitute, for as Knox remarks, 'It may have been all right in the Middle Ages, but it is a form of address only tramps use now.'[1]

What have I to do with thee? translates the Greek equivalent of a Hebrew idiom 'What to me and thee'. Its meaning depends not a little on the context in which it is found. In the

[1] *The Gospels and Epistles*, p. 55.

Old Testament it often means 'Don't bother me. Leave me alone'. On the lips of the demoniacs in Mk. i. 24 it implies 'What have we in common with you?'. Here, as has been suggested above, the probable meaning is, 'Your concern and mine are not the same.'

6. A *firkin* according to the *Concise Oxford Dictionary* is half a kilderkin which consists of 16 or 18 gallons. The waterpots therefore contained some 20 to 30 gallons each.

8. It is difficult to adopt Westcott's suggestion, which has been followed by many scholars, that this verse implies an order to the servants that they should draw up still more water after the six jars had been filled, and that it was this *further supply* which was turned into wine, and not the water already in the jars. The word translated *draw* does not necessarily mean 'draw up' (i.e. from a well) but could mean 'draw off'. Nor need the insertion of *now* convey the emphasis given it by Knox, '*Now* send the bucket down and see what will happen',[1] or imply the interpretation of Westcott, 'Hitherto they had drawn to fill the vessels of purification: they were charged *now* to draw and bear to the ruler of the feast.' Westcott's exegesis makes verses 6 and 7 somewhat pointless; and the suggestion that there would be special significance in the *seventh* act of drawing is fanciful. It is not necessary to assume that all the water in all the jars was converted into wine. Probably the miracle was enacted after the servants had drawn out some of the water from one of the jars and were conveying it to the steward in charge.

II. THE NEW TEMPLE: THE NEW BIRTH: THE NEW WORSHIP (ii. 12–iv. 54)

a. The cleansing of the temple (ii. 12–25)

The expression *After this* or *After these things* would seem in this Gospel sometimes, as here, to introduce a new section; and the present section may be regarded as extending to the end of

[1] *The Gospels and Epistles*, p. 56.

chapter iv with a minor break at iii. 21. All divisions of the narrative must however be conjectural, as the ancient manuscripts offer us no help in this matter.

After a brief notice of a visit of Jesus to Capernaum with His mother, brothers, and disciples, which lasted but a few days, the scene shifts to Jerusalem and the temple. The reader of the earlier Gospels is well aware that at the beginning of the last week of His earthly life Jesus as Messiah presented a final challenge to the Jewish authorities in the incident commonly known as 'the cleansing of the temple', and that this led directly to the passion (see Mk. xi. 18). By recording an account of a similar event on the occasion of the first visit of Jesus to Jerusalem after His Messianic ministry began, John is not correcting a supposed chronological blunder on the part of the earlier evangelists, nor deliberately altering their history in the interests of theological exposition, but, we may reasonably suppose, relating an additional 'cleansing' which the Synoptic writers had no occasion to relate, for it did not form part of the Petrine, Galilaean tradition which they were embodying. Many modern scholars have found great difficulty in supposing that Jesus twice 'cleansed' the temple. Thus V. H. Stanton wrote, 'When in different ancient documents we find two accounts in many respects so similar referring to different times, it is on the whole most probable that we have to do with different traditions about the same event.' And Bernard comments, 'apart from the fact that the duplication of similar incidents is improbable, we find it difficult to suppose that this particular incident, or anything like it, could have happened at so early a stage in the ministry of Jesus as is suggested by the traditional order of chapters in the Fourth Gospel.' But in reply it may be suggested that it was because Jesus made this early attack upon traditional Pharisaic worship at the capital, that the mission of scribes was sent from Jerusalem to Galilee, when they entered upon what was virtually a 'counter-attack' by asserting that Jesus was possessed by Beelzebub. This mission is mentioned, without any explanation of its origin, in Mark iii. 22.

John is here concerned, as always, with the light thrown by

this incident upon the Person of Jesus and the nature of His work. In narrating it in the manner he does he suggests to the reader that the first visit of Jesus to Jerusalem after His earthly ministry began was made in the spirit of Malachi's prophecy, though he does not actually quote it. 'The Lord, whom ye seek, shall suddenly come to his temple, even the messenger of the covenant, whom ye delight in. . . . But who may abide the day of his coming? . . . for he is like a refiner's fire . . . and he shall purify the sons of Levi . . . that they may offer unto the Lord an offering in righteousness' (Mal. iii. 1–3). He also desires to draw attention to one of the most distinctive and fundamental truths about Jesus, a truth implicit also, as has been suggested, in the miracle at Cana, that Jesus offered the sacrifice of His own perfect life because the ancient sacrificial system, which had come to be confined to the Jerusalem temple, was unable by reason of its many imperfections to secure remission of sins.

It would seem very inadequate to regard the action of Jesus on this occasion as something which any zealous prophet eager to reform the worship of his day might have felt moved to do. For John's narrative makes it clear that in fact Jesus was not seeking to reform the old system but to abolish it. He is not denouncing the fraudulence of the money-changers, but objecting to any business at all being transacted in the temple precincts. *Take these things hence*; *make not my Father's house an house of merchandise* (16). But merchandise there had to be, if Jews from the Dispersion who came up for the festivals were to have the opportunity of exchanging their money and buying the animals necessary for sacrifice. The evangelist also states that the disciples came to associate what Jesus was doing with the prophetic words of Psalm lxix. 9, 'Zeal for thy house will consume me' (17, RSV), thereby bringing the cleansing of the temple into close connection with the necessity for Jesus' death. He also states that the Jews demanded from Jesus a sign which would show that He had authority for doing what He did, a demand prompted by the conviction that He was in fact challenging their sacrificial system; and it is extremely significant that this request was met by Jesus with a counter-challenge which, as the disciples came to see after the resurrection, was prophetic of His own death and resurrection. *Destroy this temple, and in three days I will raise it up* (19).

In Mark's account of the later cleansing, Jesus recalls that the temple had been intended by God to be, in Isaiah's words, 'an house of prayer for all people' (Is. lvi. 7; see Mk. xi. 17), but that it had become more like what Jeremiah called 'a den of robbers', a place of imagined sanctuary where murderers, adulterers and idolaters fondly supposed they could salve their consciences by performing religious ceremonies in honour of the God of Israel! (See Je. vii. 8–11.) John records that, when the disciples reflected on the drastic action of their Master, they became more and more convinced that His zeal for purity of worship was one of the necessary reasons for His death. His zeal for God's house was bound to lead to His own destruction. Westcott denies any reference in the words 'will consume' to Jesus' death, for, he says, 'it is not natural to suppose that the disciples had at the time any clear apprehension of what the issue would be'. But the words *his disciples remembered* in verse 17 do not necessarily mean that the disciples remembered at the time of the event. They may well have the same significance that they have in verse 22. It was the failure to understand that the disciples regarded the Psalmist's words as prophetic of Christ's death and the assumption that they referred to the energy and fearlessness of Jesus on this occasion, that gave rise to the later and poorly attested reading followed by AV *hath eaten me up* in verse 17.

But the old system of worship had to be destroyed only that a new one might take its place. The mission of Jesus was far from being merely negative and destructive. He had come to make possible a more direct approach by men to God in a purer worship by offering His own body in sacrifice, an offering whose acceptance by the Father as an all-sufficient atonement would be signified by His resurrection on the third day. All believers who accepted His sacrifice would become part of His body and so enabled to offer themselves, in Paul's words, 'a living sacrifice, holy, acceptable unto God' (Rom. xii. 1). This is the truth conveyed in the somewhat enigmatical words recorded by John as Jesus' answer to the demand by the Jews for a sign. As always, Jesus refuses to give any sign other than what is already inherent in what He is saying and doing. Instead, He utters words which were destined to receive wide circulation, for they were quoted inaccurately by false-witnesses at His trial, who affirmed 'We heard him say, I will destroy (in Matthew's account, 'I am able to destroy') this temple that is made with hands, and within three days I will build another made without hands' (Mk. xiv. 58; Mt. xxvi. 61). And, according to Matthew, the passers-by taunted Jesus with the same words, as He hung upon the cross (see Mt. xxvii. 40). In John's narrative, it is made clear that what Jesus actually said was in the nature of a challenge to the Jews, *Destroy this temple, and in three days I will raise it up* (19). The Jews interpret His words in a materialistic sense, and ridicule His absurd claim to perform an architectural impossibility. What Jesus was implying, however, and what, as the evangelist records, the disciples came to see clearly after His resurrection when they recalled the incident, was the truth that His own death and the destruction of the temple are inevitably linked together. It is not without significance that it was on the eve of the passion that Jesus foretold the destruction of the temple together with the other fine buildings of Jerusalem (see Mk. xiii. 2). Indeed it would be true to say that, because the temple had to be destroyed as an act of judgment upon the unspiritual nature of the worship that had come to be offered in it, Jesus had to die. But that death was no mere passive submission to the unruly wills of sinful men; it was a voluntary surrender of life wholly acceptable to the Father, and destined to be followed within three days by the resurrection. And as a result of the resurrection a new spiritual temple could emerge —the fellowship of believers, a shrine of the indwelling Spirit (see 1 Cor. iii. 17).

During this Passover, as the evangelist notices, many were led to a belief in Jesus because of *the miracles* (RV 'signs') they had seen Him perform (23). It is clear, however, from the sequel that to *these* believers the miracles were not signs indicative of the true nature of Jesus. He did not therefore 'trust himself to them' (24, RSV). With His unique insight into human nature, emphasized by the evangelist, we may surmise that He regarded all belief in Him as superficial which does not have as its most essential elements the consciousness of the need for forgiveness and the conviction that He alone is the Mediator of that forgiveness.

Additional Notes

ii. 14. The word here translated *temple, hieron*, is used for the whole of the temple precincts, and is distinct from the word *naos* used in verses 19 and 21, which refers to the inner shrine or sanctuary.

15. A few Greek MSS followed by the Latin versions insert the word *hōs*, meaning 'as if', before *of small cords*. So Knox, 'he made a kind of whip out of cords'. The RV translation 'cast all out of the temple, both the sheep and the oxen' implies that only animals felt the whip. AV rightly has *and* where RV has 'both'. *All* must include the persons mentioned in the previous verse. RSV returns to this interpretation, 'he drove them all, with the sheep and oxen, out of the temple'.

17. *Zeal of thine house.* AV often makes no attempt to differentiate between subjective and objective genitives. Here the genitive is objective, and the translation should be 'Zeal for thine house'.

18. *Seeing that thou doest these things;* i.e. as Knox translates. 'as thy warrant for doing this'.

22. As the expression *the scripture* nearly always refers to a particular passage of Scripture, it is usually supposed that the reference here is to Psalm xvi. 10.

The word which Jesus had said is recorded in verse 17.

23. The insertion of *day* after *feast* is a mistake. The expression *the feast* refers to the whole of the festival, which included the actual Passover ceremony and the seven days of unleavened bread which followed. Knox rightly renders 'at the Paschal season'.

25. In the original, the definite article is inserted before each mention of *man* in this verse. This may be taken generically as in AV, or it may mean 'the particular man in question'. Knox takes the first reference as specific and the second as generic: 'he did not need assurance about any man, because he could read men's hearts.'

b. The interview with Nicodemus (iii. 1–21)

The supernatural knowledge possessed by Jesus of what is in man, and His refusal to recognize as His true disciples any who do not feel the need for the radical change in human nature which He came into the world to effect, are clearly brought out in His interview with Nicodemus, a member of the Jewish Sanhedrin. A learned and pious teacher, very different we may well believe from the type of Pharisee who for a pretence made long prayers and made broad his phylacteries, he was genuinely impressed by what Jesus said and did. He at least did not attribute Jesus' extraordinary powers to Satanic influence, as some other Pharisees did. On the contrary, he recognized in Jesus *a teacher come from God*, and he was anxious to know more about Him; but he was also anxious to avoid giving the impression that he intended to become a committed disciple. So he *came to Jesus bv night* (2).

It may be that the question Nicodemus intended to put to Jesus was similar to that of the rich young man about the qualifications for entering into eternal life (see Mk. x. 17), or to that of the scribe relating to the supreme commandment of the law (see Mk. xii. 28), for these were matters often debated by the Rabbis, and it would be interesting, Nicodemus may have felt, to know what Jesus thought about them. Or, it may be, he had already entertained the idea that Jesus might be the inaugurator of the kingdom of God. No doubt he was longing for that kingdom to come, for he would assume that he would have the right to enjoy its blessings not only in virtue of the privileges which belonged to his race, but also as a reward for his loyalty to Pharisaic traditions.

But as soon as Nicodemus had paid his compliments to this

unprofessional Rabbi, Jesus cut away from under his feet all ground for self-satisfaction. No-one, Jesus told him, can experience the reign of God, no matter what his race or his degree of piety may be, apart from the experience of new birth; for neither racial privilege nor the punctilious observance of religious practices can efface the sin that is inherent in every child of Adam. *Except a man be born again*, said Jesus with great solemnity, *he cannot see the kingdom of God* (3). It was a word of God 'sharper than any twoedged sword' (see Heb. iv. 12), and parallel to the equally penetrating pronouncement 'Whosoever shall not receive the kingdom of God as a little child, he shall not enter therein' (Mk. x. 15). To be born again, and to be willing to receive ungrudgingly the gifts that God offers, involves the abandonment of every attempt to become righteous by anything a man may do for himself, and the willing acceptance of the free gift of grace. Such a complete reorientation is an experience that can well be likened to physical birth, for it is an emergence from darkness into light, when the restricted and confined is at last set free.

But Nicodemus, for all his theological learning, lacks spiritual insight. He fails to see that it is a supernatural birth of which Jesus is speaking. He understands His words about a second birth in a strictly literal sense, and does not hesitate to suggest that they are absurd. He has yet to learn that God's creative power is not limited to the material and the physical. There also exists a realm of spirit in which God is at work. It is true, as Jesus points out, that there is much that is mysterious and seemingly arbitrary about the new birth of the Spirit, and something unpredictable about the behaviour of the man who experiences it. But there is also much that passes comprehension in the invisible working of the natural phenomenon of the wind, but its effects are nevertheless undeniable. One day it breathes in softness and in calm, refreshing and renewing the earth; another day it seems to go madly on its devastating way, leaving ruin and desolation in its train. Nicodemus, the distinguished *master of Israel* (10), ought not to be ignorant of the power of God to change human lives. His study of Scripture ought to have taught him that God not only *can* give men a new heart and put a right spirit within them, but that He has promised to do so (see Ezk. xxxvi. 25–27). Nicodemus, it would seem, being content with a limited knowledge of God, has an inadequate understanding of His power. But thsoe who are born again, the new men in Christ, could never restrict God's sovereignty to the natural order, for they can say with the confidence born of personal experience, *We speak that we do know, and testify that we have seen* (11).

The revelation about the new birth as the gateway to the kingdom of God inevitably becomes, as the discourse develops, a revelation about Jesus Himself. He *can*, and *does* inaugurate the kingdom of heaven, because in Him One who belongs to heaven has come down to earth. The prophet Daniel had seen in a vision one like a Son of man coming on the clouds of heaven (Dn. vii. 13). Jesus is that Son of man. But He has not come as an apparition in the sky; He has become flesh. Although heaven is His real and permanent home, He has come to live as a man among men, to reveal to them in language spoken by human lips and in actions wrought by human hands what they could never have discovered either by human intuition or by human striving. *No man hath ascended up to heaven, but he that came down from heaven, even the Son of man which is in heaven* (13).

This Son of man by becoming flesh has become subject to the death to which all flesh is subject; but the death that He is to die has unique significance. In order to explain wherein the significance lay, Jesus takes an illustration from the story of the Israelites during their wanderings in the wilderness. They had sinned by rebelling against Moses their divinely-appointed leader, and in consequence were the victims of fiery serpents. But Moses, acting on the merciful command of God, who would not 'make a full end' of His people, fashioned a serpent of brass and lifted it upon a pole for all to see; and all who looked upon it were spared the penalty of death (Nu. xxi. 9). Similarly, Jesus, the heavenly Son of man made flesh, is destined to be lifted up for all to see. He will hang on a cross like a condemmed criminal. But His subjection to that particular form of death will not be due to some mischance. He will die in that way, precisely because it is in that way that God has chosen to reveal His love for sinners. He has given His Son to pay the penalty of their sins. *Even so must the Son of man be lifted up* (14). In consequence, all who look in faith to Him 'whose blessed feet were nailed for our advantage to the bitter cross' will never be subject to the death that is sin's penalty, but enjoy eternal life.

It is a reasonable assumption that verses 16 to 21 are not part of Jesus' words to Nicodemus, but comments by the evangelist, as Jesus in speaking of the first Person of the Trinity refers to Him as 'Father' not as 'God'. RSV would seem therefore to be right in closing the marks of quotation at the end of verse 15. The primary purpose of the life and death of Jesus, God's only Son, is man's salvation, but His presence in the world inevitably divides mankind. *He that doeth truth* (21), i.e. the man of integrity, is inevitably drawn to Him, for he has nothing to fear in the exposure of his actions and motives to the divine light. On the other hand, the disingenuous shun the searchlight of Jesus' presence, and in so doing provide the evidence that they stand self-condemned. Sin invariably leads the sinner to hide himself from God, even as Adam and Eve hid themselves from Him in the garden of Eden. But in Jesus the world is faced with God's last word to man. Primarily it is a word of salvation, *for God sent not his Son into the world to condemn the world; but that the world through him might be saved* (17). But because it is *God's* word, and God's *last* word, it is also a word of judgment. *He that believeth not is condemned already, because he hath not believed in the name of the only begotten Son of God* (18).

As the evangelist enunciates these great themes Nicodemus is 'faded out' of the narrative, so that we have no record of his reaction to the challenge presented to him by Jesus. The evangelist is concerned with what the life and death of Jesus mean for *all* men and not only for Nicodemus. We learn later, however, that Nicodemus made a protest to his colleagues on the Jewish Council when they were proposing to condemn Jesus without hearing His own explanation of His actions (vii. 50f.), and that he performed the dutiful act of embalming and preparing the body of Jesus for burial (xix. 39). From these references we may reasonably infer that in the power of the divine Spirit, which like the wind blows where He will, the word of Jesus about the necessity for new birth did not, in the words of Isaiah, return empty but accomplished the task for which it had been sent; and that, although Nicodemus is not mentioned elsewhere in the New Testament as a leading member of the early Church, he nevertheless came out of darkness and error into the clear light and knowledge of God and of His Son Jesus Christ.

Additional Notes

iii. 1. *A ruler of the Jews;* i.e. a member of the Jewish council.

2. *Miracles.* As at ii. 11, iv. 54, and vi. 2 AV fails to let the reader know that the Greek word that is being translated is the peculiarly Johannine word for Jesus' supernatural works, *sēmeia* not *dunameis.* RV and RSV in all places rightly render 'signs'.

3. This is the second of many sayings of Jesus recorded in this Gospel, which are introduced by the Hebrew *amen amen*, translated *Verily, verily.* The words add solemnity to and underline the truth of what follows. The modern expressions, 'In truth I tell you', 'Believe me when I say', 'I do assure you', convey the meaning. It is a mark of the uniqueness of Jesus that He should have used so often this particular method of giving emphasis to His words.

Again. It is impossible to bring out in translation the double meaning of the Greek word *anōthen*, 'anew' and 'from above'. The second birth, of which Jesus is speaking, is a supernatural birth.

5. Some scholars suppose that the words *of water* refer solely to John's baptism on the ground that this would have been the only baptism with which Nicodemus would have been familiar, and that the contrast found elsewhere in the Gospel between John's water baptism and Christian baptism of *the spirit* is to be found here also. It is certainly probable that, as a Pharisee, Nicodemus would not have submitted to John's baptism (see

Lk. vii. 30). But in the light of the reference to the practice by Jesus of water baptism in verse 22, it is difficult to avoid construing the words *of water and of the Spirit* conjunctively, and regarding them as a description of Christian baptism, in which cleansing and endowment are both essential elements.

8. The appositeness of the comparison made in this verse is more evident in the original, where a single Greek word *pneuma* is used for both *wind* and *spirit*.

10. *A master*. Both AV and RSV fail to translate the definite article, for the omission of which there is no MSS evidence. Nicodemus is *the*, i.e. the distinguished, teacher of Israel.

11. By using the plural *we* Jesus would seem to be including His disciples, who according to the Synoptic tradition were sent out on a mission of witness early in His ministry. Similarly, by using the plural *ye* in this verse and the following, Jesus is speaking of the majority of the Jews, who disbelieved both Himself and His disciples, as Nicodemus at the moment seems to be doing.

12. By *earthly things* are probably meant spiritual truths for which a human analogy can be found, as distinct from *heavenly things*, to which there is no human parallel. The justification by God of the ungodly, and the reconciliation of men to God while they are yet sinners, are examples of such *heavenly things*. And it is significant that in the present context Jesus proceeds at once to speak of redemption.

13. The words *which is in heaven* are omitted in some ancient Greek MSS, though they have strong support in the ancient versions. It is assumed by many scholars that they were inserted into the text at an early date in the interest of the doctrine of the two natures of Christ. A decision on this variant is difficult. While there is no intrinsic reason why Jesus should not have spoken the words, there seems to be no adequate motive for their omission if they are genuine.

16. AV invariably translates *aiōnios*, used here and in six other places in this Gospel and always in association with *life*, by

between some of John's disciples and a Jew about purification. John's complete inability to provide true purification is one of the reasons why he cannot be the Christ. His function has been, as he readily admits, to go before the Christ like the groomsman despatched to make the final preparations for a wedding; to rejoice in the humble role he is called upon to play at the wedding itself; and to retire into obscurity when his appointed task is finished. And in the discharge of these functions his cup of happiness has been full. His final words are eloquent of his self-effacement. *He must increase, but I must decrease* (30). But, though John is divinely commissioned to be a forerunner of the Christ, he is, like all other human teachers, earthly in origin and forced to use the language of earth. He is unable, therefore, to speak of heavenly things with the same first-hand knowledge that can belong to Him alone who has been sent direct from heaven and is far superior to all others. Such a heaven-sent Apostle speaks God's own words; He possesses the divine Spirit to an unlimited degree; and as the Son, who is the permanent object of His heavenly Father's love, all that is to be revealed about God has been committed to Him. To accept His teaching is therefore to testify that *God is true*; on the other hand, to reject it, is in effect to make God a liar (33; cf. 1 Jn. i. 10, v. 10).

This section ends with words which re-echo the assertion made by the evangelist at the close of the Nicodemus passage. Belief or disbelief in the Son of God is a matter of life or death; for, while to the believer His coming is the supreme revelation of God's love bringing the assurance of eternal life, to the unbeliever it is the sign that he remains the object of God's displeasure.

Additional Notes

iii. 23. *They came;* better, 'people came' (RSV).

24. The other evangelists indicate that Jesus' public ministry in Galilee did not begin till after John was put in prison. Our evangelist does not regard the Galilaean incident recorded in ii. 1–11 as part of the *public* ministry of Jesus.

25. *The Jews.* In the Greek MSS the reading varies between 'Jews' or 'a Jew'. As this writer invariably uses the definite article when speaking of 'the Jews', the latter reading should probably be followed (RSV). As Westcott says, 'it gives a definiteness to the incident otherwise lacking'.

31. *Above all;* i.e. 'above all other teachers, including John the Baptist'. There is some MSS evidence for omitting the words *is above all* at the conclusion of the verse.

Speaketh of the earth does not mean 'speaks about earthly matters' but 'talks the language of earth' (Knox).

33. *Hath set to his seal that God is true;* i.e. 'has set his seal to the affirmation "God is true".'

34. *God giveth not the Spirit by measure unto him.* Many ancient MSS omit *God*; and, as the words *unto him* are an explanatory addition by AV, it is possible, following the reading which omits *God*, to regard Jesus as the subject of the verb. The evangelist would then be saying, 'Jesus speaks the words of God, as can be seen from the fact that He (Jesus) gives the Spirit in an unlimited degree to His followers.' So apparently RSV 'he whom God has sent utters the words of God, for it is not by measure that he gives the Spirit'. The meaning implied in AV is 'Jesus can speak the words of God because God has given Him the Spirit completely'. This seems to be more suited to the context. The insertion, however, of the words *unto him* may give the wrong impression that while God gives His Spirit fully to Jesus, He only gives the Spirit to others sparingly. Most modern scholars therefore take the sentence as a statement of the general truth 'God gives not His Spirit by measure', which was illustrated conspicuously in the case of Jesus. God's Spirit is in fact available for all who are called to do His work in all the fullness necessary for its accomplishment.

d. The woman of Samaria (iv. 1–42)

In all the Gospels expression is given to the anxiety of Jesus to avoid arrest at the hands of the Pharisees, before the appointed hour for the passion had struck. The reader of this Gospel is not surprised therefore to learn at the beginning of chapter iv, that when Jesus was informed that the attention of the Pharisees had been drawn to the greater number being baptized by Him than by John, He made a hurried withdrawal in the direction of Galilee. The shortest route lay through the semi-hostile territory of the Samaritans, whose relations with the Jews were strained for they were regarded as outside the covenanted mercies of Israel. It is clear that Jesus did not leave Judaea with any fixed intention of ministering in Samaria, but the wind of the Spirit blows where it will, and the true messengers of God are never slaves to fixed programmes or pre-arranged plans of campaign. So it came about that the proclamation of the gospel by early Christian evangelists to the people of Samaria, recorded in Acts viii, was foreshadowed by an interview between Jesus and a Samaritan woman and His subsequent stay of two days in a Samaritan village. The story of this interview and of its sequel makes it clear that, since the advent of the Christ, the people of God is to consist of all, whatever their race, their religious background or their moral standing may be, who acknowledge Jesus as the Saviour of the world, who have received from Him the life-giving Spirit, and who worship God in spirit and in truth.

The Samaritan woman is a timeless figure—not only a typical Samaritan but a typical human being. As she converses with Jesus, it becomes clear that like most men and women she is almost exclusively concerned with the provision of what will satisfy her physical needs, particularly thirst-quenching water which can often be obtained only by the expenditure of much time and energy. The welfare of her soul is not for her a matter of primary concern. Her reply to Jesus' request for a drink of water has sometimes been regarded as sarcastic, as though she was saying in effect 'So you Jews are not above asking help from us Samaritans when the need arises'. More probably it is an expression of bewilderment, 'Well here is a strange thing—a Jew asking a Samaritan for a drink'! Jesus at once points out to her that there can be no *rapprochement* between Jew and Samaritan, unless both accept the gift which

God is prepared to bestow but which can be received from Jesus alone, for He *is* the gift (see iii. 16). Jesus alone can supply the *living water* which can satisfy every need and become the perpetual source of life (10, 14). But when Jesus mentions *living water*, she assumes that it is of 'running' water as distinct from ordinary 'well' water that He is speaking; and she wonders how He can obtain such water, as there are no streams in the vicinity. *Jacob's well*, to be sure, was supplied by a perpetual spring; but that cannot be the source for the *living water* of which Jesus is speaking, for He has nothing to draw the water with, and being a Jew He could not use the same bucket as the Samaritan woman used. Moreover, when Jesus explains to her that the water He is able to give her will free her for ever from thirst, she still thinks that it is some magical supply of ordinary water that He is offering her, and that when she obtains it she will never have to visit the well again. *Sir, give me this water, that I thirst not, neither come hither to draw* (15). Then, suddenly and unexpectedly, Jesus penetrates her defences with the words *Go, call thy husband* (16). They are immediately effective. Her slumbering conscience is re-awakened, and the beginning of a new birth becomes apparent. She abandons any further attempt at subterfuge. She no longer tries to escape either from herself, or from the all-seeing eye of her Maker. She speaks the truth, *I have no husband* (17). And, because she is now 'of the truth', to use the language of xviii. 37, Jesus is able to appraise her honesty without in any way condoning her vice. 'You are right in saying, "I have no husband"; for you have had five husbands, and he whom you now have is not your husband; this you said truly' (18, RSV). And because she has spoken the truth, the truth makes her free—free to receive the gift that Jesus can give her.

The first sign of the change that is taking place is the woman's recognition of Jesus as a prophet, endowed with remarkable insight into human nature, *a man*, as she said later, *which told me all things that ever I did* (29). Who better qualified than He, she felt, to give a judgment in the age-long dispute between Jew and Samaritan about the proper place for worshipping God! Was it Jerusalem, as the Jews believed, or

Mount Gerizim where the Samaritans worshipped? But no sooner does she broach the subject, than 'the prophet' informs her that it is no longer relevant. Neither in the Jerusalem temple, nor in the schismatic temple on Mount Gerizim had worship pure and undefiled been offered; and the time was fast approaching, nay in a real sense it had already come, when, as Malachi had prophesied, God's name would be great among the Gentiles and in *every* place pure offering would be made unto the Lord (Mal. i. 11). Yet the worship of the Jew, for all its imperfections, was better than that of the Samaritan. The Jew had a greater horror of idolatry; and his Scripture included the writings of the prophets, and was not limited to the Pentateuch as the Samaritan Bible was; he had therefore a greater understanding of the divine will. The salvation which Jesus, Himself a Jew, had come to bring was therefore *of the Jews* (22). In Paul's words 'to them belong the sonship, the glory, the covenants, the giving of the law, the worship, and the promises; to them belong the patriarchs, and of their race, according to the flesh, is the Christ' (Rom. ix. 4, 5, RSV). Nevertheless, the animal sacrifices of the Jewish temple were offered in what the Epistle to the Hebrews calls a 'worldly sanctuary' (Heb. ix. 1); and such worship was but a shadow of the purer worship which would be possible as a result of the perfect sacrifice of Christ. His sacrifice is offered in the realm of Spirit; and all who draw near to God, accepting its benefits with grateful hearts, can worship Him *in spirit and in truth.* For *God is a Spirit,* and it is those who, born anew of the Spirit, have become His children, who can and must worship their Father, as He desires to be worshipped, *in spirit*; and it is those who accept the revelation of God in Christ as ultimate truth, who can and must worship Him *in truth* (24).

The Samaritan woman will not have to wait for the Messiah to come and solve her problem. The full solution has already been given by Jesus, who now tells her that He is the Messiah. She accepts His self-disclosure as true, and eagerly avails herself of the opportunity provided by the return of Jesus, disciples to hasten away and tell her news to others. It thus becomes increasingly evident that the advent of the Messiah makes it possible for God to be worshipped in spirit and in truth, and that such worshippers cannot be confined to one race, class or sex. While the woman is away, Jesus informs His disciples, who urge Him to eat the food they have purchased, not that He is exempt from the need of satisfying His physical hunger with material food, but that He has an inner spiritual source of sustenance. It consists in obeying His Father's will and in finishing the work that the Father has sent Him to do. He then draws their attention to the immediate results produced by the word of God He has come into the world to proclaim. There is no four-months' interval between the sowing by Him of 'seed' in the heart of the Samaritan woman and the harvest which has resulted, as there is between sowing and reaping in the ordinary course of agriculture. The prophet Amos had foretold the days when 'the plowman shall overtake the reaper, and the treader of grapes him that soweth seed' (Am. ix. 13). Those days had now arrived. Sower and reaper could now rejoice together. The disciples of Jesus will carry on the work of gathering into the new Israel of God the 'crops' of Gentile believers, of whom the Samaritan converts are the first 'sheaves'. Once more will the words of the proverb be proved true *One soweth, and another reapeth* (37). It is because others have sown, the long line of God's messengers to Israel in the past, as well as Jesus Himself, that the harvesting of converts from the Gentiles is possible.

The villagers of Sychar, as the disciples first called by Jesus and as Nathanael had done, 'come and see' for themselves the Man, about whom the woman had told them; and their faith, and the faith of many others who met Jesus during His two-days' stay in the village, becomes based on a first-hand experience of Jesus, not as a national leader of the old Israel, but as the Saviour of Jews, Samaritans, and Gentiles, in fact as *the Saviour of the world.*

Additional Notes

iv. 1. Instead of *the Lord* some ancient Greek MSS and the Latin versions read 'Jesus'. The latter is probably original, for 'the Lord' as a synonym for 'Jesus' is not found elsewhere in the narrative of this Gospel.

2. This verse corrects an inaccuracy in the information that had reached the Pharisees.

4. *Must needs go.* The necessity lay in the fact that the route through Samaria was the quickest.

6. Two Greek words in this chapter are both rendered in AV by *well.* In verses 6 and 14 the word *pēgē* 'fountain' is used, indicating that Jacob's well was supplied with running water, and that the spiritual water offered by Jesus is an inner spring ensuring a continuous supply. In verses 11 and 12 the ordinary Greek word for 'well' (*phrear*) is used. RV mg. and RSV translate by 'spring' in verse 14.

The difficult *thus* is probably rightly construed as a reference back to 'being wearied with his journey'. Tired as He was He sat down by the well. It could also be translated 'as he chanced to be'; i.e. He sat down just where He happened to be. The same difficult expression is found in xiii. 25. In both places there is some MSS evidence for omitting the word. The omission however is probably due to the fact that it was found difficult.

8. *Meat* in this verse and in verses 32 and 34, and also in xxi. 5, is an archaism for 'food' (RSV).

9. The last clause in this verse is usually regarded not as part of the words spoken by the woman, but as an explanation of the evangelist for the benefit of his non-Jewish readers. As the Jews did have *some* dealings with the Samaritans, the meaning of the Greek verb is probably 'do not share things in common', i.e. in this context 'do not use the same bucket'. (See article by D. Daube in *Journal of Biblical Literature*, Vol. LXIX, p. 2.)

The Samaritans were a half-caste people who owed their origin to the mingling of the remnant left behind when Samaria fell in 722 BC with the foreigners imported by the Assyrian conquerors. Their worship in consequence became contaminated by idolatry (see 2 Ki. xvii. 28–41 and cf. *ye worship ye know not what* in verse 22). They did their best to interfere with the rebuilding of Jerusalem when the Jews returned from the Babylonian captivity. When the Jews wished to be offensive to Jesus they called Him 'a Samaritan' (viii. 48). Jesus, on the contrary, made a Samaritan the hero of one of His parables; and this encounter with a Samaritan woman was one of the most significant incidents in His earthly ministry.

14. Instead of *a well of water springing up* we should say in modern English 'a spring of water welling up'.

24. The translation *a Spirit* is unfortunate, as it might suggest that God is one of many similar spirits. RSV rightly renders 'spirit'. There is nothing material in God's nature; therefore material worship in 'a worldly sanctuary' (Heb. ix. 1) cannot be the highest kind of worship.

27. As there is no definite article in the original, *the woman* should be 'a woman' (so RV and RSV).

What seekest thou? is addressed to the woman; and *Why talkest thou with her?* to Jesus.

29. *Is not this the Christ?* The question in the original is more tentative. So RV 'Can this be the Christ?'

35. It is probable that *Say not ye* means not 'Are you not now saying' but 'Have you not a saying', and that the following words, which in the Greek are in metrical form, are a common proverb.

42. *The Christ* is omitted in the most ancient MSS and is an early addition to the text. There was a tendency, as time went on, to elaborate confessions of belief. The expression *Saviour of the world* is found only here and in 1 John iv. 14 in the New Testament. It is most significant that it should have first been applied to Jesus by Samaritans.

e. The nobleman's son (iv. 43–54)

The two days spent at Sychar by Jesus were an exception to His general policy of confining His ministry to the lost sheep of the house of Israel (see Mt. xv. 24). Judaea was pre-eminently the 'home-county' of the land of Israel, and

Jerusalem was the 'home-town' of every true Israelite wherever he might be living; Jerusalem should therefore have been the first to welcome the coming of the Messiah. But here in the very heart of Jewry 'His own' had received Him not. Some, it is true, 'believed in his name, when they saw the miracles which he did'; but 'Jesus did not commit himself unto them', because He knew that they had not accepted the implications of His actions (ii. 23, 24). Galilee, on the other hand, was prepared to welcome Him, for the Galilaeans had been impressed by the account of what some of their members had seen when they had been up in Jerusalem at the recent Passover. News moreover of what had happened at the recent wedding at Cana would almost certainly have circulated in the district. It is not surprising therefore that the distracted father of a sick boy resident at Capernaum, when he heard that Jesus was, for the second time, visiting Cana, apparently soon after His arrival in Galilee, should have thought it worth while to make the twenty-five mile journey to try and persuade Jesus to come and visit his ailing son. The man is described as a *basilikos* (46), translated *nobleman* in AV and RV, and 'official' in RSV. He was in service, we may reasonably assume, at the Court of Herod Antipas the tetrarch of Galilee, described as 'a king' in Mark vi. 14. Others occupying similar positions were Chuza (Lk. viii. 3) and Manaen (Acts xiii. 1).

It is improbable that this narrative is a variant account of the story of the healing of the centurion's son or servant (described in Lk. vii. 2–10 and Mt. viii. 5–13), for apart from the fact that in both cases the sufferer is cured at a distance, the stories have little or nothing in common. In the Synoptic story, the father, a Roman centurion, confessing that he is unworthy to receive Jesus under his roof, bids Jesus 'speak the word only', for he is sure that that will be sufficient to effect the cure. In John's story, the father, like Jairus, makes a definite request that Jesus will visit his home. Jesus' first reaction to this request is expressed in the difficult words *Except ye see signs and wonders, ye will not believe* (48). It is usually supposed that by using the second person plural Jesus is regarding the courtier's request as typical of the Jewish demand for a sign, of which He had had a recent example in Jerusalem (ii. 18), and expressing His disappointment at their persistent attitude. On this interpretation, His words are perhaps best regarded as a question, 'Will you Jews never believe unless you see signs first?' It may be significant, however, that only here in this Gospel is the word *wonders*, 'portents', added to the word 'signs'. It is possible, therefore, as Knox suggests, that by using the second person plural Jesus is in fact not expressing disappointment with the *Jews*, but, on the assumption that the man was one of Herod's officials, rebuffing the whole entourage of that princeling, who like the petty tyrant they served were probably hoping to see miracles performed by Jesus (see Lk. xxiii. 8).[1] If this is the right way of envisaging the situation Jesus' words will carry with them the reproach, 'All you people want to see is wonder-works—miracles for the sake of miracles'. Jesus, in consequence, shows a momentary reluctance to accede to the courtier's request, in order to be satisfied that he is not like the rest of Herod's flunkies, for whom Jesus could have had little respect. But whatever may have been the reason for His hesitation, it is quickly abandoned when the father, instead of taking umbrage at any implied rebuff in what Jesus has said, repeats his entreaty in words that touch a cord in the heart of every parent of a fever-stricken child in every land and in every age. *Sir, come down ere my child die* (49).

Without obedience and trust there can be no real faith. The courtier now shows that he has both these essentials. When Jesus says to him, 'Go; your son will live' (RSV), he returns home at once, trusting that Jesus' words are true. And this incipient belief becomes the full committal of faith, when he later ascertains that Jesus' words were not merely prophetic, but restorative, for the cure had been effected at the precise moment they were uttered.

Both the miracles performed at Cana, which are closely linked by the evangelist in verses 46 and 54, are thus shown to have been prompted by trust. Mary trusted her Son to do something to relieve the embarrassment of their host at the wedding. The father of the sick boy was equally confident that

[1] *The Gospels and Epistles*, p. 255.

he could rely on Jesus' help. Both miracles are also shown to have resulted in a personal surrender to Jesus which is full Christian faith. His disciples *believed on him* after the water had been turned into wine; the father and the rest of his household *believed* as the result of the healing of the boy: and in both cases the verb in the original is an inceptive aorist 'they put their faith in Him'.

Additional Notes

iv. 43. *Two days.* AV fails to translate the definite article. RV rightly 'the two days', i.e. those mentioned in verse 40.

44. Commentators disagree as to whether *his own country* is a reference to Nazareth or Jerusalem. The word *patris* clearly has the former meaning in the other Gospels (see Mk. vi. 4; Mt. xiii. 57; Lk. iv. 24). But if it is given that meaning here, Jesus would be saying in effect that He is deliberately journeying to Galilee, because that is the region where He can expect to be treated with little or no respect. This is so difficult as to be almost impossible. It is true that Nazareth was from a human point of view His native town, the place where He had been brought up. But Jerusalem was where as Messiah He really belonged. The Messiah, as is implied in vii. 41, does not come from Galilee. Moreover, the reception that Jesus had received so far at Jerusalem from the Jewish authorities was in accord with the proverb to the truth of which Jesus is here said to have testified (see ii. 23, 24, iv. 1). The reception that awaited Him in Galilee, as the next verse shows, was very different.

50. Both in this verse and in verse 53 the verbs in the original are prophetic presents, and should be translated 'thy son will live'.

52. The colloquial Greek translated *he began to amend* implies that the fever had abated, the crisis was over, and recovery certain. The boy had in fact 'got better'.

III. THE UNBELIEF OF ISRAEL (v. 1–vi. 71)

a. Introduction

Chapters v and vi should probably be grouped together as a single section. They are connected by a common theme, which may be described as the nature and causes of Israel's lack of faith in Jesus. Chapter v is concerned with the form which this unbelief took among the Jews at Jerusalem, and chapter vi with the expression of it by the peasants in Galilee. The New Testament has much to say about the refusal of the Jews to accept Jesus as the Messiah. The theme runs through the conflict-stories and the passion narratives of the earlier Gospels; it finds poignant expression in the lament of Jesus over Jerusalem (Lk. xix. 41–44); it wrings from the heart of Paul the candid confession, 'I have great sorrow and unceasing anguish in my heart. For I could wish that I myself were accursed and cut off from Christ for the sake of my brethren, my kinsmen by race' (Rom. ix. 2, 3, RSV); and it has been the cause of bitter controversy between Jews and Christians ever since. It was very natural therefore that John should have been at pains to record in greater detail than the earlier evangelists the reasons for this great rejection, as they had found expression during the earthly life of Jesus. His Gospel has in consequence sometimes been called 'The Gospel of the rejection'.

Both these chapters begin with an account of a mighty work of Jesus; and in each case the evangelist is relating stories similar to those found in the earlier Gospels. Though the scene of the first miracle is Jerusalem, and that of the second Galilee, the background of both events is provided by a Jewish festival. Those who accept the reading 'the feast' in v. 1 naturally interpret it of the Passover, and many of them find it difficult to suppose that the incident recorded in chapter v preceded that narrated in chapter vi, for in vi. 4 it is stated that *the passover, a feast of the Jews, was nigh*, and that the feeding of the large company took place at the time when the Galilaean peasants were making preparations for the annual pilgrimage to the festival. But if we adopt the better-attested reading *a feast* in v. 1, which now has the additional support of the

Bodmer papyrus, the reference could be to any feast; and there is no need to assume as many commentators do that the chapters have been dislocated, and to attempt to restore the 'original' order by placing chapter vi before chapter v. It is true that at the end of the fourth chapter Jesus is in Galilee, and that vi. 1, *After these things Jesus went over the sea of Galilee*, might read more naturally if Jesus had remained in Galilee till the crossing was made. But the expression 'After these things' is vague and may denote any interval of time, short or long.

All four Gospels record the passion of Jesus in a Passover setting. It was also under the shadow of a Passover, John notes, that the great controversy took place in which Jesus after revealing Himself as the living Bread which came down from heaven, and promising that all who 'ate' that Bread would live for ever, added the words which were so offensive to the Jews, *And the bread that I will give is my flesh, which I will give for the life of the world* (vi. 51). The offence caused by this teaching given in the synagogue at Capernaum on the verge of Passover was one of the factors that led to the rejection of Jesus at the final Passover. The reader is thus made aware by implication, if not directly, that Jesus is the real Passover Lamb who brought redemption to mankind. Whatever else may be involved in the controversies between those who believe in Jesus and those who disbelieve in Him, it is in men's attitude to His death that their belief or disbelief most conspicuously shows itself. This was true during His earthly life, and it has been true ever since.

b. The disabled man at Bethesda (v. 1–47)

The reader who passes from the Gospel of Mark to the Gospel of John may well feel that chapter v has a general similarity to Mark ii. 1–iii. 5. Mark records in that section the healing of a paralytic carried by four men and let down through the roof, and the controversies of Jesus with the Pharisees about sabbath observance which followed it. John relates the healing of a man crippled for thirty-eight years, who had been daily frustrated as he lay in one of the five colonnades at the Sheep-Pool, a spot known as Bethesda 'the house of mercy', unable because unaided to bathe in the pool at the time when the water possessed remedial virtue. This incident gives rise to a serious conflict about the sabbath. There are differences in detail in the two narratives. The paralytic, for example, is brought to Jesus by others, who allow no obstacle to thwart their purpose. The cripple has no-one to aid him in this manner, but Jesus seems deliberately to select him from the miscellaneous group of sufferers as the one in greatest need of a physician. Both men, however, are cured by an almost identical command, *Rise, take up thy bed, and walk.* Moreover, in both cases the affliction is in some measure the consequence of the sufferer's sins. While Mark stresses the truth that the display of supernatural power by which the paralytic is healed is clear evidence that Jesus possesses the divine prerogative to forgive sins—in John's story the reference to the afflicted man's sin occurs almost incidentally. Jesus meets him in the temple after the cure and says to him *Behold, thou art made whole: sin no more, lest a worse thing come unto thee* (14).

The point that is underlined in John's narrative is that the man was cured on a *sabbath*, and in the subsequent discourse Jesus is in effect concerned to explain further what was involved in His claim, recorded in Mark ii. 28, that 'the Son of man is Lord also of the sabbath'. In Mark ii. 23–28 Jesus defends His activities on the sabbath, first by the argument that if David could 'violate' the sabbath by eating the shewbread on that day, then *a fortiori* the Christ, who was great David's greater Son, had at least the right to do as David did; and secondly by stating a primary purpose for which the sabbath was ordained. 'The sabbath was made for man', partly that he might be restored to physical strength, but also that in the spiritual refreshment provided by that day he might have a foretaste of the higher life, which he would enjoy more fully when the blessed Messianic age should come. In the discourse in John v Jesus implies that with His own coming that age has arrived. His own activity is paradoxically an expression of the sabbath 'rest' of God, who keeps no sabbath week by week, because He keeps endless sabbath. He needs no special rest on one day in seven, because His activity as the Sustainer of the world He has created, and as the living God, whose purposes and judgments are reflected in the events of human history, is ceaseless and effortless. It is this continuous and perfect activity, the unique characteristic of God, that Jesus claims to be displaying. And it is to this that He draws the Jews' attention when they attack Him both for breaking the sabbath Himself, and for causing the healed man to break it, by ordering him to carry his bed on the sabbath. 'My Father is working still', He says, 'and I am working' (17, RSV).

The Jews rightly see that by this assertion Jesus is claiming equality with God, and it rouses in them a murderous hatred. They are now more determined to have Him put to death. The way in which Jesus answers the charge of *making himself equal with God* (18) suggests that this expression was understood by His listeners in the way the Rabbis usually understood it. A man who acted independently of God, or who rebelled against God's judgments, was said to be placing himself on an equality with God.[1] Jesus therefore at once asserts that for Him to act independently of God would be utterly impossible, because the relationship between God and Himself is a Father-Son relationship; and no son can act all the time independently of his father. In His case, moreover, the relationship is unique. For, while in the ordinary father-son relationship the love of the father for his son and the obedience of the son to his father are both very far from perfect, in the relationship between God the Father and God the Son, the Son *can*, and indeed *must* be true to the Father's purposes and do the Father's work, because the love of the Father and the obedience of the Son are perfect. Such a divine Son is so completely controlled by the Father's love that He displays it in all that He does. Without this unique relationship, none of the works of Jesus would have been possible.

The actions of God which are the most complete expressions of His sovereignty are the raising of men from death to life,

[1] See W. F. Howard, *Christianity according to St. John* (Duckworth, 1943), p. 71.

and the passing of final judgment upon them. To kill and to make alive, and to be a righteous and impartial judge are the prerogatives of Almighty God (see Dt. xxxii. 39 and Gn. xviii. 25). Resurrection and judgment are in fact the *final* things, and it is these *final* things with which men and women are confronted in Jesus. This is why His revelation of God is so determinative for mankind. His first coming in human flesh is indirectly a coming in judgment, for it inevitably separates believers from unbelievers. The former pass over at once from spiritual death to eternal life. So Jesus can say not only that 'the hour is coming', but that it '*now is*, when the dead will hear the voice of the Son of God, and those who hear will live' (25, RSV). Jesus has been given this divine gift of eternal life to bestow upon others. He has also been given as Son of Man the right to pass judgment; and His present almost unconscious exercise of that right is a prelude to the final judgment which He will pronounce upon all mankind after the general resurrection at the last day. By accepting Jesus, and giving Him the honour due to God, men can here and now avoid a verdict of condemnation when that final judgment is given, and enjoy a foretaste of the eternal life which a verdict of acquittal on the last day will secure for them.

Jesus is indeed *equal with God* (18), but not in the sense that He is independent of Him. On the contrary, by Himself He can do nothing. As He hears, He judges. He makes, moreover, no proud or boastful claims on His own behalf. He gives no evidence in His own defence. Such evidence would by itself be invalid, for according to Jewish law there must be two or three witnesses (31; see Dt. xix. 15). But there is another independent witness to Jesus whose testimony is completely valid. That witness, alluded to in verse 32, is God Himself. He is the only witness in fact whom Jesus regards as important as far as His own vindication is concerned.

There are, it is true, other witnesses to Him, *human* witnesses such as John the Baptist, whose testimony He now recalls, not for His own satisfaction, but because of the part John might continue to play in bringing the Jews to salvation. John was indeed a shining light. While that light was burning the Jews had rallied round him, and rejoiced in the prospect he held out to them of a coming divine intervention on behalf of Israel. But with many of them such rejoicing lasted only *for a season*. When faced with the austerity of John's demands, as he struck at the roots of national privilege, they said he was possessed, and none of them came to his support when he was unjustly imprisoned and martyred. But important as John's witness still was, Jesus relied on a higher and greater testimony. It was to be found in the works His Father had given Him to do; and it was precisely *that* testimony that the Jews refused to see. They could not be expected to hear God's voice or see Him with their physical senses, but here was divine evidence displayed before their very eyes; and God's revelation of Himself, *his word* (38), found no home in them, precisely because they refused to accept Jesus as His appointed envoy. They pored diligently over their Scriptures, thinking that in possessing them they were in possession of eternal life. But their study of the Scriptures did not lead them to accept Jesus as the giver of eternal life, to whom those Scriptures were in fact pointing.

The essentially evil condition of the Pharisees is designated by Jesus in the other Gospels 'hypocrisy', for it was the profession of a knowledge of God wilfully limited and distorted, and therefore deceptive. In this discourse, its root cause is said to be their desire to stand well in the estimation of others. They had accused Jesus of acting independently of God; He now accuses them of displaying that independence. The motive of their actions is not love for God but the approval of their fellows. This is why they reject Him who has come to them with divine credentials, and would rather listen to teachers who are entirely self-accredited.

Jesus began this discourse in self-defence, to meet the accusation that He had contravened the law of sabbath observance. He concludes it by citing Moses as a prosecuting witness against the Jews. He reminds His listeners that embedded in the Mosaic law was a prophecy which must have led the Jews to put their allegiance in Jesus, if only they had taken it seriously. God had said to Moses, 'I will raise them up a Prophet from among their brethren, like unto thee, and will put my words in his mouth; and he shall speak unto them all that I shall command him' (Dt. xviii. 18). The tragedy however was that the Jews had regarded the Mosaic ordinances, particularly those relating to animal sacrifice, as ends in themselves; they were not therefore ready to welcome Him who was not only the supreme revealer of the divine will, the Prophet who was greater than all the prophets, but also the Priest who alone could fully atone for human sin. The law of Moses could not save sinners and give them eternal life; it could only expose their sinfulness. By such exposure Moses prepared the way for the Son of God who made forgiveness a reality and enabled men to receive praise from God. If the Jews therefore really believed Moses; if, in other words, they were really longing for divine iorgiveness and for eternal life, they would now be believing in Jesus.

Additional Notes

v. 2. AV inserts *market* and RV 'gate' after *sheep* which in the Greek is an adjective. The insertion is made on the assumption that the reference is to the 'sheep gate' of Nehemiah iii. 1, 32. But, as the word translated *pool* can be read as a dative as well as a nominative, it can be construed with the adjective which precedes it, making possible the translation 'at the Sheep-pool'. If this is correct, then it is not the pool which is called *Bethesda*, a 'house of mercy', but the place with five colonnades where the sick folk used to assemble.

3, 4. A number of important ancient MSS and versions omit the words *waiting for the moving of the water*, and others also omit the whole of verse 4. Both RV and RSV omit these passages, and they are rightly regarded by scholars as early additions to the text, inserted to elucidate further the statement in verse 7, and to give a supernatural explanation of what was a natural phenomenon.

6. *Knew.* The force of the aorist tense in the original is probably inceptive. He 'became aware'.

7. *When the water is troubled* (Knox 'stirred'). Westcott comments 'the popular explanation of the phenomenon of an intermittent spring'.

13. *Conveyed himself away* translates the Greek verb *exeneusen*, only found here in the New Testament. It means either 'turned aside' (Knox 'drawn aside') or 'slipped away'.

17. *Answered.* Jesus is replying not to a specific question, but to the charge of sabbath-breaking brought against Him by the Jews. We could bring this out by translating, 'Jesus defended Himself by saying'.

The force of *worketh hitherto* is 'has never ceased working' (so Knox). *I work* implies 'I am always at work'.

25. *The dead* in this verse means 'the spiritually dead'.

32. Some commentators equate *another* with John the Baptist. But much better sense is obtained if it is regarded as a reference to God.

34. Both *I* and *ye* are emphatic.

These things I say, that ye might be saved; i.e. 'I mention the witness of John, for it has played a part in leading others to salvation, and it may lead you to salvation'.

37. The witness of *the Father* is not different from the witness of *the works* mentioned in verse 36. This could be made clear by inserting 'in these works' after *hath borne witness of me.*

37, 38. The words *Ye have neither heard his voice at any time, nor seen his shape* can either be construed with what precedes and regarded as concessive, giving the sense 'Though you have neither heard nor seen the Father (as you could not be expected to do), nevertheless He has borne witness to me. But His word does not make its home with you, because you do not believe Him whom He sent'. Or, the words can be construed as the first half of a sentence which is continued in verse 38. In this case they contain a reprimand. So Knox, who translates 'You have always been deaf to his voice, blind to the vision of him, and his word is not continually present in your hearts; that is why you will not trust one whom he has sent'. In this interpretation the Jews are reproached, as Knox points out, for *spiritual* blindness to *all* God's manifestations of Himself. The former exegesis is preferable, as the language *neither heard his voice . . . nor seen his shape* seems unsuitable as a description of wilful spiritual blindness.

39. *Search.* The Greek verb can be taken either as imperative (so AV following most earlier English translations) or as indicative (so RV and RSV). The latter would seem to make the better sense in the context. The Jews did not need to be exhorted to study the Scriptures; and the imperative makes it difficult to understand the causal clause which follows. In fact, those who assume that the verb is imperative are obliged to regard the words *in them ye think ye have eternal life* as parenthetic, and to construe the words *they are they which testify of me* with *for*, giving the reason for which the command is given. So Field paraphrases 'Search the Scriptures, your own Scriptures, the depositories of your faith and hope, those prophecies in which ye (rightly) think ye have eternal life—search them, I say, for they are they which testify of me'.[1]

40. *And*, as so often in this Gospel, signifies 'and yet'.

42. *The love of God.* As the genitive is objective, the clause should be translated 'you have not in you any love for God'.

43. *In my Father's name* means, in this context, 'with my Father's authority'.

c. The feeding of the five thousand (vi. 1–71)

The Jews at Jerusalem rejected Jesus on the ground that, far from being the fulfilment of the Scriptures, He disregarded them. The Galilaeans, on the other hand, whose unbelief is exposed in chapter vi, failed to see that He alone can satisfy men's deepest needs, which are spiritual and not merely physical. Like the vast majority of men and women, they supposed that their needs as human beings were limited to their physical requirements. They were, in consequence, very ready to accept Jesus as a political Christ, who would be a

[1] *Notes on the Translation of the New Testament*, p. 90.

partly by inserting the remark of the more resourceful Andrew: *There is a lad here, which hath five barley loaves, and two small fishes: but what are they among so many?* (9).

The discourse results in a parting of the ways. *From that time*, the evangelist notes, *many of his disciples went back, and walked no more with him* (66). They found Jesus' language about 'eating His flesh' as a necessary condition for receiving eternal life, intolerable, and they could not understand what He meant when He said it had not been given them by the Father to believe in Jesus. The twelve, on the other hand, with one notable exception, though they have no clear grasp as yet how Jesus can be the bread which came down from heaven to bring man eternal life, or how eternal life can and must result from His death, do not leave Him, for they are very sure that His words, though difficult to understand, are vital. Moreover, they are not prepared to turn their backs upon their past experience of His saving help. They could not have failed to recall at this moment the events of the previous night recorded earlier in this chapter. They had been alone in the dark, toiling at their oars some three or four miles from shore. The sea was rough and a high wind was blowing. And their natural fears were increased by what they thought was an apparition coming towards them. But how comforted they had been to know that it was no horrific ghost but Jesus Himself; how reassured to hear His words *It is I; be not afraid*; how glad to receive Him into the boat, and in His company to come so swiftly to shore at the precise spot for which they were making (20, 21)! It was surely impossible that they could now forsake the One to whose presence they were sure they owed their safety. To whom else could they look for guidance? Peter, their spokesman, gave true expression to their thoughts when he said, *Lord, to whom shall we go? thou hast the words of eternal life. And we believe and are sure that thou art that Christ, the Son of the living God* (68, 69). His confession stands out in splendid contrast to the stark and terrible description of Judas, who so far from being 'taught of God' is stigmatized *a devil: for he it was*, adds the evangelist, *that should betray him, being one of the twelve* (70, 71).

Additional Notes

vi. 5. *Come unto him.* It is clear in the Greek that the meaning is 'was coming to him' (so RSV). In the other accounts of the feeding, the large company had been with Jesus a long time before it was ascertained that food supplies were short, and steps were taken to try and remedy the situation. Our evangelist would seem to have jumped from the question of Jesus to Philip, asked at the time when the crowd was beginning to assemble, to the intervention of Andrew later in the day.[1]

9. The *small fishes*, as the Greek word *opsaria* indicates, were dried or pickled fish.

11. The words *to the disciples, and the disciples* are omitted in RV and RSV following the reading of the most ancient authorities. The words were probably inserted at an early date to bring the narrative into closer harmony with the Synoptic accounts.

The translation *and likewise of the fishes as much as they would* is not very lucid. The meaning is 'He distributed the fish with the result that all had as much as they wanted'.

21. It is probable that the AV gives the right sense in the translation *they willingly received him into the ship*, i.e. they did so gladly because they now knew that the figure was no ghost but Jesus Himself. (So RSV and Knox.) It is possible however that the meaning is 'they wanted to take Him into the boat, but in fact they did not do so as the boat came immediately to land'. The latter interpretation is favoured by those who understand the words translated *on the sea* in verse 19 to mean 'on the seashore' as in xxi. 1 where the same expression is used. On this view, there is in *this* Gospel no miracle of Christ walking on the sea. This exegesis is difficult, however, as the disciples are said to have been a long distance from land when they saw Jesus approaching the ship.

22. The AV rendering of this verse is obscure to the point of being unintelligible. The text can only be understood if some of the verbs are taken as pluperfects. It would seem that the

[1] See R. A. Knox, *The Gospels and Epistles*, p. 104.

evangelist first states that the crowd came down to the shore on the morning after the feeding miracle, and saw no boats there at all. He then records that these people had noticed (on the previous evening) that there had been only one boat available and that the disciples had embarked on it without Jesus. But Jesus could not now be seen anywhere in the vicinity, so they surmised that He must have gone back to Capernaum by some means or other, and they decided to join Him there as soon as possible. Fortunately, the arrival of boats from Tiberias now gave them the necessary means of transport.

23. This verse should not be treated as a parenthesis, for it is in fact a direct continuation of the narrative begun in verse 22.

The word translated *other*, if differently accented, can mean 'but'. It is best taken in this latter sense, as in RV 'howbeit there came boats'. AV takes it as *other* and inserts *Howbeit* into the text.

The clause rendered *after that the Lord had given thanks*, *eucharistēsantos tou Kuriou*, is omitted in a few but important ancient authorities. They may be a later addition to the text made at a time when the eucharistic element in the Johannine story was stressed. John alone states that Jesus *gave thanks*, *eucharistēsas*, before distributing the bread; the other evangelists have 'said the blessing', *eulogēsas*. It is also noticeable that John does not use 'the Lord' in narrative.

27. *That meat which endureth unto everlasting life* could mean either 'the food which endures (in contrast to the bread which perishes) and results in eternal life', or 'the food which lasts to eternity'.

Sealed. When a document is sealed it possesses the authority of a warrant. Hence the meaning here is that the Father has authorized the Son of man to be the giver of eternal life.

31, 32. In verse 32 Jesus is not denying that Moses had anything to do with the giving of the manna. He is in effect commenting on the quotation in verse 31, and telling His listeners that now that He Himself has come bringing men *the true bread from heaven*, the words of Psalm lxxviii. 24 have a wider and deeper significance.

34. *Kurie* should probably be translated *Sir* in this verse rather than *Lord*, as it is clear from verse 36 that these Galilaeans did not believe in Jesus.

40. *Which seeth the Son.* The Greek verb used here for 'seeing', *theōrō*, suggests that the meaning is 'who reflects who the Son really is'.

45. *In the prophets;* i.e. in that part of the Old Testament known as 'the prophets'. The reference is to Isaiah liv. 13.

46. *He which is of God* means 'he who came from God', i.e. Jesus.

50. *This;* i.e. 'the bread I am speaking of'.

57. *By the Father* and *by me* are better rendered, with RSV, 'because of the Father' and 'because of me'.

58. The meaning of this verse is 'The true bread from heaven is different from the manna which your fathers ate, for they died although they had eaten it. On the other hand, whoever eats the true bread will live for ever'.

60. *Who can hear it?* is better rendered by RSV 'who can listen to it?', and by Knox 'who can be expected to listen to it?'

Hard means 'offensive'.

69. *Christ, the Son of the living God* is the reading of the later MSS, and is probably due to an attempt to harmonize the present passage with Matthew's account of Peter's confession at Caesarea Philippi (see Mt. xvi. 16). The oldest MSS read here 'the Holy One (*ho hagios*) of God' (so RV and RSV). The demoniacs possessed this particular insight into the supernatural character of Jesus (see Mk. i. 24); and they knew that His essential holiness and their own evil nature were eternally opposed. Here the significance of *ho hagios* seems to be that the apostles have recognized Jesus as 'dedicated' by God to convey *the words of eternal life* to mankind.

IV. JESUS THE APOSTLE OF GOD: THE GIVER OF SIGHT: THE SHEPHERD OF THE SHEEP (vii. 1–x. 21)

a. The Feast of Tabernacles (vii. 1–13)

In this Gospel Jerusalem is the storm-centre of the Messiah's ministry, where He vindicates His claims before consummating His work by suffering outside its walls. So in the seventh chapter, after a reference to the temporary shelter provided by Galilee, the scene at once shifts back to Jerusalem at the time of the autumn festival of Tabernacles; and this festival provides the background of the narrative till x. 21, just as the Passover supplied the background to the incidents and teaching recorded in chapters v and vi.

At Tabernacles the Jews not only kept Harvest Festival, but also commemorated with thanksgiving the divine protection afforded to their ancestors during the long sojourn in the wilderness, when God tabernacled with Israel in the tent of meeting as they journeyed from place to place. After the time of Solomon the Jerusalem temple came to be regarded more and more as the exclusive spot, where the divine presence could be encountered; and it was part of the religious decline of Judaism that it tried to localize the presence of God by an exaggerated emphasis on the temple. But neither in the tent of witness nor in the temple was the divine presence fully or finally manifested. Both were shadows of something better to come. Both pointed forward to the day when God would dwell not only in the midst of the congregation of Israel, but in the hearts of all believers, after a new covenant-relationship between God and the individual had been made possible by the removal of the barrier that sin had erected. It was precisely such a new covenant-relationship that Jesus had come to bring into being by the sacrifice of Himself, for only so could He make the permanent indwelling of God in the believer's heart a reality.

The approach of Tabernacles was of significance therefore for Jesus in the working out of His unique vocation. His brothers were in a sense perfectly right when they challenged Him to go up with the other pilgrims to the festival, and make a public manifestation of Himself at the very centre of Jewry, so that the faith of His disciples living at the capital might be strengthened; for it was true that it was at Jerusalem that the full and final display of His glory must be publicly made; upon it true faith depended, and without it God could not tabernacle in men's hearts. The brothers were wrong however in what they understood the glory of Jesus to consist. Like the Galilaeans in chapter vi, they imagined His glory to be limited to demonstrations of His miraculous powers, whereas in reality it could only be supremely displayed by His crucifixion. Just because the request of His brothers was based on so false a conception of His vocation, it was in fact another sign of their unbelief, and Jesus could not yield to it. When the proper time was come, when His predestined hour should strike, and the hatred of the world for One, who was exposing the evil nature of its life, should reach its climax, then He would manifest His glory at Jerusalem on a cross, but not at the present festival of Tabernacles. The brothers of Jesus are still part of the evil world, which organizes itself without reference to God's purposes. They can therefore move about freely within it, at any time, without any risk or danger. They can take their full part in the festival, for they are unaware of its limitations and its imperfections. Jesus must walk more circumspectly, and not force the issue before the time was come; He would not therefore take any part in the present pilgrimage to Jerusalem. And when He does make the journey, after the others have gone, he travels *as it were in secret* (10). His presence in the city could not, however, remain unknown, and attempts were made to discover where He was hiding; there was also much whispering among the crowds about Him. 'He is a good man' was the verdict of some; others were convinced that He was leading the people astray; but there was no public expression of their views for fear that the Jewish authorities might take action against His sympathizers.

Additional Notes

vii. 2. For details about the feast of Tabernacles at the end of September see Lv. xxiii. 39–43 and Dt. xvi. 13–15.

3. For a discussion of the meaning of *His brethren* see the introduction to the author's commentary on James.[1]

Thy disciples means in this context 'thy disciples at Jerusalem'.

4. *If thou do these things;* i.e. 'If you really are performing miracles'.

6. The word *kairos*, translated *time*, means 'the right, or proper time', 'the fitting occasion'. Here it denotes 'the predestined time'.

8. For the reading *go not up yet* many ancient MSS have 'go not up'. The latter reading, adopted by RSV, is perhaps more likely to have been changed to the former than *vice versa*. On the other hand, *not yet* is very strongly attested, and it may be that it was altered to 'not' in the light of the interpretation given to the passage in some parts of Christendom (e.g. by Ephraem in the fourth century) which virtually construes *unto this feast* as 'at this feast'. In the literal sense Jesus did go up to the feast, but His real 'ascent' was not made till the final Passover when He was crucified.

b. Jesus the Apostle of God (vii. 14–52)

We learn from the earlier Gospels that the congregation in the synagogue at Capernaum was astonished at the authoritative character of Jesus' teaching (see Mk. i. 22); and that later in the synagogue at Nazareth people were at a loss to discover the source of the young carpenter's knowledge, for they were well acquainted with those responsible for His upbringing (see Mk. vi. 2). Now, in the temple, where Jesus began to teach again when the festival was half over and excitement had begun to wane, the Jews show amazement that a man with no professional training as an interpreter of the law should dare

[1] *The General Epistle of James* (*Tyndale New Testament Commentaries,* 1956), pp. 22-24.

to expound the Scriptures. If He was merely self-taught, then (so they appeared to have argued) His teaching, so far from possessing authority, was boastful and impertinent. Jesus refuted this charge by drawing attention to the *divine* source both of His claims to be a teacher and of the content of His teaching. He was no upstart, puffed up by His own self-gathered knowledge, nor did He aim at winning honour for Himself; He was sent by God, and His supreme object was to reflect the glory of Him that sent Him (16). That was the hall-mark of honesty and sincerity.

It is characteristic of many of the outstanding men of the Bible that they are convinced that they must do what they are doing, and say what they are saying, because they have received a divine commission. They are, in a word, God's apostles. Moses is *sent* by God to Pharaoh to bring forth His people out of Egypt (Ex. iii. 9f.). Ezekiel is *sent* to the children of Israel to convey to them God's message, whether they will hear or whether they will forbear (Ezk. ii. 3ff.). Similarly Jesus, who is significantly described in the Epistle to the Hebrews as 'the Apostle . . . of our profession' (Heb. iii. 1), was conscious of being *sent* to Israel as Messiah and Saviour. He told His disciples that He must preach and work in other towns as well as at Capernaum, for it was for that purpose that He had 'come forth' (Mk. i. 38); and from Luke's narrative it is clear that 'come forth' implies 'come forth from God', for his version of the expression is 'for this purpose was I *sent*' (see Lk. iv. 43). Throughout John's narrative, and particularly in this debate with the Jews at Tabernacles, great emphasis is laid by Jesus upon the Father who *sent* Him, as the primary source of His authority; and He indicates that only those who are eager to do God's will can recognize in His teaching the marks of divine origin and truth (17).

The Jews might pride themselves on being interpreters of the Mosaic law, and blame Jesus for breaking the law of sabbath observance; but the fact that they were looking for an opportunity to murder Him showed that they were breaking the sixth commandment (19). The prohibition of murder belonged to that part of the law which was a permanent and final revelation of moral truth. On the other hand, the laws relating to circumcision, and some of the details of the laws relating to the sabbath were of a more temporary nature. Their purpose was to prepare Israel for something better. The command to practise circumcision, given by God to the patriarchs and later enshrined in the Mosaic legislation, was important not least because it was a type of the greater circumcision of the heart, by which evil would be cut away from what is the mainspring of human conduct. This circumcision of the heart the law could never effect; it was destined to be God's gift to man when the blessed messianic age should dawn. In the same way, the sabbath, from one point of view, was a weekly preparation for the sabbath-rest of God which the Christ alone would make available for believers. Jesus had in fact made it clear by healing the disabled man that He, the Christ, had come not to make *part* of a man whole, as circumcision did, but to recreate his entire being. This was essentially divine work, the work of God who is perpetually at work and yet keeps endless sabbath. If therefore permission was given by the law to practise on the sabbath circumcision, which only conveyed *limited* benefits, how much more fitting was it that the work of *complete* restoration should be undertaken on that holy day (23)! To try to murder Jesus for such an action as this was to be guilty of a wholly superficial judgment; on the other hand, to see in what He was doing signs that He was fulfilling God's purposes as set forth in the laws relating to both circumcision and the sabbath would be to form a judgment that was just.

The threats of the Jews to kill Jesus do not deter Him, and He continues to teach unmolested. Some of the inhabitants of Jerusalem are so astonished at this that they begin to wonder whether some of the authorities may not have accepted Him as the Christ (26). But such an idea is soon dismissed when they recall His earthly origin. He had not come unexpectedly and from somewhere unknown as they had been led to believe the Christ would come. To these bewildered folk Jesus speaks once again about the divine nature of His mission. He admits that they know where He has come from; He has come, it is true, from Galilee; but Galilee is not His original provenance. He has come from God. The God who is ultimate reality, the God of whom He has direct knowledge, has sent Him (29). Many of the crowd, though unimpressed by His claim to be of divine origin, nevertheless believe in Him because of the great number of signs He has performed; and the expression of their belief alarms the chief priests who hear of it, and leads them to take drastic action against Him. They send some of the temple-police to arrest Him (32). But, however much they may attempt to get rid of Him, they are powerless to do so till the appointed hour has come; and *a little while* remains before that hour is destined to strike (33). The death of Jesus, moreover, which the Jews will ultimately succeed in bringing about, will not mean His complete disappearance, but will be the prelude to His return to the Father who sent Him, and in that heavenly state He will be beyond the reach of all unbelievers.

The Jews completely fail to grasp the meaning of Jesus' words *I go unto him that sent me. Ye shall seek me, and shall not find me: and where I am, thither ye cannot come* (33, 34). After discussing it among themselves they can only conclude that He is speaking about leaving Judaea and going to teach among their brethren dispersed throughout the Hellenistic world, a mission which would not be confined to Greek-speaking Jews but would be for Gentiles as well. Here, as more than once in this Gospel, the Jews are unconsciously prophesying. The departure of Jesus in death would indeed be beneficial, but not because it would remove from the earth a false Messiah, as they supposed, but because, as a result of the proclamation of the gospel which would follow His death and resurrection, Gentiles would be brought into the people of God.

The departure of Jesus in death would also make possible that baptism of the Spirit, which was to be the supreme gift of Jesus to all who believed in Him. This truth is proclaimed once again on *the last day, that great day of the feast*, when water from the pool of Siloam was solemnly offered (37). Jesus promises to all believers, who are conscious of their need of it, the gift of thirst-quenching water which would become in them a perpetual source of refreshment both to themselves and others.

Though no specific passage of Scripture is quoted, this would in fact be a fulfilment of such prophecies as that of Zechariah that one day a fountain would be open to the house of David, and living waters would go out from Jerusalem (Zc. xiii. 1, xiv. 8); and of Isaiah that God would pour water upon the thirsty (Is. xliv. 3, lv. 1). The evangelist makes it clear that these words of Jesus about *living water* flowing *out of his belly*, i.e. from the inmost nature of the believer, refer to *the Spirit, which they that believe on him should receive:* and, he adds, *the Holy Ghost was not yet given; because that Jesus was not yet glorified* (38, 39). Only when Jesus is glorified in a death, which, though brought about by the Jews, is none the less a death of His own choice, will the cleansing and refreshing power of the Spirit come in all its fullness to those who accept Him as Saviour.

The people of Jerusalem remain bewildered and divided by this teaching. Some are prepared to accept Jesus as the expected prophet like unto Moses; some as the Christ, though presumably a Christ after their own pattern; while others, ignorant apparently of His birth in the royal town of Bethlehem or of His legal descent from David, find his Galilaean origin a stumbling-block to belief; and there were also those who would have liked to arrest Him. But no-one, not even the temple police, can in fact lay hands on Him (44).

The excuse given by the police for their failure to make an arrest is the unprecedented character of Jesus' words and His manner of speech (46). This exasperating report is taken by the authorities as evidence that these servants of the Sanhedrin have been led astray, and have rejected the judgment of their employers about Jesus in favour of the whims of some of the crowd, who in their ignorance of the law are under the curse of God. Their exasperation is increased, when one of their own number, *Nicodemus*, who, as the evangelist reminds his readers, *came to Jesus by night*, reminds them that it is contrary to the law to condemn anyone without first giving him a proper judicial hearing and attempting to obtain accurate information about what he has done (50, 51). But Nicodemus seems, to his fellow-counsellors, to be behaving as though he too were a despised Galilaean, who would accept forsooth a Galilaean Christ! Let him read his Bible again and produce the evidence that any prophet, much less the Messiah, would come from Galilee!

Additional Notes

vii. 15. *Having never learned;* i.e. having never graduated n the rabbinic schools.

17. *I speak of myself;* i.e. make up what I say out of my own head.

19. The first reference to *the law* is to the law as a whole; the second to the specific law against murder.

20. *Thou hast a devil;* i.e. 'You are possessed, and therefore mad'. The same was said of John the Baptist (see Mt. xi. 18).

21. *One work;* i.e. one work on the sabbath at Jerusalem, *viz.* the healing of the cripple described in chapter v.

22. *Therefore* translates *dia touto* (lit. 'because of this'). By their position in the Greek these two words could be attached to the last sentence in verse 21; so RSV, 'You all marvel at it'. But as there is no previous mention that the healing of the impotent man caused wonder, they should probably be taken with the opening clause of verse 22, as in AV. The logic of the passage seems to be: 'One of the reasons why Moses gave you circumcision was that you might learn not to take too narrow a view of sabbath observance, for circumcision is permitted on the sabbath.'

Because, though a possible translation of the Greek *hoti*, is here almost certainly wrong. It should be rendered 'that', the general sense being 'I say that Moses gave you circumcision, but in fact the command to circumcise was first given to Abraham'.

23. *The law of Moses;* i.e. the law relating to circumcision, which made circumcision obligatory on the eighth day after birth, even if that was a sabbath.

Every whit whole; i.e. healthy in every part, not merely in a single member.

26. The particles introducing the question in the Greek (*mē pote*) give the sense 'Can it possibly be that the rulers have information?'

28. The second *and* in this verse has, as it so often has in this Gospel, the meaning 'and yet'.

True translates *alēthinos* which denotes genuineness rather than veracity. Here the meaning is that God is the ultimate reality.

34. *Where I am;* i.e. in the heavenly sphere.

38. Some MSS and commentators, both ancient and modern, attach the words *He that believeth on me* to the previous sentence, giving the sense 'let him that believeth on me drink'. If this is done, it is probable that the words of Scripture mentioned (it is not a definite quotation) refer to Christ, out of whose *belly*, i.e. from the centre of whose being, flows living water. It is better however to punctuate as in AV, and to take *his* as a reference to the believer. This is in keeping with the teaching given in iv. 10–14.

Belly is, in fact, 'the womb', the sphere of generation.

41. The way the question is introduced in the original conveys a marked note of surprise; 'Why surely the Christ is not going to come from Galilee?'

42. For the descent of the Messiah from *the seed of David* see 2 Sa. vii. 12; and for His coming from *Bethlehem* the key text is Mi. v. 2, quoted in Mt. ii. 6.

48. *Have any of the rulers* is better rendered 'Is there a single one of the rulers?'

49. Cf. Dt. xxvii. 26, 'Cursed be he that confirmeth not all the words of this law to do them.' The Pharisees do not understand that they, as well as the despised rabble, were under the same curse.

51. See Dt. i. 16, 17 for what the law says about just judgment.

[Jesus and the woman taken in adultery (vii. 53–viii. 11)]

Scholars are agreed that this section did not originally form part of St. John's Gospel, though it records a genuine incident in the life of Jesus. Not only does the overwhelming majority of ancient Greek MSS omit it at this point, but many of the later MSS which include it here mark it with asterisks denoting that there was doubt about its position. One group of MSS, moreover, inserts it after Luke xxi. 38; one MS has it after John vii. 36; and a few others after John xxi. 24. All this evidence suggests that scribes were often ignorant of its exact position, though anxious to retain it as part of the four Gospels. This consideration becomes more probable in view of the large number of variant readings which are found in this short section. Apart from numerous minor changes the following explanatory additions found in the text followed by AV are omitted in most ancient authorities: *as though he heard them not* (verse 6); *being convicted by their own conscience*, and *even unto the last* (verse 9); *and saw none but the woman*, and *those thine accusers* (verse 10); while some later MSS add at the end of verse 8, 'the sins of each one of them'. All this suggests that the story was constantly repeated verbally and that varied versions of it were current. In its present position it clearly interrupts the discourse at the festival of Tabernacles; and it contains phrases, such as 'the scribes and Pharisees', which occur nowhere else in this Gospel. The general style of the passage is more Lucan than Johannine.

It may have been inserted here as an illustration of Jesus' words in viii. 15, *I judge no man*; or possibly to show that, while the Jews could not convict Jesus of sin (see viii. 46), Jesus could and did, particularly on this occasion, convict them. The mention of *the mount of Olives* would naturally account for its presence after Luke xxi. 38; and its insertion after John xxi. 24 is evidence of the desire to keep it as an addition to the narratives of the four Gospels, even though the scribes were ignorant where it should be inserted. Incidentally, the fact that these particular MSS placed it after xxi. 24 and not after xxi. 25 is some indication that this Gospel was once in circulation without verse 25, for it would have been somewhat unintelligent to insert a passage of this length between the two closing verses of the Gospel, but perfectly intelligent to add it as an appendix to the Gospel as a whole (see further the note on xxi. 25).

The unnamed woman in this story is guilty of the same sin as the Samaritan woman in chapter iv, though from the reference to the law in verse 5 it might seem that she was liable to this particular punishment because she had sinned during the period of betrothal, fornication during that time being regarded as adultery (see Dt. xxii. 23, 24). The scribes and Pharisees who report the case to Jesus seem roused to righteous indignation at the sin that had been committed; but it is clear from the evangelist's comment in verse 6 that the question they put to Jesus was prompted not by religious but by political motives. It was asked as a test question to enable them to form a charge against Him. They hoped, as in the case of the tribute-money (see Mk. xii. 13–17), to put Jesus in a dilemma; and by making Him uphold the validity of the Jewish law about stoning to cause Him to challenge the Roman authority which had reserved for itself the sole right to inflict a capital sentence.

Jesus is fully aware of their intentions. He knows that the zeal for righteousness of these Pharisees is 'not according to knowledge'. Their interest in complying with the letter of the law goes hand in hand with a failure to recognize the truth about their own nature and their own status with God. They see clearly the evil that is in others, but are blind to the evil in themselves. Ready at all times to class as sinners all who cannot or will not keep the law, they fail to see that their own self-righteousness is sin. Eager to discover whether Jesus shares their own enthusiasm for the moral law by passing the death sentence upon those who violate it, they are ignorant that they themselves have a death to undergo, if they are to receive salvation. That death, to be sure, is a spiritual death, but none the less a radical death, such as only the God who kills and makes alive can effect, the death of the proud sinful ego which leads men to thank God they are not as other men, when all the time God's face is turned away from them.

Jesus will not therefore tell His questioners whether He approves either of the law they invoke or of the action of the Roman power in preventing the Jews from enacting the penalty it prescribed; nor will He pass judgment on the woman, and displays His unwillingness to do so by stooping and scribbling with His finger on the ground. The words *as though he heard them not* in verse 6, though probably not original, correctly interpret the meaning of Jesus' action. When the Pharisees press their question, Jesus sits up straight as though about to give a judicial decision, but His words instead of being a sentence upon the woman are like a sword driven deep into the hearts of her hypocritical accusers. *He that is without sin among you, let him first cast a stone at her* (7). 'Judgment', He seems to say, 'must begin at the house of God' (see 1 Pet. iv. 17). It begins with those who claim to speak in God's name, to be defenders of His justice, and to administer His laws, but who know not that their own vision is blinded by sin. And, as Jesus stoops down again and leaves His words to accomplish the task for which He uttered them, those who were *tempting him, that they might have to accuse him* (6) become themselves accused. *They which heard it, being convicted by their own conscience, went out one by one, beginning at the eldest, even unto the last* (9). When Jesus sat up again and saw that all her accusers and would-be condemners were gone, He uttered the words with which the story ends, *Neither do I condemn thee: go, and sin no more* (11).

This saying, so characteristic of what Paul calls the 'gentleness of Christ' (2 Cor. x. 1), is liable to be misunderstood; and it may well be that fear lest it should be misunderstood was one of the reasons why it was some time before the story had a settled place in the Gospels. Jesus does not in fact imply that the woman's sin can be glossed over, or that it can be lightly forgiven without any payment of the penalty it deserved. On the contrary, Jesus Himself was going to pay that penalty, the penalty not only of the woman's sins, but of the sins of her accusers, and indeed the sins of all mankind, by suffering in her place and in theirs a criminal's death. In the meantime He gives this particular sinner an insight into the blessed truth proclaimed in i. 17, 'The law was given by Moses, but grace and truth came by Jesus Christ.' Only in Him are mercy and truth met together; only in Him do righteousness and peace kiss each other (see Ps. lxxxv. 10).

T. W. Manson ends a discussion of this section with words which may well give us food for thought. 'Once more Jesus refused to back Jewish nationalism against Roman imperialism. And he did something more, which is, I think, not irrelevant to present-day discussions about marriage, divorce, and second marriage: he gave a plain hint that the mechanical and rigorous administration of laws, however lofty the ideals they embody, is not, in the last resort, the best way of dealing with sinners as persons; particularly when the administrators themselves cannot be expected to have perfectly clean hands.'[1]

c. Jesus the Light of the world (viii. 12–30)

During this same visit to Jerusalem for the festival of Tabernacles, while teaching near the treasury in the temple, Jesus made the further revelation of Himself as *the light of the world* (12), who opens the eyes of men's spiritual understanding and guides them into the truth about themselves and about what God has done to satisfy their most urgent needs. Such a revelation at this time was in keeping with the symbolism of the festival. The Israelites had been guided during their journey across the wilderness by a pillar of light in the sky; and this phenomenon was recalled to the minds of worshippers at Tabernacles by the ceremony of lighting the golden candelabra. Jesus, the Word of God, whose life, as the Prologue has stated, is 'the light of men' (i. 4), gives illumination to all who follow Him. The nature of this illumination becomes more explicit in the controversy that follows the gift of sight to a man blind from birth recorded in chapter ix.

At the moment, the Pharisees hearing the pronouncement *I am the light of the world* raise once again the question of the authority by which Jesus acts and speaks (13). Is He not, in fact, a witness in His own defence, giving invalid testimony to

[1] T. W. Manson, *Jesus and the Non-Jews* (The Athlone Press, 1955), p. 10

Himself? In the discourse in chapter v He made it clear that the real witness to Himself was God. He now claims that His own knowledge of His divine origin and of His divine destination gives Him the right to bear witness, if need be, to Himself; and asserts that it is precisely because the Jews refuse to recognize where He came from and where He was going, that their judgment of Him is superficial and based solely on external considerations. In any case, true and perfect judgment is God's sole prerogative. Even Jesus Himself does not exercise that judgment during His earthly life (15). His presence in the world, it is true, leads men to pass judgment on themselves; but He is not at the moment passing judgment on anybody, though He claims that were He to do so His judgment would be true because of the unbroken unity between Himself and Him that sent Him (16). If the Jews then demand *two* witnesses in order to satisfy the Jewish law of evidence, those two witnesses exist; they are Jesus and His Father (18). In reality, however, the testimony of these Two is single and undivided. The Jews now understand that He is referring not to a human father but to God, but they are unwilling to allow the validity of an invisible witness who cannot appear and give evidence before them. So they formulate their next question in a manner which might appear to show ignorance on their part as to whether He is speaking of a divine or human father. *Where is thy Father?* they ask. Jesus, in reply, admits that God cannot be a visible witness in the same way as human witnesses, but insists that He can nevertheless be known and understood; for to know Jesus is to know God. In their blindness as to the nature of Jesus the Jews reveal how limited is their knowledge of God. *Ye neither know me*, Jesus tells them, *nor my Father: if ye had known me, ye should have known my Father also* (19).

The Jews, moreover, are as ignorant of the destination of Jesus as they are of His origin. They hope by murdering Him to be rid of Him for ever. In fact, however, He will go back to His Father after making atonement for sinners, without which they will die unforgiven; and in the heavenly sphere where He is going He will be beyond the reach of all unbelievers (21). The Jews, for all their religious pretensions, are essentially strangers to that higher realm of spiritual realities; they belong to the world below. Consequently they fail entirely to understand that, when He says He will go where they cannot follow, He is not speaking of suicide, but of a glory to be reached by Him in and through death. Nor can they grasp that nothing except faith in Him and in His atoning sacrifice can save them from dying in their sins, i.e. unredeemed (24).

The teaching that Jesus is now giving, and has been giving since the beginning of His earthly ministry, reveals fully and finally the nature of God as He has been from all eternity, and as He has been shown to be through the words of His inspired prophets. Such would seem to be the meaning of the difficult words with which Jesus answers the question *Who art thou?*, which the AV translates *Even the same that I said unto you from the beginning* (25). Because His hearers, for the most part, fail to accept His teaching as a revelation of God, which He has been commissioned by His Father to unfold, the Father who is always with Him and to whom He is always obedient, they stand under His judgment. But, as Jesus prophesies, these truths will come home to them in all their stark reality when they have lifted Him up on a cross and discovered that that will not be the end of His influence. Such a clear statement that He is in fact not just a man but the supernatural Son of man, whose knowledge is no product of his own human wisdom but divine truth, leads many to commit themselves unto Him in faith (30).

Additional Notes

viii. 12. This verse resumes the discourse broken off after vii. 52. *Unto them* refers, therefore, to the Jews addressed in chapter vii.

The light of life could mean 'the light which comes from Him who is life', or 'the light which results in life' or 'the light which is itself life'. In view of i. 4 the last would seem to be the primary, though not necessarily the exclusive meaning.

13. The rabbinical law of evidence held that a man's testimony on his own behalf was invalid.

14. No *man* knows either his origin or his destiny. Such knowledge is a mark of divinity.

15. *After the flesh;* i.e. superficially, judging by appearances only.

I judge no man; i.e. during My earthly life. All judgment is in fact committed to the Son of man, but the exercise of that prerogative will be at the final judgment.

16. *True.* The best attested reading is *alēthinos*, 'valid'.

17. The expression *your law*, found again at x. 34, does not imply that Jesus in any way dissociates Himself from the law. He speaks in this way that His hearers may understand that the law, to which they appeal in order to condemn Him, also contains much in the light of which they stand condemned. The passage of the law here referred to is Dt. xix. 15.

20. The *treasury* was not a building but the receptacle for offerings visible to all (see Mk. xii. 41).

24. The absolute *I am* found also in verses 28 and 58 without a predicate in the Greek signifies, 'I am what I really am', or 'I am what I am telling you that I am'.

25, 26. RV margin gives an alternative translation 'How is it that I speak to you at all?' This is a possible rendering of the Greek, and was the interpretation of Chrysostom and the Greek Fathers generally. If this is adopted Jesus gives no answer to the question *Who art thou?*, but rebukes His hearers and proceeds at once to tell them that He has much to say to them in judgment, but that He does not pronounce such judgment now, but limits His teaching to what He has heard from His Father. The translation of AV, RV and RSV seems preferable, though it is not without difficulty, as the verb translated *I said* (RV 'I have spoken') in the Greek is in the present tense.

28. The word *lifted up* has a moral as well as a physical connotation. On the cross the Son of man is exalted to high honour. The cross is the throne from which He reigns, and His continued influence after His resurrection, and the fulfilment of His prophecies (e.g. that Jerusalem would be destroyed), will be evidence even to His opponents that He is no self-appointed human teacher, but sent from God.

d. Christian freedom (viii. 31–59)

It is clear that a new paragraph in this long debate begins at verse 31. Jesus now turns to address certain Jews whose belief in Him would seem to have been merely nominal and intellectual, and therefore short-lived. The evangelist very significantly uses a different Greek construction to distinguish the belief of this group from the fuller belief of the many who are mentioned in verse 30, a point noticed in RV but not in AV. This belief was inferior because it lacked personal commitment. It was similar to the belief of those mentioned in ii. 23, who believed when they saw the miracles that Jesus did, but Jesus did not trust Himself to them, the reason clearly being that they had not made the self-commitment that is an essential ingredient of true faith. The Jews addressed in this section of chapter viii were prepared, we may suppose, to give assent to many of the statements of Jesus but not to accept their implication for themselves. They were, in a word, nominal disciples.

True discipleship, as Jesus says clearly in verse 31, means abiding in His word, i.e. welcoming it, being at home with it, and living with it so continuously that it becomes part of the believer's life, a permanent influence and stimulus in every fresh advance in goodness and holiness. Christ's word is indistinguishable from Christ Himself. He is the Word. To abide in His word is therefore to abide in Him, to be always within earshot of His voice; and when a believer abides in Christ, Christ abides in him, and Christ's life invigorates and sustains the believer's life. This is genuine discipleship, as Jesus makes clear in verse 31, *If ye continue in my word, then are ye my disciples indeed.*

It is apparent in this section that what prevents men and women from making the personal surrender to Christ, which is the essence of true belief, is their exclusive and intense reliance on other things, and a failure to understand that those other things are blinding them to the truth about themselves. It may be reliance on ancestry, or national privileges and traditions; it may be a blind trust in the rites and ceremonies of religion, or a slavish obedience to some external law or rule of life—but the result is always the same, a failure to grasp the truth about themselves. Man's greatest need, it has been well said, is to know what *is* his greatest need.

The Jews to whom Jesus is now speaking have no understanding of their real predicament. They imagine that spiritually they are free. They are pathetically content with the knowledge that they are physically descended from Abraham. *We be Abraham's seed*, they confidently assert in verse 33; *Abraham is our father* they repeat in verse 39. The righteousness of Abraham, they assume, is a sufficient guarantee for their own; and they presume that they have been made free from slavery to the evil impulses of human nature by the covenant made by God with their forefather. *We be not born of fornication*, is their self-righteous claim in verse 41. 'We are not like the Samaritans', they imply, 'descended from an unholy union between Jews and heathen. Nor are we guilty like them of the idolatry, called in our Scriptures "fornication", which combines the worship of Israel's God with the recognition of other deities. We are God's servants, keepers of His law. How then can we be in servitude to anyone? We may have been politically in slavery at certain periods in our history, but spiritually we are free.' They are bitterly indignant when Jesus tells them that they are out of touch with reality and blind to the truth about themselves, and when He points out to them that only the truth which comes from full surrender to Himself can liberate them, for as long as His word *hath no place* in them (RV 'hath not free course' in them) they remain spiritually enslaved.

The bitter truth was that for all their imagined freedom there were fetters in these men's souls which no amount of nominal belief or external religion could remove. The evidence that they were in slavery is given by Jesus in verse 34, *Whosoever committeth sin is the servant of sin*, or, if we follow the ancient authorities which omit *of sin*, 'whoever commits sin is a slave'.

Jesus does not mean, 'Whoever commits *a* sin', but whoever habitually asserts his own will, priding himself on his own independence, following his own inclinations, and primarily concerned with pleasing himself—whoever, in a word, is living a self-centred life—is a slave. Such a person is confined within the limits of his own self-interest.

That this was in fact the state of these men who had professed to believe in Him is clear, Jesus tells them in verse 40, because instead of whole-heartedly accepting His words, which embody the truth He has heard from God, they are now trying to put Him to death. They may claim to be Abraham's children, and physically they are, but Abraham never behaved like that! On the contrary, he welcomed the divine messengers sent to him (see Gn. xviii. 2ff.). To be in the grip of the lust to kill is to be a slave indeed, and to be spiritually neither a child of Abraham nor a child of God, but rather, as Jesus states plainly in verse 44, a child of the devil, who was *a murderer from the beginning*, the instigator of the first recorded murder when Cain slew his brother. Similarly, to refuse to understand and come under the influence of the truth, which was God's truth, spoken by Him who was sent from God to proclaim it, is in fact to give unmistakable evidence of spiritual descent from him whose very nature is falsehood, and whose entire object is to deceive the human heart—the devil himself. When the devil tells a lie, Jesus says in verse 44, he is speaking his native language, for he is a liar and the father of lies.

The first step therefore towards true spiritual freedom is to recognize our slavery, and to know that we have no power to liberate ourselves. Slaves cannot emancipate themselves. A slave cannot have the status of a son or live as a son. His position in the household is moreover but temporary. *The servant abideth not in the house for ever* (35). So the slave of sin cannot by himself change his status. He cannot convert himself, nor can he be converted by any fellow-sinner. He may long to be free; he may feverishly strive to be free, and others may help him in the struggle; but any freedom that he may enjoy by such efforts will be but the temporary exercise of an impotent will and therefore short-lived. It will not be the real freedom of which Jesus speaks in verse 36, where the word *indeed* shows that there is also a spurious kind of freedom. A man may be really free, even when outward appearances point to the contrary. Jesus was really innocent, said the centurion at the foot of the cross (Lk. xxiii. 47), though He looked like a criminal paying the penalty for his crime. On the other hand, a man may appear to be free, when inwardly he is the slave of wayward passions and uncontrolled desires.

The liberator from our bondage must come from outside the ranks of enslaved humanity. He must be a new Man, a second Adam, wholly free from the chains forged for the human race by the first Adam. He must be no temporary dweller in His Father's home but the eternal Son who lives for ever in His Father's presence, fully cognizant of His Father's will, ever seeking to reflect His Father's glory, speaking only what He has heard from His Father, and guiltless of human sin. Such a Liberator, Jesus in this great passage claims Himself to be. *The servant abideth not in the house for ever: but the Son abideth ever. If the Son therefore shall make you free, ye shall be free indeed* (35, 36).

Because Jesus denies that the Jews who oppose Him have the freedom of sons, and because He implies that they are not members of the true Israel, they try to dismiss Him as *a Samaritan* (48) challenging their right to be God's children, and as a madman obsessed with a sense of His own importance, glorifying Himself and making Himself out to be greater than Abraham (53). How absurd was His claim that all who obeyed what He said would never die, when Abraham was dead, and the prophets! But they stand condemned, Jesus says in effect, by the very patriarch whose spiritual, as well as whose physical, descendants they claim to be. Abraham had a vision of the messianic age, and rejoiced in the knowledge of what was going to be the climax of the divine revelation, which began with his own call to be the progenitor of the elect people of God (56). Jesus knows of Abraham's joy, for Abraham's mind is known to Him in virtue of His own divine nature and pre-existence. *Before Abraham was*, He asserts, *I am* (58). This claim to pre-existence leads the Jews to attempt to stone Him on the spot, but Jesus evades them and disappears from their sight.

Additional Notes

viii. 31. *Believed on him.* The Greek translated here is a different construction (*pisteuō* with the dative) from that similarly translated in verse 30 (*pisteuō* followed by *eis* with the accusative). The latter, in the usage of this evangelist, denotes a fuller and less formal belief than the former. As it is clear from the subsequent narrative that these men had now ceased to be believers, the perfect tense should probably be translated 'had believed'.

37. The verb translated *hath no place* (*chōrei*) usually has the transitive sense, 'make room for', 'contain' (see ii. 6), but is here used intransitively. Hence the RV translation 'hath not free course in you'. The meaning, however, is not that these Jews have received the word but not allowed it to make progress, but that they have never really made room for it at all.

39. According to the reading adopted in AV, Jesus denies that the Jews are *Abraham's children* in the sense that children should reflect the qualities of their sire. Another ancient reading, which may well be original, gives the sense 'If you are Abraham's children do the works of Abraham'. If this is correct Jesus admits that they are legitimate descendants of Abraham, but challenges them to behave in a manner worthy of their lineage.

43. By *cannot hear my word* Jesus means that though the Jews hear it they do not entertain or pay attention to what they hear. RSV, 'cannot bear to hear', and R. A. Knox, 'you have no ear for the message', bring out the sense better.

44. The Greek *estēken*, taken as an aorist in some MSS and here translated *abode not*, should be aspirated and read as *hestēken*, which has a present meaning. So RSV 'has nothing to do with the truth'.

Of his own; i.e. what is natural to him.

Of it; i.e. of lying.

46. *Convinceth* is archaic. Modern English requires 'convicts' to convey the sense.

The unexpressed answer to the rhetorical question is 'Nobody'. Therefore, Jesus proceeds to argue, His opponents have no ground for not believing Him when He tells them the truth. *If*, as very often, has a temporal sense.

50. Jesus does not spend time defending His reputation. His Father is ever eager to promote His Son's honour, and in doing so He passes judgment on those who wilfully misrepresent Him.

55. Different words are used in this verse for *know*. The Pharisees have not 'come to know' God for what He really is. Jesus does not have to 'come to know' the Father for He has immediate knowledge of Him. The former sense is expressed by *ginōskō* and the latter by *oida*.

56. The Greek does not mean 'rejoiced in the hope of seeing My day' when it actually came, and when Abraham would be in the abode of the blessed; but 'rejoiced in that he actually saw' it while he was still on earth. There was a rabbinic tradition that when God established His covenant with Abraham (Gn. xv. 9ff.), the latter received a vision of the messianic age. It is interesting also that the Hebrew expression in Gn. xxiv. 1, which stated that Abraham 'went into the days' (an expression translated in our Bible 'was well-stricken in age') was taken by some Rabbis to mean that he saw into the distant future.

58. *Was.* The Greek *egeneto* should be rendered 'came into being'. The fact that the Jews attempted to stone Jesus after hearing the words *I am* shows that it suggested to them the divine name so translated in the LXX version of Ex. iii. 14.

59. The words *going through the midst of them, and so passed by*, should be omitted with many ancient authorities (so RV and RSV). They seem to be an echo of Lk. iv. 30.

e. The man born blind (ix. 1–41)

The record of the failure of the Jews because of spiritual blindness to recognize Jesus as the Apostle of God and the Light of the world is followed by the story of the miraculous gift of sight to a beggar born blind. This miracle is a sign that Jesus can open the eyes of the spiritually blind so that they can receive the complete sight which constitutes perfect faith. Faith means passing from darkness to light; and to bring men this faith, to give them the opportunity of responding when the divine Spirit draws them to Himself, is the primary purpose for which Jesus has been sent into the world. Through Him the activity of God is at work in those who, apart from Him, would be as devoid of spiritual sight as the blind beggar was of physical sight. As long as Jesus is in the world He must reveal Himself in word and deed as the world's Light.

Christian faith begins when men and women come to see that sin has robbed them of spiritual vision, that in this sense they are all blind from birth and are wholly unable to free themselves from their predicament; and faith comes to maturity when they accept Jesus as the One who alone can recreate in them the faculty sin has destroyed. It is very significant that the man confronted by Jesus in this story was a *beggar* and that he was *born* blind. The reason for this misfortune, Jesus asserts, was neither the man's own sin in a pre-natal condition nor the sins of his parents. In this instance the question of whether the sins of the father had been visited upon his child, or whether the physical suffering was a direct consequence of the sufferer's own sin, is wholly irrelevant. The man's condition is what it is, because in the divine providence what is to happen to him is to be a permanent revelation of divine truth. The glory of God which Jesus will display by changing the man's physical condition is to be a sign for all time of the glory of God which shines forth in human life whenever He opens the eyes of the spiritually blind. Accordingly, the blind beggar's physical need is a symbol of all men's spiritual needs. To obtain physical sight he must not remain passive, but must wash in the pool of Siloam; and to receive the gift of spiritual sight all men must wash in the cleansing water that comes from the crucified Christ, because it is only made fully available by His atoning death. Christian experience is first and foremost a willingness to accept the gift of cleansing, a truth symbolized in baptism, the initial sacrament of the believer's life. In a word, true faith begins in obeying the command, given by Elisha to Naaman, 'Go and wash' (2 Ki. v. 10).

The change wrought by regeneration in the converted Christian is so great that other people often find it difficult to believe he is the same person; so it was with the physical change effected by Jesus in the blind beggar. Some of his neighbours, when they met him after he had been given his sight, remained at first unconvinced of his identity. Moreover, the manner in which regeneration is brought about is a great mystery to the converted man and others, just as the way in which the physical change had taken place in the beggar was beyond his own and his friends' understanding. When questioned about this, all he could do was to describe his experience in very matter-of-fact terms. He cannot explain it. *A man that is called Jesus made clay, and anointed mine eyes, and said unto me, Go to the pool of Siloam, and wash: and I went and washed, and I received sight* (11).

What the beggar knows for certain is that he has undergone a unique experience. He cannot therefore accept the verdict of the Pharisees that Jesus was not a godly person because He had technically 'broken' the sabbath by making clay; and when asked for his own opinion of his benefactor he replies *He is a prophet* (17). Later, the Pharisees learn from the man's parents that he really was born blind, but they fail to obtain from them any explanation as to how the change had taken place in their son, but are merely reminded that he is old enough to speak for himself (21). So they recall him, and urge him to speak the truth in the presence of God and to admit that he has been mistaken about Jesus, for in their view (and they are very sure that they have the prerogative to pass judgment upon their fellows, and that they possess all the information needed to formulate it) He is no prophet, but a sinner. The cocksureness, the petty-mindedness, and the legalistic spirit of Pharisaism at its worst find eloquent expression in the words *we know that this man is a sinner* (24). But the patient whose eyes have been opened will not be bullied into accepting a judgment about Jesus which conflicts with what he himself has come to know about Him; and he repeats the plain unvarnished tale of the experience by which he has been given a new faculty.

It becomes increasingly clear, as the narrative proceeds, that the Pharisees for all their claims to be spiritual leaders are in fact spiritually blind. Unable to explain this unprecedented phenomenon of a man born blind being enabled to see, they will not admit that it has really happened. Much less will they acknowledge that He who has achieved this miracle, so far from being a sinner, must be, as the man himself admits, One to whose prayers God has listened, who is obedient to His will, and who is Himself from God. *Why herein is a marvellous thing*, the man tells them in words that express his scorn for their spiritual pretensions, *that ye know not from whence he is, and yet he hath opened mine eyes* (30). By being content with the law that came by Moses and by shutting their eyes to the grace and truth which came by Jesus Christ, the Pharisees are being plunged into the darkness of unbelief as surely as the once-blind beggar is walking more and more towards the illumination of faith.

'To him that hath shall be given.' This is especially true of the believer who makes room in his heart for the word of God. Faith which begins in trustful acceptance reaches maturity in adoration and worship. The redeemed man, whose eyes God has opened, and who has washed in the water of regeneration, is inevitably led to worship his Saviour. The ultimate reason for the decline of Christian worship is, and must always be, a failure to recognize or experience the redeeming work of Jesus; for it is not as a social reformer, nor as an ethical teacher, but as Saviour that He claims and receives the adoration of the faithful. The Pharisees, the victims of a narrow legalism, expel the man who does not fit into their ecclesiastical system on the ground that he was *altogether born in sins* (34), utterly tainted from birth onwards, and yet was claiming to teach his superiors. But Jesus, hearing of his excommunication, goes at once to look for him, and hears from his lips a full confession of faith. *When he had found him, he said unto him, Dost thou believe on the Son of God? He answered and said, Who is he, Lord, that I might believe on him? And Jesus said unto him, Thou hast both seen him, and it is he that talketh with thee. And he said, Lord, I I believe. And he worshipped him* (35–38).

The last three verses of chapter ix make it clear that this incident has been recorded primarily because it is an acted parable of faith and unbelief, and therefore of judgment, a theme that is never absent for long from this Gospel. When Jesus speaks, His words are truth and judgment. For though He does not deliberately take upon Himself the function of judge, yet, because He is the real Light (see i. 9) which shows up the hidden motives and the darkest secrets of men, the inevitable consequence of His presence in the world is a separation between those who claim to have religious insight though they are in fact spiritually blind, and those who, conscious that they are blinded by sin, pray that they may be given the sight of which the sin inherent in their nature has robbed them. To awaken in men a sense of their spiritual blindness is a primary work of Jesus the Apostle of God, and the performing of it puts all who remain ignorant of their deepest need upon the defensive. Hence the indignant and touchy question of the Pharisees in verse 40, *Are we blind also?* But, as Jesus proceeded to point out to them, it is precisely when men say that they see, and *because* they say that they see, that their *sin remaineth.* They continue to be guilty men, however unconscious of their guilt.

Additional Notes

ix. 2. The disciples wrongly assume that the man's blindness must be due to sin, either his own sin or his parents'. It is not absolutely certain that they were thinking of the possibility of the man having sinned in a pre-natal condition. As R. A. Knox points out, they may not have known that the man was born blind, and the Greek might be understood to mean, 'Did this man sin? or did his parents commit some sin with the result that he was *born* blind?'

3. The ellipse after *but* in the original should be made good in translation 'but it happened that'.

4. Many ancient MSS read 'we' for *I.* If 'we' is original Jesus associates His disciples with His ministry, for there was a sense in which they too were the light of the world (see Mt. v. 14). It is perhaps more likely that 'we' would have been altered by scribes to *I* than *vice versa.* On the other hand, if *I* is original, the change to 'we' could have arisen later, when the saying became detached from its context and was used to inculcate the truth that daylight is given to make work possible, and that its opportunities should be grasped.

7. The pool received its name *Sent* from the fact that it was not a natural spring, but water was conveyed to it artificially.

14. It is clear that making clay constituted work, and rendered the worker a sabbath-breaker.

16. *This man* is contemptuous; 'This fellow'.

17. *That* is causal, 'seeing that'. Both *thou* and *thine* are emphatic in the original. 'What have *you* to say about him? After all it was *your* eyes that he opened!'

24. *Give God the praise* is literally 'Give glory to God', an expression sometimes used for giving thanks to God as in the case of the Samaritan leper who alone returned to Jesus for that purpose (see Lk. xvii. 18); and sometimes of speaking the truth as though to God Himself. For the latter sense, which is the meaning here, cf. Jos. vii. 19, 'Joshua said unto Achan, My son, give, I pray thee, glory to the Lord God of Israel, and make confession unto him; and tell me now what thou hast done.'

28. The abuse hurled at the man for daring to suggest that the Pharisees might want to become disciples of Jesus is better expressed in R. A. Knox's translation, 'Keep his discipleship for thyself'. The sense is 'You are his disciple—and you may stay so'.

31. As a well-brought-up Jew the man regards it as axiomatic that a miracle wrought in answer to prayer is proof that its worker is no sinner. No divine help is available for impenitent sinners. God has told His people when they offered Him vain oblations with hands stained with blood, 'When ye spread forth your hands, I will hide mine eyes from you: yea, when ye make many prayers, I will not hear' (Is. i. 15). And the Psalmist was well aware that if God saw iniquity in his heart He would not hear him (Ps. lxvi. 18).

35. Many ancient MSS read 'Son of man' for *Son of God.* It is clear, however, from the context, as R. A. Knox notes, that Jesus is asking the man to confess Him as a supernatural divine Person, whichever title He may have used.

36. There is an ellipse before *that.* The sense is 'I want to know that—'.

36, 38. The words translated *Lord* in these verses can also mean 'Sir'. It is probable that it should be translated 'Sir' in verse 36 before the man is aware who the Son of God is, and 'Lord' in verse 38 where He confesses his belief.

39. *They which see not* means 'they who have no spiritual vision but are conscious of their need of it'; and *they which see* means 'they who wrongly suppose that they already possess spiritual vision'.

41. *Blind,* i.e. involuntarily afflicted with physical blindness. *Now ye say, We see,* i.e. when in fact you suffer from the blindness of stupidity that results from sin.

f. Jesus the Good Shepherd (x. 1–21)

The indictment of the Pharisees by Jesus for spiritual blindness is followed very naturally by the parable of the sheepfold and the good Shepherd. Because the Pharisees are blind leaders, they are also bogus shepherds, and come under the category of those designated in x. 8 *thieves and robbers.* All who claim to be caring for God's flock but who do not enter into the sheepfold through the door which is Christ Himself—all, in other words, who hold out before men and women the prospect of a higher and better life apart from the necessity of redemption through the blood of Jesus, are deceivers, spiritual charlatans depriving men of the salvation that might otherwise be theirs. Those who have heard the authentic word of God, and who by obeying it have become members of God's flock, His elect people, will no more listen to such shepherds, however much they may claim to be speaking with divine authority, than sheep will take notice when a stranger calls to them (5).

In the Old Testament, the relationship between God and His people is often symbolized as that of a shepherd and his flock. The flock is always regarded as belonging to God though the care of it may be temporarily entrusted to others. Some of those guardians of the flock, such as Moses and the genuine prophets, tend the sheep with care, and in this respect are forerunners of Christ Himself. Others, such as the prophets who prophesy falsely, care not for the sheep; they come into the fold only to plunder, and they stand under divine judgment (see Je. xxiii. 1, 2). Like the hireling shepherds in this parable they afford the sheep no protection in the hour of danger (12). Their misdemeanours are many. They bid God's people rely upon political alliances with foreign powers rather than upon God Himself. They give 'religious' support to the policies of reigning monarchs for the sake of personal gain in a manner contrary to the divine will. They encourage men to trust in themselves, as though, forsooth, sinful men could ever justify themselves in the eyes of a holy God. The opposition of God to all such false prophets finds clear expression in the writings of the genuine prophets, especially in Ezekiel, who predicts the day when God will search for His sheep and bring them out from among foreign peoples and gather them from distant countries, whither they have been driven for lack of trustworthy leaders (see Ezk. xxxiv. 11). This prophecy is now being fulfilled in Jesus who has been sent by God as His good Shepherd, and who will gather together the sheep at present scattered far and wide.

The presence of this good Shepherd inevitably separates the sheep who belong to God's flock from those who do not. Jesus brings about this separation not only because He knows what is in *man* and shows it up in its true light, but because He knows the will and purpose of *God* His Father, and is the object of that Father's love because He is ready and willing to lay down His life in perfect obedience as a voluntary sacrifice for the sheep

(15). He has come to 'His own'—to the Israel of God. But, in Paul's words, 'they are not all Israel, which are of Israel' (Rom. ix. 6). Those who are really 'His own' listen to His voice. They recognize that He has been sent from God, and are ready to follow Him as the good Shepherd, who by His sacrificial love rescues His flock from evil and death, and leads them into the best of all pasturage where they can enjoy a richer and a fuller life (9, 10). He does not offer them an extension of physical life nor an increase of material possessions, but the possibility, nay the certainty, of a life lived at a higher level in obedience to God's will and reflecting His glory.

These genuine members of God's flock Jesus calls forth, many by name, during His earthly ministry to form the nucleus of a transformed Israel. To their number will be added, as a result of the Gentile missions which will inevitably follow after Jesus has laid down His life and taken it again, *other sheep . . . not of this fold* (16). As a result, the flock will be universal in character. Such believers, as they listen to the good Shepherd's voice, will be united to one another in virtue of their common faith in Him who loved them and gave Himself for them; and they will be under the care of shepherds conscious that they have been sent by Jesus, as Jesus was conscious that He had been sent by God. Such shepherds will never use illegal means of entering the fold, as the false shepherds in the parable did in order to carry out their murderous designs, but will go in and out through the door which is Jesus Himself. They will not, in Paul's language, preach themselves, their own philosophies or ideas, but Christ crucified as the power of God unto salvation, for faith in the good Shepherd and the desire to reflect something of His sacrificial love must always be the characteristics of those worthy to be called pastors of God's people.

The claim of Jesus to be the supreme arbiter of His destiny, to lay down His life and take it again (17, 18), is a further proof to some of the Jews that He is a megalomaniac, to listen to whom is the mark of a fool. Others see signs of sanity in His words, and cannot regard the gift of sight to a man born blind as the act of a madman (20, 21). None of them, however, sees the true significance either of the creative miracle or of the words of eternal life spoken in the parable, and so they remain blind to the essential truth about Jesus, which is that He is the Saviour of the world.

Additional Notes

x. 3. The picture is of many flocks sheltered for the night within the same fold. In the morning each shepherd collects his own flock by calling out the names of his sheep, eastern shepherds being accustomed to giving names to their sheep. In this Gospel, Jesus calls the following 'sheep' by name, Philip, Mary of Magdala, Thomas, and Simon Peter; and on each occasion it is a turning-point in the disciple's life (see xiv. 9, xx. 16, xx. 29 and xxi. 16).

6. It is perhaps not surprising that the parable was found difficult by Jesus' listeners, for it is not easy for the legally minded to think pastorally. Moreover, they probably tried to allegorize what He was saying, by attempting to find a single equivalent for each character mentioned. Some of the figures are, however, of no particular significance, e.g. *the porter*, while Jesus Himself is both *the door* and the *good shepherd*. It is significant that the word translated *parable* in this verse is not *parabolē* but *paroimia*, elsewhere translated 'proverb' (see xvi. 25, 29). In Westcott's words 'it suggests the notion of a mysterious saying full of compressed thought, rather than that of a simple comparison'.

8. The *all that ever came before me* must be limited to the false prophets that had troubled Israel at various times in their history, and to the false Messiahs, many of whom had arisen within the living memory of Jesus' hearers. Fear lest this very comprehensive expression might be supposed to include the true prophets of Israel, culminating in John the Baptist the immediate forerunner of Christ, led to the omission in some MSS of the words *before me*. Some scholars maintain that the use of the present tense *are* is evidence that only the recent false Messiahs were included by Jesus in this expression, but in view of the constant denunciation in the Old Testament of false prophets and treacherous shepherds this would seem improbable.

10, 11. These verses are closely connected in sense. It is because the good Shepherd lays down His life for the sheep that abundant life is made available for them.

11. The reading *giveth*, though it has some ancient Greek attestation both here and in verse 15, would seem to have come into the English version through the influence of the Latin Vulgate. The variant 'lays down' (RSV) is almost certainly original in both places, for it is a characteristic thought of this evangelist that Jesus lays aside His life, as a man lays aside his clothes, the same verb *tithēmi* being used in xiii. 4 as is used in x. 11, 15.[1]

14. The word here translated *good* (*kalos*) very often carries with it the sense of 'attractive'. Many inherently good people are not always attractive, and their goodness is not always seen to be good. The goodness of Jesus, on the other hand, has been found attractive even by some who have been unable to accept His claims; and no picture of Him has drawn believers to Him with such magnetism as the picture of Him as the good Shepherd who cares for His sheep and surrenders His life for them.

16. Two different words in the Greek are translated in this verse by the same word *fold*. The reason is that by an error in the Vulgate, by which in many places the makers of the early English versions were influenced, the same word *ovile* is found twice. The first Greek word *aulē* is rightly translated *fold*, but the second word *poimnē* should be rendered 'flock'.

The sheep *not of this fold* are non-Jewish Christians. Only when all that are Christ's, in whatever fold they may be found, have responded to the gospel will the ideal of one flock under one Shepherd be a reality. The early Jewish Christians erred in supposing that all believers in Christ should be included in the fold of the Jewish Christian community by submitting to circumcision and being compelled to keep the Jewish law.

[1] For a discussion of the variant readings in x. 8 and x. 11, and some other variants in Jn. x. 7–xi. 57 see the author's article 'The Readings of the Chester Beatty Papyrus in the Gospel of John' (*The Journal of Theological Studies*, Vol. xxxvi, No. 144).

V. JESUS THE GIVER OF ETERNAL LIFE (x. 22–xii. 50)

a. The Festival of Dedication (x. 22–42)

These is uncertainty about the original reading at the beginning of x. 22. Some MSS have the temporal particle *tote* 'at that time', giving the sense, 'It was at that time that the feast of dedication was being held', while others have the particle *de*, implying 'and the time came for the feast of dedication'. The AV, probably rightly, follows the latter, but has produced an ambiguous sentence. If *tote* is read, then this section should be attached to what precedes it, and it must be assumed that the parable of the sheepfold was given while the Dedication festival was in progress. With the alternative reading, the mention of this winter feast would seem to mark the beginning of a new section. In either case, these verses can be regarded as forming a link between the preceding parable and the subsequent story of the raising of Lazarus. They carry on the imagery of the shepherd and his sheep, and they prepare the way for the record of the seventh and last 'sign' of Jesus recorded in this Gospel, which marks the climax of those *works*, to which He has so often appealed as evidence not only that His heavenly Father has sent Him, but also of the unity of purpose that exists between His Father and Himself. They are, in fact, the works of His Father (see x. 38).

The Pharisees, confined within a narrow legalism, still fail to see in Jesus the fulfilment of their Scriptures. It is indeed the 'winter' of their discontent. In consequence, they are not only untrustworthy shepherds of God's people, but are showing that they ought no longer to be classed among the sheep that pay attention to His voice. He who had so carefully shepherded Israel in the past was now calling to 'the sheep of his pasture' through Jesus the good Shepherd; and to disregard that call was evidence of defection from the flock. That nothing less than this is implied in their unbelief is stated by Jesus, when the Jews crowd round Him in Solomon's porch and impatiently request Him to give them a plain answer to the plain question, 'Are you the Christ?' (24). Jesus does not reply to them with a direct affirmative. An unambiguous answer would fall on deaf ears in the case of those who are unwilling to accept the evidence of the works performed by Him as His Father's representative.

It is increasingly clear as the long controversy goes on, that the presence of Jesus is in fact effecting a purge in the old Israel, and that the people of God are being consecrated to Him afresh as a transformed community of believers who acknowledge Jesus as the Christ, and accept at His hands the gift of eternal life. It is as inevitable that this should happen as that the Jerusalem temple should have been rededicated after the desecration perpetrated within its sanctuary by Antiochus Epiphanes in 168 BC, the event which was now being commemorated.

If the unbelieving Jews are outside the flock of God, other sheep are coming into it to enjoy the blessings the good Shepherd has to offer them. Prompted by the Father to pay heed to the voice of Jesus and follow Him, they will be rescued from evil and death and be given eternal life. This must be so, because their care and protection has been entrusted by the Father to the Son, who is so united in purpose with the Father that His actions are in effect the Father's actions; and as the Father is *greater than all*, His actions can never be thwarted or made ineffective (29).

Once more the Jews attempt to stone Jesus as a blasphemer who makes claims to divinity which no man is permitted to do (33). Jesus points out to them that even within their Scriptures, whose validity is permanent and beyond dispute, men in the persons of the judges receive from God Himself the title *gods* (Ps. lxxxii. 6). They were entitled to be so designated, for they represented, however imperfectly, the divine will in so far as they were called upon to administer God's word. In the light of this verse from the Psalms, Jesus cannot therefore be legitimately denounced as a blasphemer for calling Himself by what is nominally the lesser title *Son of God* (36). It is, to be sure, only *nominally* a lesser title, for the judges as well as the lawgivers and prophets of the old dispensation, as is pointed out in verse 35, were those *unto whom the word of God came*, while Jesus is *Himself* sent by God, the very Word of God made flesh. The Old Testament, nevertheless, here envisages the possibility of a very close association between the divine and the human in the execution of the divine will, such as is found to perfection in the man Christ Jesus.

If the deeds of Jesus were not essentially *good*, possessing a goodness that was so unmistakably good that it could only be an expression of *God's* goodness; or if there were a radical contradiction between what He was doing and the claims He was making; or if there were no evidence that He had been set apart and commissioned by God for the discharge of His holy mission, then He would indeed be a blasphemer and a pretender, unworthy to demand or to receive the homage of mankind. *If I do not the works of my Father, believe me not* (37). A man is known both by his words and his deeds. And Jesus is perceived, with a perception which becomes a permanent understanding, to be living in unbroken union with the Father by all who are not blind to the evidence that God's creative and redemptive power is present in all that He says and does—not in what He says apart from what He does, nor in what He does apart from what He says, but in His words which interpret His deeds and in His deeds which corroborate His words.

Although the witness of John the Baptist is secondary to the witness of God given directly through the works of Jesus, yet there is nothing in Jesus' claims which is not implicit in John's testimony. This section therefore ends with a visit by Jesus to the district beyond Jordan where John originally baptized (40). Here many are now prepared to testify that in the light of the ministry of Jesus John's witness to Him has proved true; and they express their faith in Jesus, in striking contrast to the unbelief of the Jews at Jerusalem.

Additional Notes

x. 29. *And* is inferential, and means 'and so'. Many ancient MSS have the words *which* and *greater* in the neuter, giving a sense which is well brought out in Knox's translation, 'The trust which my Father has committed to me is more precious than all.' For a similar use of the neuter with reference to the flock entrusted to Christ's care cf. vi. 39 and xvii. 2. On the whole the reading followed in the English versions seems to fit the context best.

30. *One* translates the Greek neuter *hen*. This verse was much quoted in the Aryan controversy by the orthodox in support of the doctrine that Christ was of one substance with the Father. The expression seems however mainly to imply that the Father and the Son are united in will and purpose. Jesus prays in xvii. 11 that His followers may all be one (*hen*), i.e. united in purpose, as He and His Father are united.

32. The same word (*kala*) is used to describe the 'goodness' of Jesus' works as is used to denote the goodness of the good Shepherd. See note on x. 11.

From my Father. The power to achieve the works has come from the Father.

Do ye stone. The force of the present tense is conative 'do you try to stone Me?'

34. *Law* is used here in the sense of the *torah*, i.e. the entire revelation embodied in the Old Testament. Hence the Psalms are regarded as part of the 'law' though they are not legal documents.

35. *The scripture*. In the singular *hē graphē* usually means a single passage of Scripture, and the verb translated *broken* (*luō*) is used in v. 18 of disregarding the letter of the law. The meaning here is 'this passage of Scripture cannot be set aside as irrelevant to the matter under discussion'.

36. *Hath sanctified* is better rendered 'consecrated' as RSV. The Father does not need to render the Son holy, but He dedicated Him to discharge His earthly ministry as His Apostle.

38. *Know, and believe*. The best attested reading has the same verb *ginōskō* here twice, first in the aorist tense and then in the present—giving the sense 'that ye may come to understand and continue to understand'. In the thought of this Gospel belief precedes knowledge. Only the man of faith can understand the relationship that exists between Jesus and His Father.

b. The raising of Lazarus (xi. 1–57)

The claim of Jesus to be working in complete and conscious union with His Father led the Jews to attempt unsuccessfully to stone Him. But it was His claim to bestow upon believers the gift of eternal life by raising them from spiritual death which led, according to the Johannine narrative, to His crucifixion. In order to emphasize the truth that this gift was made possible by Jesus' own death, the evangelist records an incident which took place in Judaea on the eve of the passion during a period about which the other Gospels are silent. In the perspective of this Gospel, the raising of Lazarus from death to life is seen to be the event which led the Jewish authorities to take decisive action against Jesus; and it is also the 'sign' which discloses more clearly than any other the meaning of His death and resurrection.

The other Gospels record two examples of how Jesus used His divine power to restore the dead to life. The raising of Jairus' daughter (Mk. v. 22–43) and of the widow's son at Nain (Lk. vii. 11–17) are in fact, though they are not explicitly stated to be such, signs that with Jesus the messianic age has come. That the dead were being raised by Him to life was part of the reply given by Jesus in answer to John the Baptist's question 'Art thou he that should come?' (Mt. xi. 3). The raising of Lazarus was, more unmistakably, a display of His supernatural power; for, while the reader of the other Gospels might conceivably, though wrongly, suppose that the daughter of Jairus and the widow's son were not really dead but only in the sleep of coma, the 'death' in each case having but recently occurred, the sleep from which Lazarus was awakened could not by any stretch of the imagination be regarded as a temporary sleep. On the contrary, it was the sleep of a man four days dead, whose body was already in the process of dissolution.

The statement that Lazarus *had lain in the grave four days already* (17) is of great importance for the understanding of this meaningful event. The sin which results in death, from which Jesus by the exercise of His redemptive power raises men to eternal life, is no temporary misfortune, no passing ailment, no sad accident, but a deep-seated malady perpetually corroding and disintegrating human life. It is a 'sickness unto death'. Jesus raises Lazarus not solely out of sympathy with Martha and Mary the bereaved friends of Jesus, though His sympathy was great, nor merely because Lazarus was especially dear to Him, though that was equally true, but because through the miracle of his restoration Jesus desires to manifest Himself as *the resurrection, and the life* (25). In a deed which speaks more eloquently than words He expresses the primary truth about His Father—that He desires to bestow eternal life upon all who have faith in His Son.

In spite of His love for Martha, Mary, and Lazarus, when Jesus hears of the illness of His friend, He stays where He is for two days. Such behaviour is unnatural from a purely human point of view, but very necessary if it is to be made clear that the illness, which is not destined to result in spiritual death, must nevertheless lead to physical death, so that through it the glory of God the Father may be reflected in the action to be taken by His Son. When the two days are over, and Lazarus is now unmistakably dead, the time for the display of that glory has come. Consequently, when His disciples now attempt to dissuade Him from returning to the district where the Jews were but recently trying to stone Him, Jesus points out that their well-meant solicitude is unnecessary, for while the time allotted to Him by His Father for the display upon earth of divine power is still present, no harm can come to Him. He can travel safely, as a man walking in the sunlight, unmolested by the powers of darkness (9, 10). Moreover, He wishes the disciples to learn that faith in Him is essentially faith in Him as the vanquisher of death which came into the world through sin; and He would teach them this lesson during the brief remaining period of His ministry. This is why He tells them that He is glad that He was not present when the death of Lazarus occurred, for had He been present and acted at once, that lesson would not have come home to them so forcibly. As it is, their faith in Him as the Giver of life will be increased by knowing that He has power to raise a man from a state of obvious corruption to incorruption. The disciples, however, can think only of the danger their Master is incurring by returning to Judaea; and Thomas utters a cry of loyal despair, *Let us also go, that we may die with him* (16).

When Martha hears that Jesus is on His way to Bethany she goes out to meet Him, and her first words to Him express her conviction that if only Jesus had been present at the crisis of her brother's illness he would not have died. But great as her disappointment is, she has such confidence in Him who is known to herself and her sister as *the Master*, that she is very sure that, even though humanly speaking the time for action seems to have passed, any petition He may yet address to His heavenly Father will be granted (22). Jesus at once tries to comfort her with the assurance that her brother will rise again. But she understands this as no more than an expression of the formal Pharisaic belief in the resurrection at the last day, an article of faith to which she assents, but, it would seem, without much enthusiasm. In times of bereavement present sorrow dims the prospect of future bliss; and when the imagination is overwrought, death, not life, is apt to seem the ultimate reality. Jesus now completely reorientates the faith of Martha by telling her that *He* is *the resurrection.* Let her look trustfully to Him; for to believe in Him is not only to be assured about the resurrection at the last day, but to experience here and now something of that eternal life to which resurrection is the prelude. Such a believer, though he must pass through physical death, as Lazarus has done, will go on living; and no-one who has faith in Jesus can ever perish. Martha may not understand all the implications of this momentous revelation, but she voices her belief that Jesus is *the Christ, the Son of God*, for whose coming God's people have been waiting (27).

The truth that Jesus is the resurrection is not apparently passed on by Martha to her sister; but Mary hastens at once to Jesus when she hears that He is asking for her. As she prostrates herself at His feet, she repeats Martha's complaint that if only Jesus had been with them all would have been well with

Lazarus. How often must those words have come to the lips of the two sisters since their brother's death; and their repetition now by Mary, and the sight of her and her sympathizers in tears deeply move Jesus. His emotional disturbance cannot, however, be adequately explained either as an expression of human sympathy or as due to sorrow caused by the limited faith of His friends. The words in which His distress is recorded, translated *he groaned in the spirit, and was troubled* (33) are, in the original, unusually intense. They could be rendered 'He was enraged in spirit and troubled Himself'. There would seem to be indignation and even anger in this sorrow. The presence of the grief-stricken sisters, to whose faith bereavement is presenting its sharpest challenge, brings vividly home to Him, so we may suppose, the iron grip in which mankind is held by what Paul calls 'the last enemy that shall be destroyed' (1 Cor. xv. 26). To bring about his destruction was the chief purpose for which the Son of God had entered the human arena. B. B. Warfield's comment on this passage may therefore well be right, 'It is death that is the object of his wrath, and behind death him who has the power of death, and whom he has come into the world to destroy. Tears of sympathy may fill his eyes, but this is incidental. His soul is held by rage: and he advances to the tomb, in Calvin's words, "as a champion who prepares for conflict". The raising of Lazarus thus becomes, not an isolated marvel, but . . . a decisive instance and open symbol of Jesus' conquest of death and hell. . . . Not in cold unconcern, but in flaming wrath against the foe, Jesus smites in our behalf. He has not only saved us from the evils which oppress us; he has felt for and with us in our oppression, and under the impulse of these feelings has wrought out our redemption.'[1]

Jesus suffered much agony of spirit as He approached the grave of Lazarus with tears in His eyes and anguish in His heart, to expend the divine power which would release him from death and so exhibit *the glory of God* (40); and He was destined to suffer the same agony in Gethsemane before moving on to Calvary to perform the redemptive act by which the

[1] *The Person and Work of Christ*, p. 116. Quoted in the *Westminster Theological Journal*, Nov. 1950, p. 76.

sting of death would be for ever drawn, and in which believers would always see 'the glory of God'.

Jesus is able to be the resurrection, the vanquisher of sin and death, because the union between Himself and His Father is so close and indestructible that the life of God is His life. Faith in Jesus is in fact faith in God. For this reason, before He utters the creative word *Lazarus, come forth*—a word as powerful and effective as the divine fiat at the creation 'let there be light', Jesus offers audibly, for the benefit of those standing by Him, a thanksgiving that His prayers are always heard and that therefore He is able to exercise the creative and redeeming power of His Father (41–43).

As is made clear so often in this Gospel, the deeds of Jesus invariably divide mankind into believers and unbelievers. So it was after the raising of Lazarus. Some of the Jews who had come primarily to sympathize with Martha and Mary, believe on Him. Others with malicious intent report the incident to the Pharisees (45, 46). At a hastily-summoned meeting of the Sanhedrin anxious fears are expressed lest the crowds, very naturally impressed by the story of the miracle, should accept Jesus as the leader of yet another messianic rising, and so bring about the fall of the holy city and the end of the Jewish nation as a privileged and largely independent people within the Roman Empire. The members of the council applaud the advice of Caiaphas that it is expedient for the nation as a whole that Jesus should be put to death. The words of Caiaphas, uttered as the reigning high priest during that memorable year in which the salvation of the world, and not of the Jewish people only, was brought about by the death of Jesus, were in the nature of unconscious prophecy. It was indeed expedient that one man should die for the people of God; and the Passover was at hand, at which this prophecy was to be fulfilled. The evangelist therefore notes that many of the pilgrims, who had now arrived at Jerusalem from the country in time to make preparations for the festival, were eager to know where Jesus was, for they had the feeling that this particular Passover was likely to be memorable, if Jesus were present. Indeed, the news that He had raised Lazarus had become so widespread that the authorities had ordered that anyone who knew where He was should give the necessary information to secure His arrest. But Jesus could not be found; He had withdrawn with His disciples to Ephraim, a town north-east of the capital. His hour, though very near, had not yet come.

Additional Notes

xi. 4. The disciples clearly understand Jesus to mean by the expression *not unto death* that the illness is not serious. Hence their optimism in verse 12.

9. The *twelve hours in the day* signify the time allotted by the Father for the earthly ministry of Jesus. During those 'hours' neither He nor His disciples can come to any harm. When darkness falls, another 'hour' will have come, the hour for the passion (cf. ix. 4 and xiii. 30).

12. *He shall do well* translates *sōthēsetai* (lit. 'he shall be saved'). Hence 'he will recover' (RSV). The disciples regard Lazarus' sleep as a sure sign that he will get better.

16. It is significant that Thomas is the only one of the twelve apostles mentioned by name in this incident. It is probable that Peter, the usual spokesman of the twelve, was not present, and this would account for the absence of any mention of this event in the other Gospels which are based ultimately on the Petrine tradition.

49. The pronoun *that* (*ekeinos*) is a favourite one with our author, and is not always emphatic. Here, however, and in verse 51 and xviii. 13 it would appear to be so, probably stressing the truth that this was *annus mirabilis*, being the year of man's redemption.

c. The supper at Bethany (xii. 1–8)

While the Jewish pilgrims were at Jerusalem making preparations for Passover, Jesus arrived at Bethany, where a supper was given in His honour at which Martha served and Lazarus sat with Jesus as a fellow-guest. At this supper Mary, who had but recently prostrated herself at Jesus' feet in tears, anointed

His feet with a very expensive perfume, oil of pure nard, and wiped them with her hair. In Mark's account of what would appear to be the same incident, an unnamed woman anoints the head of Jesus; and the reader is meant to infer that she is in fact anointing Him as a king, though a king who is to be laid in a tomb, before He enters fully into His kingdom. Her action, revealing such sympathetic insight, is clearly contrasted in Mark's narrative with the treachery of Judas 'one of the twelve' (see Mk. xiv. 3–11). In John's version, the woman, identified with Mary the sister of Lazarus, is also pictured as consecrating her Master to death and burial, though it is His *feet* over which she pours her perfume; and Judas Iscariot, *one of his disciples*, who is destined to betray Him and so bring about that death, voices the disciples' disapproval of her extravagance.

The reading adopted by AV in verse 7 in the reply of Jesus to Judas, when the latter asks why the perfume had not been sold for ten pounds or more and the money given to the poor, is translated *Let her alone: against the day of my burying hath she kept this* (Gk. *tetērēken*). This reading is usually, and probably rightly, regarded as a later simplification of the original reading which has *hina tērēsē* for *tetērēken*. It probably however conveys the correct meaning better than either the RV translation of the original reading 'Suffer her to keep it against the day of my burying', or the RSV rendering of the same reading 'Let her alone, let her keep it for the day of my burial'. Both these versions presuppose that the woman still has some of the perfume left, which Jesus wants her to be allowed to keep for the anointing of His body when the day for the laying out of the body comes. In Mark's narrative, however, the woman crushes in her hand the alabaster phial containing the scent, so that all the contents must have been emptied. John would also seem to imply that the woman made use of all the perfume, and that she was behaving as if she were *now* preparing the body of Jesus for burial. In the subsequent narrative, moreover, it is Joseph of Arimathaea and Nicodemus, not Mary of Bethany, who embalm the body on the actual day of burial. It is, however, most probable, as Hoskyns maintained, that there is an ellipse in the Greek before *hina tērēsē* which should be made good in translation, so that Jesus' words become what they were surely meant to be, a reply to Judas' question. Jesus therefore is saying in effect, 'Leave the woman alone; (she has not sold her perfume and given the money in charity) in order that she might be able to use it now with a view to My burial.' She is in her present action anticipating that event. If we suppose that *tetērēken* is original, then we must suppose that the scribe who altered it to *hina tērēsē* meant his alteration to mean 'Let her alone! Let her keep what is left for My burial'. As F. F. Field remarked, 'The *correction* (supposing *tetērēken* to be the original reading) may easily have been made by some critic-scribe, who did not understand how *that* day could be said to be the day of his "laying out" (not "burying"); or who failed to see how the ointment could have been *kept* already, as it might more naturally be supposed to have been just purchased.'[1]

John states that Mary poured the perfume over Jesus' *feet*, a detail which stresses her humility. Her action like all acts of true Christian devotion is prompted by an understanding of the love of God revealed in the death of Jesus. It is indeed an extravagant act; the scent permeates the whole house; nevertheless it is offered in a spirit of humility, without the least trace of ostentation. Mary of Bethany is in fact another of the timeless, representative figures so wonderfully portrayed in this Gospel. She is a type of the true Christian worshipper, even as the sinful woman in the very different anointing story in Luke vii. 36–50 is a type of the true Christian penitent.

The two women do one thing in common. They both prostrate themselves at Jesus' feet, and anoint them with ointment. But the woman in the Lucan narrative wets His feet inadvertently with tears wrung from her in gratitude for the forgiveness she has received before she wipes them with her hair and anoints them with her ointment. Mary in the Johannine story *at once*, and *deliberately*, anoints Jesus with ointment and wipes them with her hair. As Westcott well comments, 'The sinner and the friend were equal in their

[1] *Notes on the Translation of the New Testament*, p. 98.

devotion, yet widely separated in the manner in which they showed it.' The identification of the unnamed woman in Luke with Mary of Bethany, though often favoured by Christian writers both ancient and modern, seems *prima facie* improbable, and is based, it would seem, solely on the fact that both stories speak of a woman anointing the feet of Jesus, and wiping them with her hair, though in the one case *before* and in the other *after* the anointing. And the view of Bernard, adopted by Temple, that Mary at the supper at Bethany 'did actually reproduce her former gesture (of wiping Jesus' feet with her hair), then dictated by a sudden impulse of penitence, now inspired by adoring homage of her Master', seems unduly fanciful.

Mary understands that the words 'extravagance' and 'waste' are irrelevant where Christian devotion is concerned because the death of Jesus was no waste; and she knows instinctively that 'high heaven rejects the lore of nicely calculated less or more'. Her character in the Gospels is wholly consistent. She understands better than her sister Martha that, when Jesus of Nazareth is visiting their home, every possible moment must be spent in His presence (see Lk. x. 38–42). And she understands now that, when Jesus is with them for the last time before His passion, nothing could be less wasteful than offering Him a sacramental token of loyalty, understanding and devotion, however costly that offering may be. Jesus commends her for her loving insight, as He reminds His disciples that they will always have the poor as the possible recipients of their charity, but they will not always have Himself.

Additional Notes

xii. 1. On the assumption that the Passover began on the Thursday evening of what we call Holy Week, *six days before the passover* would signify that Jesus arrived at Bethany on the previous Friday evening, presumably just before the Sabbath began. John does not state that the supper at Bethany was held immediately after His arrival. Mk. xiv. 1 and Mt. xxvi. 2 imply that it took place two days before Passover, i.e. on the Tuesday evening of Holy Week.

2. *They made him;* i.e. 'a supper was given in His honour'. John does not state, as do Mark and Matthew, that the host at Bethany was Simon the leper. In the story of Lk. vii the host, Simon the Pharisee, is almost certainly a different Simon from the one mentioned in Mark. Simon was a very common Jewish name.

3. *Ointment* is better rendered 'perfume' as it was more liquid in substance than 'ointment' implies.

6. John alone tells us of the dishonesty of Judas. We learn from the other Gospels of his avarice which led him to betray his Master for thirty pieces of silver, and avarice often leads to dishonesty.

The bag was more properly 'a box' (see 2 Ch. xxiv. 8). So RSV 'money box'. It is clear that Judas was the keeper of the common purse, when Jesus and the twelve were travelling together (see xiii. 29).

The Greek word translated *bare* (*bastazō*) means both 'carry' and 'carry off'. Judas did both!

d. The triumphal entry and the final rejection (xii. 9–50)

The Jewish authorities were justified in thinking that the news of the raising of Lazarus might lead to a rising among the Passover crowds, for a large number of enthusiasts assembled at Bethany, when it became known that Jesus was there. They were anxious to see not only Jesus but Lazarus; and, in consequence, the chief priests now resolved to have Lazarus put to death as well as Jesus (9, 10).

The next day, presumably the day after the anointing, as Jesus journeyed on to Jerusalem, He was met by a company of pilgrims who had left the city after hearing that He was on the way up to the capital. They had been fired with enthusiasm by the news of the raising of Lazarus, and, as the evangelist tells us in a delayed footnote in verse 18, this was the main reason why they had come out to meet as quickly as possible both the Man who had achieved this miracle and those travelling with Him, many of whom had been eyewitnesses of the stupendous event. These pilgrims were waving palm branches in Jesus' honour, and shouting words from a psalm often sung as pilgrims made their way to the temple at Passover. The English versions do not make it clear that the actual words from the Psalm were 'Hosanna. Blessed be he that cometh in the name of the Lord' (Ps. cxviii. 26). On this occasion, the excited throng added to the customary quotation the words *the King of Israel* (13). They greeted Jesus as a king, though ignorant of the nature of His kingship. It would seem that they looked upon Him as a potential nationalist leader, with whose help they might be able to become wholly independent of foreign powers. The Galilaean peasants after the miraculous feeding of five thousand people had tried from similar motives to make Jesus an earthly king, but He immediately left them (see vi. 15). On this occasion, however, no such flight was possible, for the predetermined hour of the passion was imminent, and Jesus must journey on to Jerusalem. So instead of attempting to escape He makes a symbolic entrance into the city as a king of peace in the manner Zechariah had predicted that one day a king would come. The fact that the word 'meek' (inserted in Mt. xxi. 5) is here omitted from the prophecy concentrates the reader's attention on the words *sitting on an ass's colt* (15). Moreover, reference to the book of Zechariah reveals that the passage quoted by John concludes with the words, 'And I will cut off the chariot from Ephraim, and the horse from Jerusalem, and the battle bow shall be cut off: and he shall speak peace unto the heathen' (see Zc. ix. 10). In stating that Jesus *found an ass* the evangelist seems anxious to suggest that it was the jubilant shouting of the undiscerning crowd that led Him deliberately to take this action. The significance of what Jesus did, as John frankly admits, was not understood by the disciples, until they recalled the event after Jesus was glorified in death (16). At the moment, He seemed to be enjoying an earthly triumph; and His continued popularity with the people as a miracle-worker was creating a dangerous situation for the authorities, who are forced to admit that their counter-measures have not yet proved effective. It almost seemed as if Jesus had the world at His feet!

The Pharisees were of course exaggerating, but the words *the world is gone after him* (19), like the words of Caiaphas in xi. 50, were unconsciously prophetic. Indeed, they received a partial fulfilment almost at once in the desire expressed by certain Greek proselytes, who had come up for the festival, to see Jesus. The evangelist does not tell us whether the Greeks in question were interviewed by Jesus, but he records that as soon as Philip and Andrew reported to Him the wish of these men to see Him, He announced that the hour for His own glorification in death had come. His sacrifice alone would open up the kingdom of heaven to *all* believers, Greeks as well as Jews. It would bring within the flock of the new Israel the elect children of God at present scattered throughout heathen lands, and enable them all to enjoy eternal life. For what is true in the natural world, Jesus goes on to say, is also true in the spiritual. The same divine principle that life comes through death is operative in both spheres. God kills to make alive. The grain of wheat must fall into the ground and die that it may produce fruit. Even so, eternal life for the many comes through the sacrifice of the One. And the same providential law is applicable to each individual believer. He must disown the imperious authority of his selfish ego, if he is to live the life of an integrated person; he must abandon ruthlessly a self-centred existence lived in conformity to the standards of the world, if the higher element in him is to be preserved unto life eternal. This he cannot do by himself. He must have an example to follow. Jesus is that example. By looking to Him, a life of service to Him is made possible; and that life of service constitutes the 'dying in order to live' which is the theme of Jesus' teaching in this passage. The servant who continually keeps close to his Master is under His abiding influence; and the disciple who here and now lives *in* Christ is being prepared to live *with* Christ for ever in that higher sphere to which Jesus passes after His death. Moreover, the honour that the Father will bestow upon the Son in virtue of His unique self-sacrifice will be shared by all who follow Him along the road of unselfish service.

The immediate prospect of abandoning His life and of

feeling in so doing the whole burden of human sin and the horror of evil in its most blatant form throws the soul of Jesus for a moment into turmoil. He knows not how to give expression to His feelings. He either prays, or is tempted to pray, *Father, save me from this hour* (27). A decisive judgment on this is difficult, for these words can be construed either as a prayer actually prayed, or as a contemplated prayer, 'Am I to say, Father, save me from this hour?' In either case, it would seem that the expression *save me from this hour* means 'help me to come safely out of this hour' rather than 'enable me to avoid this hour altogether', as the preposition translated *from* is *ek* and not *apo*. But whether He prays this prayer or not, Jesus at once becomes aware that it is in fact unnecessary, for it is inevitable that having come to *this hour* He should be brought safely out of it. The last sentence of verse 27 is well paraphrased by Alford, 'I came to this hour for this very purpose—that I might be safe from this hour. The going into and exhausting this hour, this cup, is the very appointed way of my glorification.'[1]

But Jesus' own glorification is also the Father's glorification. The two are inseparable. Accordingly, He now prays that His Father's name may be glorified, i.e. that in and through His forthcoming suffering His Father will be recognized as being what in truth He is, the lover of sinners. In answer to this prayer, the Father states that He has already shown His divine love in the splendour of Jesus' action in raising Lazarus from death; and a similar and more transparent revelation that His name is love will be made when He raises Jesus from the dead. That will provide unmistakable evidence of the truth of such words as those recorded in iii. 16, 'God so loved the world, that he gave his only begotten Son, that whosoever believeth in him should not perish, but have everlasting life.' The form in which the answer to Jesus' prayer *Father, glorify thy name* (28) is conveyed (apparently a loud noise, interpreted by the materialists as a clap of thunder and nothing more, and by the more spiritually-minded as an angelic utterance) brings home to those standing near Jesus (for this, He states, was its primary

[1] *The Greek Testament*, p. 829

purpose) the truth that Jesus really is engaged upon His Father's business. And He now tells them how critical that business is. It is nothing else than *the judgment of this world* (31). By His own forthcoming conflict with evil in His passion, the situation created by the fall of Adam will be reversed. It was because of disobedience that man was driven by God out of the garden of Eden for having submitted to *the prince of this world* (31); now by the perfect obedience of Jesus on the cross the prince of this world will be deposed from his present ascendancy. That world remained God's world, even though it had become disintegrated by sin and had tried to organize itself without reference to its Creator, and in consequence stood under His judgment. But Jesus lifted on the cross, the supreme expression of the invincible power of divine love, would draw to Himself like a magnet all who accepted in faith His victory over sin and evil; and over against all such believers the world and its prince would be impotent.

The people who had been ready only a short time before to accept Jesus as a *national* king are unwilling to follow Him as a *crucified* king. They pour scorn on His words about the 'lifting up' of the Son of man, for they see in them a reference to His crucifixion (34). *This* Son of man, whoever else He may be, cannot, they feel sure, be the Christ predicted in their Scriptures. For had not Ezekiel said that God's servant David would be a prince *for ever*? (Ezk. xxxvii. 25.) And had not the Psalmist foretold that God would establish David's seed *for ever*, and build up His throne *to all generations*? (Ps. lxxxix. 4.)

But Jesus can stay no longer to argue His claims with the unbelieving Jews. Instead, He makes a final appeal to them to recognize the Light while it is still shining in their midst, and to believe the truth which He, the Light of the world, is disclosing, that they may be able to live honestly and sincerely as *the children of light* (36). But they still disbelieve what He is saying about Himself; and even His numerous miracles fail to convince them that here is the hand of God outstretched in love and mercy. Jesus therefore parts company with them. He hides Himself from them. Meanwhile, before the evangelist proceeds to relate the story of the passion, he pauses to notice that this rejection of Jesus by the Jews is no isolated phenomenon, but the climax of Israel's unbelief. In consequence, the complaint of Isaiah about his contemporaries is seen to be not only relevant to, but prophetic of Jesus' contemporaries. *Lord, who hath believed our report? and to whom hath the arm of the Lord been revealed?* (38). Moreover, the vision of Isaiah recorded in Isaiah vi is interpreted by John as a vision of the Godhead as a whole. The prophet saw Christ's glory as well as the Father's glory. So it was Christ who said to the prophet, in Hoskyns' paraphrase of the words quoted in John xii. 40, 'that God would blind the eyes of the Jews, lest they should perceive the significance of His miracles, and lest He, the Christ, would then of necessity heal them, and consequently obscure the judgment of God in unbelief.' This quotation from Isaiah vi. 10, found also in the other Gospels as part of the explanation of the teaching of Jesus by parables, is notoriously difficult; and in trying to understand it we have to remember the Hebrew idiom, which so often states what God foresees is going to happen as though it was inevitable. The Jews *did* not believe, therefore they *could* not believe. But, as Hoskyns commented, 'The purpose of this final summary of the public ministry of Jesus is not to deny the whole tenor of the narrative, as though it was impossible for the Jews to recognize Him as the Son of God, but to point out that the rejection of the Messiah by His own people ought not to surprise those familiar with the Old Testament Scriptures.' In fact, the unbelief was not total unbelief, for there were many who believed, but for fear of excommunication, and desiring at all costs to stand well with their fellows, they made no open confession of their faith (42, 43).

In the closing verses of chapter xii Jesus loudly and openly emphasizes once again the serious nature of unbelief. They are His last public words to His fellow-countrymen, 'His own' to whom He came and who for the most part have not received Him. To reject Him, He solemnly reaffirms, is to turn one's back upon the true light, and to go on living in doubt and with the certainty of dying unforgiven; it is to pass judgment upon oneself instead of accepting a Saviour who can take away all fear of judgment. Rejection of Jesus is, moreover, rejection of

Him who sent Him, the God who offers men in Jesus the gift of eternal life, and at whose command Jesus utters words which, because they are God's words, will prove to have been words of judgment when the last assize is held and time is no more. It is by obedience to those words that man will then be justified, and by disobedience to them that he will stand condemned.

Additional Notes

xii. 10. *Consulted.* The Greek probably means 'came to a decision', 'resolved'.

13. *Cried.* The imperfect tense in the original signifies that the shouting was persistent.

Hosanna meant originally 'Save (us) now'. It is not certain whether it has this significance here, or whether it is a shout of acclamation, as it appears to be in Mt. xxi. 9.

14. Although diminutives are not always strictly used as such in the New Testament, *a young ass* is almost certainly the meaning here, as Mark calls the animal a foal, and emphasizes that it had not yet been broken in (see Mk. xi. 2).

24. Jesus is *alone* till after the crucifixion and resurrection in the sense that no-one can help Him in world evangelization before those events, which release the power of the Holy Spirit necessary for the work (see vii. 39).

26. *Let him follow.* The sense is that a man *must* follow Jesus if he would serve Him; he must follow the *exemplum Christi*, for his service must be inspired by and in some degree a reflection of Christ's supreme service.

28. Three times in Jesus' earthly life *a voice from heaven* was heard, at His baptism, at the transfiguration, and here before the passion. The significance of what was said, as is made clear in this passage, was only intelligible to those who had 'ears to hear'.

30. The form of expression *not because of me, but for your sakes* is probably an example of the Semitic way of expressing comparison, rather than a strict contrast—i.e. 'more for your sake than Mine'. It is clear that on this occasion the voice had considerable significance for Jesus Himself.

31. *Prince of this world* is John's usual synonym for Satan, the latter word being used only in xiii. 27. It is also found in xiv. 30 and xvi. 11. The princely authority of Satan in the present temporary world order is described in Mt. iv. 9 and Lk. iv. 6.

32. *If*, as often, has the force of 'when'. There is no doubt in Jesus' mind that He will be crucified.

34. A passage in *the law* (i.e. in the canonical Scriptures considered as a whole) in which the *Son of man*, here equated with *Christ*, was regarded as exercising a dominion unbroken by death, is Dn. vii. 14.

36. *Children of light.* The Semitic idiom 'sons of' describes men who possess the characteristics of what is said to be their 'father'. In our idiom, we should probably say 'men of light', cf. our expression 'a man of integrity'.

40. *Be converted.* The verb in the original probably has a middle, not a passive force, giving the sense 'turn for me to heal them' (RSV).

VI. THE UPPER ROOM (xiii. 1–xvii. 26)

a. The feet-washing (xiii. 1–17)

At chapter xiii the second part of the Gospel begins. I would suggest that verse 1 should be separated from the incident which immediately follows it, and regarded as an introduction to the whole of the remaining chapters. As Passover approached, Jesus became aware that His public ministry to the Jews was over, and that the time for His supreme 'work', His death, had come. What the evangelist is in effect saying in verse 1 is 'Jesus had always loved those whom His Father had given Him, the small company of believers, who are now designated *his own*, and form a group distinct from those who are given the same title in i. 11. The latter had for the most part rejected Him, and so it is to the former that He now showed the completeness of His love by laying down His life for them. And it is the story of this final submission of Jesus to death of which the feet-washing was an acted parable and for which the teaching that followed the feet-washing was a careful preparation, that I am now going to record in the second half of my Gospel.' The expression translated *unto the end*, *eis telos*, can equally well mean 'completely'; and that is the sense which should probably be given to it here: cf. Knox's translation 'he gave them the uttermost proof of his love'. If verse 1 is regarded in this way, it is not necessary to suppose that the events in the upper room took place *before the feast of the passover*, or to conclude in consequence that the last supper could not have been the Passover meal.

It will be suggested later when the concluding words of xiv. 31 are discussed, that in all probability everything that is recorded in chapters xiii–xvii is regarded by the evangelist as having taken place in the upper room. It is obvious therefore that information about it must have come from one of the twelve apostles, for there is no evidence that anyone else was present with Jesus on that momentous occasion.

The evangelist does not give any account of the solemn distribution by Jesus to His disciples of the bread which He had symbolically broken and the wine which He had symbolically outpoured, because some record of that was probably recited every time the Christians met for the service known as 'the breaking of bread', and John's readers would be very familiar with it. In the ceremony of the feet-washing and the teaching that follows it the meaning of the death of Jesus is conveyed to the disciples in an equally dramatic manner. It is clearly inadequate to regard this symbolic action solely as a striking example of the nobility of serving others, such as might have been given by any good ethical teacher. It may well be that it was the strife that had arisen among the apostles at the supper table as to which of them should be accounted greatest, that led Jesus to decide upon this particular method of emphasizing the truth of His words 'but I am among you as he that serveth' (see Lk. xxii. 24–27). But the fact that the washing of the feet took place at Passover with all the implications of that festival for this evangelist; that it was enacted during or after the meal, and not before it as though it were a substitute for the customary washing by slaves of the feet of guests; and the significant way in which the incident is related, all tends to show that in this sacramental action Jesus is illustrating the cleansing power of His death.

By the time that Jesus and His disciples were assembled in the upper room He was aware that Judas had already yielded to the devil's suggestion that he should betray his Master. He was also very sure that His Father had laid upon Him the task of making effective the divine plan for man's salvation with all the suffering and utter self-oblation which that involved. Accordingly, it was not *in spite of* but *because of* His consciousness of His divine origin and destination, that He rose from supper, and assumed the dress and posture of a slave; for a servant in truth He was, being none other than the ideal Servant delineated in Isaiah's prophecy who was destined to 'pour out his soul unto death' (see Is. liii. 12). He *laid aside his garments* (4) even as He was to 'lay aside' His life. He tied a slave's apron round Him, poured water into a basin, and proceeded to wash His disciples' feet and wipe them clean wtih the towel, the outward badge of His servitude.

Peter resisted the attempt of Jesus to wash his feet, precisely because he failed to associate what his Master was doing with His death, but regarded it merely as an act which any slave might perform before a banquet. In making this protest Peter was in fact displaying the pride of unredeemed men and women, who are so confident of their ability to save themselves that they instinctively resist the suggestion that they need divine cleansing. They desire to do everything for themselves. Peter would much rather wash Jesus' feet than that Jesus should wash his feet; he would prefer to lay down his life for Jesus than that Jesus should lay down His life for him. Jesus points out to him that the full significance of this washing will become clear to Peter *hereafter*, i.e. after the crucifixion and resurrection. But Peter persists with his impatient protest, 'You are never going to wash *my* feet.' Whereupon Jesus tells him plainly that there can be nothing in common between them, and that their companionship must be for ever abandoned, unless Peter allows Him to do what He desires to do (8). With characteristic exuberance Peter now declares that he will gladly permit his Master to render him menial service to a degree beyond what was usually expected of a slave before a meal, if that would prevent their separation; he will allow Him to wash his *hands* and *head* as well as his *feet*. Peter is right in thinking that it is a more complete cleansing that Jesus wishes to effect, but he does not understand that the washing by Jesus of his feet is in fact a symbol of that total cleansing. Jesus therefore (on the assumption that the words *save his feet* in verse 10 are not part of the original text) reminds him that a man who has bathed (the literal meaning of the word *leloumenos*, misleadingly translated in AV *he that is washed*) has no need of further washing, but is entirely clean (10). Those who are humble enough to receive what Jesus in His humility is ready to do for them, those, in other words, who are willing to accept the cleansing which His own submission to death makes available for them, are wholly clean. No other washing is required; no further means of salvation are necessary. It is clear that Jesus knows that Peter will in the end let Him do what He had all along intended to do, for He proceeds to state that all who are present in the room with Him are clean, with the single exception of the man who is betraying Him.

But such total cleansing at the hands of Jesus lays upon all who receive it the obligation to reflect the love which has been so graciously shown to them, in their relations with other believers. The primary basis of Christian ethics is the example of Christ Himself. *If I then, your Lord and Master, have washed your feet; ye also ought to wash one another's feet* (14). The servant, who has been rendered such a supreme act of service by Him whom he rightly calls *Lord and Master*, cannot be exempt from the duty of loving his fellow-servants; for to claim such exemption would be to assert that he was greater than his Lord. But, as Jesus reminds His disciples at the close of this section, the recognition of their obligation is insufficient. It must be followed by action if they are to be blessed.

Additional Notes

xiii. 2. Some MSS read *being ended* (*genomenou*) and others 'while still in progress' (*ginomenou*). Both readings are well-attested.

4. It is most significant that the verb (*tithēmi*) translated *laid aside* is also used for the 'laying down' of His life by the good Shepherd in x. 15.

6. There is nothing in the text to show in what order Jesus washed His disciples' feet. It may be that He came to Peter first as he was *primus inter pares* in the apostolic band; but it may also be that Peter made his lone protest after the others had readily submitted.

Thou and *my* are both given great emphasis in the original. Cf. Knox's translation, 'Lord is it for thee to wash my feet?'

8. *My* is very emphatic, and it perhaps has more significance if Jesus had already washed the feet of the others. 'Whatever you may have done to the others, I will never let you wash my feet.'

10. Though the majority of ancient authorities for the text insert the words *save his feet* (*ei mē tous podas*) it is probable that they should be omitted with RV margin on the authority of the fourth-century Codex Sinaiticus, what is probably the earliest text of the Latin Vulgate, and some early Greek Fathers. The use of two different verbs in this verse for 'wash', the former *louō*, meaning to 'bathe' the whole of the body, and the latter *niptō*, to wash a part of the body, suggests that what Jesus means is, 'The man who has bathed has no further need of washing'. If, as seems probable, He intended His own washing of the disciples' *feet* to be symbolic of the *total* washing of salvation, it is unlikely that He would have obscured this truth by adding the words *save his feet.* On the other hand, these last words may well have been added at an early date (they are found in the Bodmer papyrus, *circa* AD 200) by a scribe who failed to understand the spiritual significance of what Jesus was doing, and imagined that He was merely drawing attention to the social custom that the man who arrived for a banquet after having bathed at home needed only to have his feet washed on arrival at his host's house. Or it may be that the shorter text seemed to suggest that the baptized needed no further forgiveness. Many of the early Fathers thought of post-baptismal sins as similar to the dust that adhered to the traveller's feet as he journeyed through life. The stains of these offences had to be removed by confession and absolution, but they in no way diminished the effects of baptism. The total immersion of baptism symbolized the complete cleansing of conversion; it was therefore a sacrament that could never be repeated.

b. The traitor (xiii. 18–35)

The new Israel consists of all who are cleansed by accepting in faith the sacrifice of Jesus offered on their behalf. But in the upper room is one who, although a chosen apostle of Jesus, is not destined to remain in the company of those who can be for ever designated 'His own'. Judas can never be among those who find their blessedness in serving the servants of Christ.

The treachery of Judas does not come as a surprise to Jesus. *I know*, He says, *whom I have chosen* (18). Westcott remarks about the problem of the choice of Judas to be both an apostle and a traitor (a problem which must largely transcend our finite comprehension), 'Jesus knew the thoughts of men absolutely in their manifold possibilities, and yet as man not in their actual future manifestations.' It was inevitable in the mysterious working out of the divine plan of salvation that the Saviour of the world should be betrayed by human agency; and the words of verse 18 imply that Jesus knew it to be in accord with divine revelation that the traitor should come from among His most intimate friends. Some time before Judas took the decisive step, described by Jesus in the Psalmist's words as 'lifting up his heel' against Him, Jesus was aware of the manner in which the treachery of Judas would show itself. But, just as Judas had been careful to conceal his intentions from his fellow-apostles, so Jesus kept the knowledge of the part that Judas would play strictly to Himself; for to have divulged it to the others might have led them to attempt to prevent the traitor from carrying out his designs. But the betrayal is now so certain and so imminent that there is no longer any need for silence. Jesus therefore decides to break the unwelcome news that the traitor is at that moment eating bread with them. Two purposes are served by this disclosure. First, Judas is given the opportunity of withdrawing from the fellowship of the children of light, and entering the realm of darkness to which he belongs. And, secondly, the further evidence of Jesus' foreknowledge, which would be available when His prophetic words about the traitor have been proved true, will strengthen the faith of the rest of the apostles that Jesus is the Christ in whom David's prophecy in Psalm xli is fulfilled.

Verse 20 stresses the high calling of the apostles. To welcome them would be to welcome both Jesus Himself and the Father who sent Him. Inevitable though the defection of Judas was, it grieved the heart of Jesus that there should be among the twelve one who could no longer fill such a high position; and as He uttered the words *one of you shall betray me* He bore witness to His distress (21). The disciples are bewildered by this staggering, and, it would seem, wholly unexpected announcement; and except in the case of the disciple whom Jesus loved, their bewilderment is not removed till after Judas has left the upper room. When Jesus offers Judas a special morsel from the common dish, such as it was customary for a host to offer to an *honoured* guest, it is a mark of divine love which ever seeks to overcome evil with good; but at this critical hour in human destiny divine love is temporarily impotent, for it is the hour of darkness and the prince of this world is allowed to marshal his forces for the final combat unmolested. In accepting *the sop* Judas shows himself completely impervious to the appeal of love; and from that moment he is wholly the tool of Satan (27). Jesus knows that this is so, and He at once bids him in effect to hasten the execution of his murderous design. One who is wholly evil cannot remain in the company of those who belong to Christ; and now that the hour for His baptism in death is at hand He is sore straitened till it is accomplished (see Lk. xii. 50). *After the sop Satan entered into him. Then said Jesus unto him, That thou doest, do quickly. . . . He then having received the sop went immediately out: and it was night* (27, 30). The Passover moon was in all probability shining brightly overhead, but it was nevertheless the hour of darkness; and the hour of darkness it would remain till the gloom was banished by the glory radiant in the self-offering of Jesus and in the acceptance of that offering by the Father.

The moment when Judas left the upper room and Jesus made no attempt to bring him back, but expedited his departure, is the moment which brings supreme honour to Jesus Himself, for He is now irrevocably committed to the death which Judas has gone out to make certain. Hence He can say *Now is the Son of man glorified* (31). It is also the moment when God is supremely exalted, for the passion of the Son of man is the most splendid expression that the world can ever see of God's love for mankind; and that passion has now virtually begun. But even as God is exalted in the sacrifice of Himself for sinners offered by the Son of man, so in His turn the Son of man must share in this divine exaltation. He cannot be left in the corruption of death, but must be raised from the dead, and that without delay. Such would seem to be the meaning of verse 32. The glory of the Father and the glory of the Son are inseparable; so too the glory of the cross and the glory of the resurrection are inseparable.

But, while the death of Jesus and His return to the Father are the occasions of His own supreme glory, for the immature disciples, now tenderly called *little children*, they bespeak grievous bereavement and interminable separation (33). Jesus therefore explains to them that the forthcoming *physical* separation need not mean *spiritual* separation. It is true that they will not be able to follow Him at once into the heavenly sphere where He is going, for they will not die immediately; but it is also true that, inspired by His own love for them, they will be able to love those for whom He is laying down His life; and in so far as they do that they will be dwelling in Him and He in them. The world, moreover, confronted by the mutual love of Christ's disciples will take note that they have been and still are 'with Jesus' (see Acts iv. 13). In obeying Christ's *new commandment* the disciples will find the sting of separation drawn. The old commandment enacted that men should love their neighbours as themselves; and this old commandment is by no means annulled by the new. But to love others not because we like them, or are bound to them by family, social or national ties, nor because they happen geographically or in some other way to be our neighbours, but solely because they are fellow-sinners redeemed by Christ, this is indeed obedience to a *new* commandment, for it is new not only in the sphere of its exercise and in the motive which inspires it, but also in the degree of self-sacrifice it evokes. In Hoskyns' words 'whereas the Old Testament demanded that men should love their neighbours as themselves, the New Law is that they should love the brethren better than themselves, and die for their friends (see xv. 13)'.

Additional Notes

xiii. 18. As so often, there is an ellipse before *that.* The sense is 'There has to be this exception that the scripture might be fulfilled which says. . . .'

For *bread with me* some ancient MSS have 'my bread' (so RV and RSV). The latter is found in the Hebrew original of the quotation from Ps. xli. 9, and is probably the correct reading here. To eat a person's bread was a sign of loyalty. *Lifted up his heel against me* implies that Judas is behaving like a treacherous horse, kicking out violently at its master.

19. *I am.* As in viii. 24, no predicate is expressed, but the sense in both passages is 'I am what I claim to be, *viz.* the Christ'. Here, as Knox points out, 'the context seems to imply that our Lord is the Christ inasmuch as He is the person in whom David's prophecy is fulfilled.'

21. *Testified*; i.e. gave evidence that He was troubled in spirit. This is well brought out in Knox's translation, 'Jesus bore witness to the distress in his heart. Believe me, he said, believe me one of you is to betray me.'

23, 24. It would seem clear that the disciple whom Jesus loved was occupying the second place of honour, i.e. on the right side of Jesus, and that he was reclining on his left side leaning back with his head in the fold of Jesus' garment, here called His *bosom*. It is often supposed that the chief place of honour, on the left of Jesus, was occupied by Peter the leading apostle. But the fact that Peter *beckoned* to the disciple whom Jesus loved in an attempt to obtain information about the identity of the traitor suggests that he was not next to Jesus; otherwise he could have spoken to Him directly. It is more probable that Judas was given the place of honour; and so Jesus was able without rising from the table to hand him *the sop*. RV follows a variant reading in verse 26 which inserts the words 'and took it', between 'dipped the sop' and 'gave it'. This is probably an addition to the original text based on the assumption that Judas was not close to Jesus, and that Jesus had therefore to carry the sop to him. RV also follows a different reading in verse 24 and translates, 'beckoneth to him, and saith unto him, Tell us who it is of whom he speaketh'. But as the word translated *beckoned* (*neuō*) invariably implies a movement of the body unaccompanied by verbal utterance, the reading followed by AV, which has the support of the Bodmer papyrus, would seem preferable. The disciple whom Jesus loved was not given the opportunity of announcing the name of the traitor to the assembled company.

25. For *lying on Jesus' breast* RV has 'leaning back, as he was, on Jesus' breast', 'as he was' translating the Greek *houtōs* omitted in the MSS followed by AV. This word is also found in iv. 6 where it is translated 'thus'. If original, its presence here suggests that we are reading the personal evidence of the actor concerned in the incident. The disciple remembers that without moving his position he leaned back further, till he actually touched the breast of Jesus and was thus in a position to whisper to Him.

26. The word translated *sop* (*psōmion*) is used in modern Greek for a piece of bread. It was *dipped* in a dish containing broth. The best attested reading both here and at vi. 71 makes *Iscariot* agree with *Simon*. So RV 'Judas, the son of Simon

Iscariot'. The word means 'the man from Karioth'. When 'Iscariot' came to be virtually a surname for the traitor, to distinguish him from others of the same name, it was natural that the word should be made to agree with him in these passages.

27. The words construed literally in AV *that thou doest, do quickly* are more idiomatically rendered by Knox 'Be quick on thy errand'.

29. The fact that some supposed that Judas was being sent out to buy what was necessary *against* (RV 'for') *the feast* is often regarded as evidence that Passover had not yet begun, and that therefore the events described by John in the upper room could not have taken place at the Passover meal. This is not, however, an inevitable conclusion, as the festival lasted for seven days.

33. Jesus had said to the Jews 'Ye shall seek me, and shall not find me' (see vii. 34). It is significant that the words 'and shall not find me' are here omitted. Unlike the Jews, the *little children*, the new-born members of Christ's family learning from Him the graces of Christian living, would in no unreal sense 'find' Him even though they could not follow Him at once into the heavenly sphere.

c. The disciples' questions (xiii. 36–xiv. 31)

The remainder of chapter xiii and the whole of chapter xiv are occupied with difficulties raised by individual disciples; and in reply to their questions Jesus explains more fully the meaning of His forthcoming departure and the nature of the destination to which He is journeying. Peter now exhibits a further sign of impatience. He cannot believe that it is of departure in *death* that Jesus is speaking when He talks of going away. How could the Christ enter into His glory and leave 'His own' behind Him, unable to follow Him immediately, and unable to enjoy His company except in the somewhat indirect manner of which Jesus has spoken! So Peter asks directly *Lord, whither goest thou?* (36), convinced that it must be an *earthly* goal to which He is journeying. It becomes clear however in the dialogue which follows that the destination of Jesus can be reached only through *death*. Peter, as his Master prophesies, will reach the same destination eventually by the road of martyrdom, the road which Peter rashly asserts he is prepared to take, if need be, at once. But for all his professed readiness to lay down his life for Jesus, Peter is in fact far from ready for the role of martyr. On the contrary, he has still to learn by bitter experience the vital lessons of penitence and humility. Before the cock has heralded the dawn of another day, Peter will have three times disowned his Master. After his restoration, as the reader of the last chapter of the Gospel will be informed, the time will have come for him to undertake the exacting task of feeding the flock of Christ; and it will be only as the consummation of such witness and service, and not as an impulsive act of fanatical heroism, that Peter will in the end lay down his life for his Lord.

Jesus now assures all His disciples that each one of them, whether called to lay down his life for Him or not, will be able sooner or later to follow Him where He is going; for to make ready their ultimate reception in the heavenly sphere is the prime purpose of His departure, and the essential sequel to all the previous revelations of God that He has given them. Jesus is going to *prepare a place* for them, so that they may permanently abide with God and enjoy Him for ever (xiv. 2). This thought should banish all feelings of distress and anxious fears from their hearts, and enable them to renew their faith both in God and in Jesus. When provision has been made for them in the many rooms of the Father's house, Jesus will return and take the disciples to Himself so that where He is they may be also. This was a very precious promise to the early Church, and Paul may well be echoing it when he informs the Thessalonians 'by the word of the Lord' that Jesus will descend from heaven and gather believers unto Himself to be with Him for ever (see 1 Thes. iv. 15–17).

The distress of the disciples at the prospect of Jesus' departure should also be removed by what they have learned from Him about the way that leads to the Father. They know the way to where He is going. Thomas, however, questions whether it is possible for anyone, who has no definite knowledge of the final goal of a journey, to know the way that leads to it. *Lord, we know not whither thou goest; and how can we know the way?* (5). His bewilderment is due to a failure to understand that, though the necessity of human language compels Jesus to speak of 'going away' and of 'a way to the Father', these terms have no spatial or material significance. The way to God lies in the knowledge of the truth about Him and in the experience of His life. It is precisely this knowledge and this experience which Jesus throughout His incarnate life, and supremely in His atoning sacrifice, is bringing within men's reach. Jesus Himself is therefore *the way*, because He is the embodiment of *the truth* about God and His relationship with men; and by reason of this, *the life*, that is inherent in His own words and actions, the very life of God Himself, is available for mankind. Because to know Jesus is to know the Father, the disciples in fact already have knowledge of the way to the Father.

But such indirect knowledge of God, obtainable only through an intermediary, even though that intermediary be Jesus, fails to satisfy Philip. Why, he asks in effect, cannot they be given here and now a more direct vision of the Father, such as Moses and the elders of Israel had been given when 'they saw the God of Israel' (Ex. xxiv. 10), or such as was granted to Isaiah when he saw 'the Lord sitting upon a throne, high and lifted up' (Is. vi. 1)? To see God with his physical eyes, to know Him by what men tend to regard as the sure evidence of the senses, that will indeed satisfy Philip and remove his doubts, and he asks for nothing more. But the very fact that he makes such a request after having been so long with Jesus reveals a pathetic misunderstanding both of the Person and the work of his Lord. Because Jesus lives in perpetual union of purpose and will with His Father, His words and actions are God's words and actions. To have faith in Jesus as *such* a revealer of God will moreover enable the disciples to do even *greater works* than Jesus Himself had been able to do owing to the enforced restrictions of His human life, during which He was confined to the land of Palestine and was able to minister for the most part only to 'the lost sheep of the house of Israel'. It will enable them to carry the gospel of redemption to the heathen world, and to make the reign of God a reality in the hearts of thousands who never knew Jesus on earth. Their proclamation of this gospel will be attended by 'signs following' (see Mk. xvi. 20), miracles of the same kind that Jesus performed. Moreover, in the strength and reality of this faith, the prayers which the disciples will pray will be prayers such as Jesus Himself would pray, prayers offered He tells them *in my name*, such as He could present before the throne of grace. In a word, His own departure to the Father, so far from ending His influence on earth, will mean its continuance under wider conditions and with results rendered possible by the power of effective prayer.

The prayers that Christ prayed on earth were the prayers of One whose chief characteristic was obedience to His Father. Prayers that are offered 'in Christ's name' must therefore be the prayers of those who are obedient to His commandments; and such obedience will be made possible, not by the cold exercise of the will, but by the warm love of the disciple for his Lord. This love will be fully reciprocated, and as a result the Father will send at the request of the Son another Advocate, the Spirit who reveals the truth and abides for ever in the heart of the believer. This other Advocate, to whose coming after the sacrifice of Jesus has been offered the narrative has so often pointed, though He has not been designated by this title before, will be the disciples' reservoir of power and their unfailing guide when Jesus has left them. While Jesus has been with them, He Himself has been their Advocate. He has stood beside them like counsel for the defence summoned to the side of a prisoner to plead his cause and strengthen him in the hour of trial. He has prayed for Peter that his faith may not utterly fail (Lk. xxii. 32). He has defended the disciples against the charge brought against them by the Pharisees of breaking the sabbath (Mk. ii. 23ff.). He has befriended the blind man, upon whom He bestowed sight, after his excommunication from the synagogue (ix. 35). And at His forthcoming arrest He will plead with His adversaries to allow His followers to go free, so that the whole weight of the enemy's attack may fall upon Himself (see xviii. 8). After Jesus has returned to the Father, the Holy Spirit which is His Spirit will continue to perform, in a manner unrecognizable by and unintelligible to the world, the same office He has Himself discharged for them so lovingly while He has been with them on earth.

But before Jesus returns to the Father and this other Advocate is sent to represent Him in the hearts of believers, Jesus after *a little while* will come to them Himself in the glory of His resurrection body (19), and bring them the assurance that they are not left desolate like orphans in the storm at the mercy of a cruel and hostile world, but that they are sharers in His own risen life. Any doubts they may have had during His earthly life about the reality of the intimate communion between His Father and Himself will be banished *at that day*, when He will show Himself alive to those who, because they love Jesus with the love that expresses itself in obedience, are also the objects of the Father's love. The evangelist in due course will record instances of this self-revelation of the risen Christ; but Jesus assures His disciples that a spiritual knowledge of Himself as risen will in fact be possible at all times to all believers, for He will manifest Himself to those who love Him (21).

Such a confinement of the appearances of the risen Jesus to *believers* seems to Judas (the other Judas, not Judas the traitor who has already left the company) a serious limitation of Jesus' power. Surely, he objects, a Christ risen from the dead should manifest Himself to *all*, whether believers or not. *Every* eye should see Him. So he asks what has happened that Jesus will reveal Himself only to His friends and not to the wider world (22). His question recalls the request of the brothers of Jesus that He should go up to Jerusalem at Tabernacles and show Himself to the world (see vii. 4). But Jesus insists that the unbelieving world would be insensitive to any such manifestation. They would not believe though one rose from the dead (see Lk. xvi. 31). The heart that does not love Jesus with the love that is expressed in obedience cannot be an abiding place either for Jesus or His Father. Faith in the promises of God made known in 'Moses and the prophets', and love for Him in whom those promises are fulfilled, must always be the keys that unlock the door, through which the divine presence can be experienced in the human heart.

The resurrection of Jesus, in spite of the present misgivings of Judas, will in fact remove from the disciples the sense of bereavement and the fearfulness that the separation caused by the crucifixion will inevitably foster; and under the inspiration and in the illumination of the other Advocate the words spoken to them by Jesus on earth will not only be recalled, but become radiant with hitherto unsuspected meaning (26). The very existence of this Gospel of John, and indeed of the entire New Testament, would have been impossible apart from this aspect of the Holy Spirit's work. At the moment, the disciples imagine that Jesus by His departure is leaving them in a state of turmoil and distress, and at the mercy of a cruel world. In reality, He is leaving them with an endowment, such as the world has no power to bestow, for it is His sole prerogative to bequeath it. That endowment is the gift of *peace* (27).

All men, even, as Augustine pointed out,[1] the revolutionary and the warmonger, desire peace; they are always striving for what they imagine would be a more settled condition of life. There is, as Jesus implies, a peace which the world can give. Temporary freedom from distraction, anxiety, and strife is often obtainable, enabling men to settle down for a short time at least to do what they want to do, and live their lives in their own way with relatively little interference. There is also the peace of momentary flight from the unpleasant things of life sought in day-dreams, pleasure and amusement, the peace of escapism. And there is the peace of false security, when men cry 'Peace, peace where there is no peace', the peace that is so often the prelude to disaster. The peace which Jesus offers His disciples is something very different. It is *His* peace. *My peace*, He tells them, *I give unto you*. He Himself enjoyed this peace, for He was never for one moment unmindful of His Father's will, and was ready in obedience to it to drink the cup of suffering and endure a penal death for man's salvation.

[1] See *The City of God*, Book XIII, chapter 10.

In His own life of constant victory over every temptation to follow any other course; in His abandonment of all temporal security and earthbound hopes; in His refusal to settle down and live His life in His own way, He had come to know the divine peace, the peace of inward quiet which no distress of mind or body was able to destroy. And now He would bequeath that same peace to those who, refusing to compromise with the world, are willing to accept the sacrifice He is making on their behalf; to enjoy the assurance of forgiveness that of necessity accompanies such acceptance; and to follow Him along the same road of loving obedience and service.

The disciples had witnessed something of what Jesus calls *my peace* when they had seen Him restoring calm to human lives racked by the misery of sin and disease; and they had more than once themselves sheltered in the security of His presence as they heard His reassuring words 'It is I. Be not afraid'. His return to the Father, He now assures them, would mean, not the lessening, but the heightening of the experience of this peace, because, exalted to the right hand of God, He would be able to communicate to them from the original source of divine power and authority, His Father being *greater* than He, the very peace of God Himself (28). He would come back to them on the third day with the words 'Peace be unto you' on His lips (xx. 19); and among the fruit of His Holy Spirit there would be the gift of peace, the peace of the justified sinner (see Gal. v. 22 and Rom. v. 1). But without the victory of Jesus over *the prince of this world* (30), and apart from the final expression of His own love in the surrender of His life, no further manifestation of this peace would be possible. The forces of evil were already mustered for their final assault upon Him, and He is ready to go and meet them.

It is not necessary to suppose that Jesus led the company out of the upper room at this point, and that the discourses recorded in chapters xv and xvi, and the prayer of chapter xvii, were spoken on the way to the garden where He was arrested. The words *Arise, let us go hence* do not necessarily indicate that the upper room was left at that moment. As C. H. Dodd has recently pointed out, the verb *agōmen*, translated *let us go*, implies in normal Greek usage 'let us go to meet the advancing enemy'; and to bring out this sense this sentence should be construed with what has preceded it in verses 30 and 31. He would therefore paraphrase the passage, 'the ruler of this world is coming. He has no claim upon Me; but to show the world that I love the Father, and do exactly as He commands, up, let us march to meet him'. Jesus is here giving expression to His *spiritual* determination to meet the prince of this world, not as a matter of compulsion, but as a voluntary action reflecting His obedience to God's command and His desire to express His love. No *physical* movement from the upper room at this moment is implied. It is because the words *Arise, let us go hence* have been construed as a separate sentence instead of being taken as the apodosis of the previous sentence, that readers of the English Bible have been given the impression that an immediate withdrawal from the upper room is indicated at this point.[1]

Others have not hesitated, in spite of the lack of any manuscript authority, to rearrange the material so that the words *Arise, let us go hence* form the conclusion of the entire collection of the last discourses. Such a drastic and unwarranted expediency is unnecessary in order to safeguard what would seem to be on general grounds the right inference, that the evangelist believed that the whole of the revelation contained in these chapters was given by Jesus to His disciples secretly in the quiet seclusion of the upper room.

Additional Notes

xiv. 1. The verbs translated *ye believe* and *believe* can each be taken either as indicative or imperative. AV and RV take the former as indicative and the latter as imperative, giving the sense 'You already believe in God, now make the additional venture of faith and believe in Me'. But the disciples already believed both in God and in Jesus. It is better therefore, with the Latin and old Syriac versions, to take both verbs as imperative with the force of continuous presents. 'Go on believ-

[1] See C. H. Dodd, *The Fourth Gospel*, pp. 406–409.

ing in God and go on believing in Me' in view of the future blessings that I am going to make possible for you.

2. *Mansions*, *monai*, came into the AV and RV through the influence of the Vulgate *mansiones*, which can mean 'stations' or 'temporary lodgings' where travellers may rest at different stages in their journey. In the light of this, many scholars, especially Westcott and Temple, following Origen, assume that the conception of heaven in this passage is that of a state of progress from one stage to another till the final goal is reached. This was not however the interpretation generally given to the word by the ancient Fathers, and by derivation it would seem to denote much more the idea of permanence. It is found once more in the New Testament, in xiv. 23, where the permanent dwelling of the Father and the Son in the hearts of loving disciples is stressed. The thought here is that there are many dwelling-places in heaven, where there is room enough for all believers. It is a permanent home, from which eviction is impossible, and where no notice to quit can ever be served!

Many ancient MSS insert the word *hoti* before *I go to prepare*, meaning either 'because' or 'that'. If this reading is followed with the meaning 'that', it is possible to take both parts of the verse as a single sentence and translate with RSV 'Would I have told you that I go to prepare a place for you?'. This probably gives the right sense. As R. A. Knox says, 'Our Lord's thought appears to be "there are places waiting in heaven for others besides myself, as you may infer from my saying that I am going to prepare a home for you".' The AV rendering gives no explanation of why *if it were not so* Jesus *would have told* them. And, if we follow the reading *hoti* and translate it 'because', we get the somewhat irrelevant sense, 'I would have told you because I am going to prepare a place for you'.

4. The best attested reading has 'the way' instead of *and the way ye know*. Hence RV 'whither I go, ye know the way'; and RSV 'you know the way where I am going'. The AV reading was probably an alteration made to adapt the words of Jesus more closely to the subsequent question of Thomas.

12. The literal rendering of the word translated by AV *greater works* is 'greater things'; and probably this should be retained. The works of the apostles after the resurrection were not greater in kind than those of Jesus, but greater in the sphere of their influence.

15. Some MSS have the verb in the apodosis of this sentence in the future indicative, 'you will keep' (so RV and RSV); and some in the aorist imperative *keep*. The former is preferable, and is more in accord with the psychological truth that, when we love a person, we are the more ready to do what is pleasing to either him or her. Jesus assumes that if a disciple has a strong personal love for Him, he will almost inevitably keep His commandments. The imperative would suggest the sense 'you must, by a further effort of will, keep My commandments'.

16. *Comforter*, in its more original sense of 'strengthener', is the AV and RV translation of *paraklētos*, a passive adjective designating one summoned to the side of another to befriend him, advise him, and if necessary plead his cause. The word is also used in 1 Jn. ii. 1 of Christ as the believer's 'advocate' in heaven. Probably this is the dominant thought underlying the use of the word in these last discourses, where it is a title of the Holy Spirit (see verse 26). It has often been pointed out that *another* implies that the Spirit is a different Person from the Son, while *Comforter* indicates similarity of nature.

18. *Comfortless* renders a word meaning 'orphans'; and the sense of bereavement should be retained in translation. Neither 'desolate' (RV and RSV) nor 'friendless' (Knox) wholly succeed in doing this.

22. *Judas* is called 'Judas of James' in Lk. vi. 16 and Acts i. 13; and on each occasion AV translates 'the brother of James', and RV and RSV, more naturally, 'the son of James'. He seems to be identical with the Thaddaeus of Mt. x. 3 and Mk. iii. 18. Some of the apostles clearly had more than one name.

How is it is more accurately rendered by RV 'what is come to pass'. Judas thinks something must have happened for the Christ so unnaturally to limit His sphere of influence. Surely the Messiah would wish to reveal Himself publicly.

26. *In my name*, i.e. 'on My account', to instruct the disciples further in *all* the *things* that Jesus had begun to teach them, particularly about His Person and His atoning sacrifice.

28. The words *greater than I* were frequently appealed to by the Arians to support their doctrine of the creaturely subordination of the Son to the Father. They do not, however, mean that the Father was greater in power or in divinity, but that the Son, being begotten of the Father, is 'inferior' to Him in the sense that He that is begotten is secondary to Him who begets (see i. 14).

30. *Hath nothing in me* is a literal construe of the Greek. RSV 'has no power over me' indicates the sense. As Westcott comments, 'There was in Christ nothing which the devil could claim as belonging to his sovereignty. In others he finds that which is his own, and enforces death as his due; but Christ offered Himself voluntarily.' In other words, Christ did not belong to the world, over which the devil was temporarily supreme.

d. The allegory of the vine (xv. 1–16)

Before Jesus engages in the last and fiercest strife against the prince of the world, He teaches His disciples by means of a simple allegory the demands their discipleship imposes upon them and the conditions under which it can become effective. As they are not a collection of individuals, but a corporate society, the new Israel of God—it is natural that Jesus should frame His allegory in language that had been used to describe the people of God under the old dispensation. Israel had often been pictured under the figure of a vine; 'a noble vine', Jeremiah called it, 'a right seed' (Je. ii. 21). This vine had been brought out of Egypt by God and planted by Him in a goodly land, as the author of Psalm lxxx so graphically describes; but it had very often failed to yield to its Owner the fruit He had a right to expect. More than once Isaiah's words had proved true: 'He looked that it should bring forth grapes, and it brought forth wild grapes' (Is. v. 2). Moreover, as Jesus reminded His listeners in the parable of the wicked husbandmen, the Israelites had on numerous occasions ill-treated the messengers sent by God to collect what was His due (see Mk. xii. 1–10).

Jesus' description of Himself as *the true*, or 'genuine', *vine*, implies that Israel had been an imperfect foreshadowing of what was found to perfection in Himself. He is what God had called Israel to be, but what Israel in fact had never become. With Him therefore a new Israel emerges, the members of which draw their spiritual sustenance from Him alone. Believers in Jesus are 'limbs' of His body, and share in the life which results from the sacrifice of that body on the cross, a truth which was underlined in the words 'Except ye eat the flesh of the Son of man, and drink his blood, ye have no life in you' (vi. 53). The same truth is now emphasized in the allegory of the vine. Believers are brought into the closest union with their Lord, as Jesus had indicated very clearly to His disciples when He bade them drink the outpoured wine which symbolized His blood shed for their redemption. And it is most probable that it was after His reference to the 'fruit of the vine' at the institution of the Eucharist, that Jesus spoke the present allegory (see Mk. xiv. 25).

The relationship of a vine to its branches leaves the believer under no misapprehension about his need for constant 'cleansing' if he is continually to enjoy the eternal life which Jesus offers him. This further 'cleansing' is different from the initial cleansing of the disciple which is symbolized in baptism, the sacrament of initiation which can never be repeated. It is the 'cleansing' to which expression is given in the prayer of humble access in the Communion service in the Book of Common Prayer. 'Grant us therefore, gracious Lord, so to eat the flesh of thy dear Son Jesus Christ, and to drink his blood, that our sinful bodies may be made clean by his body, and our souls washed through his most precious blood, and that we may evermore dwell in him, and he in us.' The branches of a vine are not self-centred or independent. They have no source of life within themselves. And the fact that they need constantly to be pruned makes it apparent that their life is drawn not from a source outside themselves, nor from themselves in isolation, but from the stem of the vine to which they belong. The ancients spoke of pruning as a 'cleansing' of the branches, just as we speak of 'cleansing' the land.

The verb *kathairō* translated *purgeth* in verse 2 is better rendered, as in RSV, 'prunes'. Unwillingness, through a proud sense of self-sufficiency, to draw spiritual strength from Jesus, or to submit to the discipline which alone makes possible the flow of this vitalizing power, renders the so-called believer a dead branch unable to bear fruit. There is no permanent place for him in the fellowship of the redeemed, and Jesus asserts that his destiny is as surely determined as that of a withered branch which is removed from the tree and burned. Judas Iscariot, though one of the original twelve apostles, is the outstanding example of the truth set forth in verse 6. On the other hand, when the believer relies completely and continuously upon his Saviour and is obedient to His commands, then the life of Jesus inevitably flows into his life, so that he can truly say with Paul 'I live; yet not I, but Christ liveth in me' (Gal. ii. 20). Two consequences flow from this divine indwelling. The believer's prayers, whatever their content, are effective (7), for they are in fact the prayers that Christ is praying; and the divine love shown in the death of Jesus is reflected in the believer's love for all for whom Christ died (12).

In the closing verses of this section Jesus reminds His disciples of the dignity and the joy of their vocation. They are apostles of Him who was sent from God, and chosen servants of One whose destiny it was to lay down His life for His friends. Their love for others must therefore be a sacrificial love. But the practice of that love would never be a joyless duty. Jesus endured the cross for the joy that was set before Him, and part of that joy lay in the knowledge that His disciples, in obeying the commands He had given them, would find in their obedience the fullness of their own joy. He had already told them that a servant was not greater than his lord: neither he that is sent greater than he that sent him (xiii. 16). But, though they must of necessity be His servants and express their love in service, He now prefers to call them *friends* (14), as He had at least once called them before (see Lk. xii. 4). This designation is singularly appropriate in view of all that He has been telling them about the loving purposes of God. Such an intimate disclosure of what was in His mind could never have been made to slaves, but only to friends who were chosen and ordained to pass on to others the revelation they had received (15). They would set out upon the great Gentile missions after the death and resurrection of their Lord, not under the impulse of their own initiative, but with a sense of divine commission, and with the assurance that they had available the strength with which to discharge it. This was the abiding fruit which, as members of the real Vine, Jesus expects them in the power of effective prayer to bring forth (16).

Additional Notes

xv. 1. The word translated *true* (*alēthinos*) is almost certainly used here in its Platonic sense of antitype as opposed to type. The vine of Israel is a symbol of Him in whom the symbol becomes a reality—Jesus the 'genuine' Vine. Similarly, in i. 9 John's light is contrasted with Jesus, the 'real' Light; and in vi. 32 the manna in the wilderness is typical of the 'real' Bread from heaven, which is Jesus Himself.

2. There would seem to be a play on the Greek words *airei*, *taketh away*, and *kathairei*, *purgeth*. If pruning is implied by *kathairei*, the play on the words could perhaps be brought out by translating the former word 'cuts away' and the latter 'cuts back'.

3. The eleven disciples are now in the position of pruned branches ready to bear fruit. *The word*, i.e. the entire revelation of God's will made known to them in Jesus' teaching, has had a cathartic effect upon them. Every discourse they heard from His lips, every answer He gave to their questions, every rebuke they received from Him for their stupidity, faithlessness and arrogance, had been in the nature of a pruning. It had removed some of the more exuberant excrescences of their pride.

8. *So shall ye be* translates the reading *genēsesthe*, and suggests that, until the disciples have borne fruit, they would not really deserve the name of disciples. The variant *genēsthe*, translated in RSV 'that you bear much fruit, and so prove to be my disciples', implies that the Father is glorified not only in their bearing fruit, but also in the proof that that affords of the reality of their discipleship.

9, 10. *Continue ye* translates an aorist imperative, the authoritative note of which can perhaps be brought out better by the translation 'You must continue'. Love and obedience go hand-in-hand. Jesus obeys His Father because there is mutual and permanent love between Father and Son. Similarly, the disciple can obey Jesus only when he responds to the love Jesus has shown to him.

11. The words translated *that my joy might remain in you, and that your joy might be full* probably mean 'that you may continue to share the joy I already possess (*viz* the joy that accompanies loving service) and so find your own joy completed'. They could also mean 'that I may have joy in you, and that, because of this, your joy may be complete'.

e. Persecution (xv. 17–25)

The power of effective prayer will indeed be essential to the apostles, for during the time they will be witnessing to the love of God both by preaching the gospel of the cross and spending their lives in the service of others, they will be continuously confronted by a hostile world. Jesus reminds them of what He had already told them (xiii. 16) that if a slave cannot expect to render less service than his master, neither can they, as the apostles of Him who had to face the world's impassioned hatred in its most virulent form, expect to be immune from that hatred themselves. It is true that by their natural birth they belong to the world; by nature they are part of the sin-stained race of men and women who, for the most part, have forgotten their creaturely estate, and are arrogant and selfish, organizing their lives without thought of God. There was indeed a time when they would not have been the objects of the world's hatred at all. But Jesus has separated them from the world (19). He has incorporated them into His body; and as members of that body they must expect to be the objects of the hatred that the world in its ignorance of His divine origin is always directing against Himself.

The persecution of Christ's disciples by the world would be suffered in the first place, as the Acts of the Apostles makes abundantly clear, at the hands of the Jews. Herein lay the tragedy of the situation. For however excusable the ignorance of God that provokes hostility to Christ and His followers may be in the *heathen*, it is unpardonable in God's own people, to whom Jesus was primarily sent and before whom He displayed the works of God. Their sin is fundamentally disbelief in Jesus (see xvi. 9). His very presence among them, and their wilful refusal to recognize His divine origin and nature, remove all possibility of excuse; and their unreasonable hatred both of Himself and His Father is inexplicable except as a corroboration of the truth of the Psalmist's words *Thev hated me without a cause* (25; Pss. xxxv. 19, lxix. 4).

Additional Notes

xv. 18. *Ye know* can also be read as an imperative *know ye*. The sense therefore is either 'Ye are aware', or 'Be very sure', so that (on either interpretation) the hatred of the world for them will not take them by surprise.

19. *Of the world*; i.e. worldly, exhibiting the characteristics of the world. *Out of the world*; i.e. separated from the world.

20. The force of the last clause in this verse is well brought out by Knox 'they will pay the same attention to your words as to mine; that is, none'.

21. *For my name's sake*; RSV, rightly, 'on my account'.

24. The last clause could also be translated 'but now they have actually seen these works of Mine, and yet have hated both Me and My Father'.

f. The work of the Advocate (xv. 26–xvi. 15)

In spite of the hostility of the world, testimony to the truth as it is in Jesus will continue to be given after His departure both by the Advocate sent by the Father at the instigation of the risen Jesus, and by the apostles who have been with Jesus from the beginning of His ministry. The witness of the Advocate and the witness of the apostles are in effect a single witness; and the testimony of the eyewitnesses of the ministry of Jesus given under the inspiration of the Spirit is of paramount and permanent importance, for the apostles are the sole link between all subsequent believers and the historic Christ. It is therefore an essential part of the Advocate's work to see that their witness is unimpaired by opposition and persecution. There is also another guarantee against any such weakening of their testimony. When persecution comes, their faith will not be taken unawares but will remain unshaken, for they have been forewarned by their Master of its nature and its cause (xvi. 1). Not only will they be excommunicated from the synagogues of the old Israel, but the hour is not far distant when to murder them will be regarded as an act of worship acceptable to God, so ignorant will their persecutors show themselves to be of the true character both of Jesus and His heavenly Father (2).

During the earlier part of His ministry Jesus had spoken comparatively little to His disciples about the persecution which awaited them, because He had been in their company, and as long as He was with them the world's hatred must inevitably be drawn to Himself as the Head of the body of the new Israel, rather than to the other members. But because His departure is now imminent, and His friends seem obsessed by a sense of their own personal loss and unconcerned about the destination for which He is bound, He is constrained to comfort as well as warn them. It is true that persecution awaits them, but it is also true that once Jesus has reached His destination He will be able to make available for them the help that only the divine Spirit can bring them (7). As they bear their witness they will be aided, He once again reminds them, by the Advocate, who while acting as their defendant will also expose the world's errors. This great Advocate for the defence will also act as counsel for the prosecution. His conviction of the world will be threefold (8). First, He will expose the naked truth that the root of sin lies in the desire of men to live their lives in self-centred independence, disowning any allegiance to Jesus. Secondly, He will show that all that Jesus said and did was right, because He will have been vindicated by returning to the Father after being withdrawn from His disciples' sight. And thirdly, He will make it clear that there is such a thing as judgment, because the prince of this world already stands condemned. When Jesus was sentenced to death by the judgment of Pilate, it looked as if His cross would be His scaffold, but it proved to be the place where judgment was passed on the prince of this world by whom Judas had been diabolically inspired.

The disciples had always found it very difficult to understand why Jesus must suffer, and their grief-stricken hearts could not endure any further words on the subject at present (12). But what Jesus had been unable to make fully clear to them during His earthly life, the Spirit of truth, speaking from the ultimate source of truth, would expound to them further after His departure. It would, however, not be any new truth that He would unfold, but the truth that was implicit in what Jesus had said and done. He would explain in greater detail the divine plan of salvation, and disclose the eternal significance of the crucial events that were now imminent—the death and resurrection of their Master. And every fresh insight into such truth would enable the apostles to have a more complete vision of the glory of God to be seen in the face of Jesus Christ.

Additional Notes

xv. 26. Although the coming of the Advocate is clearly stated to be dependent upon the initiative of the Son, He is only said to 'proceed' from the Father. Hence the long controversy between East and West over the *filioque* clause in the Nicene Creed. R. A. Knox pertinently remarks that 'if our Lord had said "who proceeds from the Father and from me", He would have been speaking as God, without reference to His Incarnate state, which was not His habit. The Holy Spirit does not proceed from the Incarnate Christ as such.'[1]

[1] *The Gospels and Epistles*, p. 149.

Which in Jacobean English could be masculine as well as neuter, and its use here in AV does not militate against the doctrine of the personality of the Spirit. RSV translates 'who'.

xvi. 1. The word *skandalizō*, translated *offended*, is one of the most difficult words in the Greek Testament to translate into English. A *skandalēthron* was not a stumbling-block which might trip you up, so RV, 'that ye should not be made to stumble', is no improvement upon AV. It is used of the spring of a trap which might 'go off' when you were least expecting it. The sense here is 'taken by surprise' or 'caught unawares'. So Knox 'that your faith may not be taken unawares'. The RSV 'to keep you from falling away' misses the note of unexpectedness which is inherent in the word.

2. *That* should be translated 'when' as in RSV.
Doeth . . . service. The Greek *prospherein latreian* means more specifically 'perform an act of worship'.

5. Simon Peter had in fact asked 'Lord, whither goest thou?' (xiii. 36); but the apostles are now so absorbed in their own sorrow that they have lost interest in the question of the destination of Jesus.

13. *Into all truth* is misleading, for it can be taken to imply that the Church will be guided by the Spirit into the truth about all subjects; and in fact the Church has often claimed, most disastrously, to know the truth about many matters about which it is not really competent to speak. The Greek means 'all *the* truth', i.e. the specific truth about the Person of Jesus and the significance of what He said and did. The existence of the New Testament is permanent evidence that the apostles were guided into the truth about this.

Things to come is again apt to be misleading. The apostles were not given by the Spirit power to predict the future. The Greek means 'the things that are coming', i.e. the unique events which are imminent and with which the last discourses of Jesus are primarily concerned, His death and resurrection. About these matters, so central to the Christian religion, the minds of the apostles were illuminated by the Spirit after Pentecost.

g. The 'little while' (xvi. 16–33)

During His ministry Jesus had on several occasions told His disciples that the Son of man must suffer and go the way that was appointed for Him in Scripture (see Mk. viii. 31, xiv. 21); but this startling paradox, which identified the suffering Servant of Isaiah with the supernatural Son of man of the book of Daniel, had bewildered them. After the resurrection, however, it became clear to them, as Jesus had foretold, not only that He was the culmination of the previous revelation of God to Israel, and that in Him 'the last things' of Jewish prophecy found their fulfilment, but that part of those 'last things', and indeed the most essential part, was His death and resurrection. Until the power of sin had been broken and salvation accomplished, the new age He had come to inaugurate could not become a reality. The hours of the passion and the period of anxious waiting between the crucifixion and the resurrection were, in consequence, the most tense in the entire history of revelation. Then the final birth-pangs were endured, in which the new age was born. This appears to be the significance of the expression used by Jesus in verses 16 to 22 *a little while*, which seemed to the perplexed disciples an unspecified time reference with a double meaning, rendered more mysterious by their Master's previous reference in verse 5 to His going away to Him who sent Him. *What is this that he saith unto us, A little while, and ye shall not see me: and again, a little while, and ye shall see me: and, Because I go to the Father?* (17).

It is improbable that two 'little whiles' are envisaged, though Tyndale translated 'After a little while you will not see me, and again after a little while and ye shall see me'. The AV retains better the ambiguity of the original. Many commentators, however, have followed Tyndale, assuming that *again* implies a further period also designated *a little while.* Thus R. A. Knox paraphrases 'There will be a short period (of some eighteen hours) from now, after which you will no longer be able to fix your eyes on me as you are fixing them now. But it will only be a short interval after that (of some fifty-six hours) before I shall appear in your company again (on the evening of Easter Day)'.[1] Others, also assuming a double 'little while', interpret the second as the period between the crucifixion and the ascension, on the ground that in the Greek a different verb for *see* is used in the two parts of the sentence, the first denoting 'physical' and the second 'spiritual' sight; and it was only after the ascension that further 'physical' sight of Jesus by His disciples became an impossibility. It is doubtful however whether the evangelist, who uses synonyms very freely, is necessarily contrasting two types of sight, and the Vulgate translates both verbs by the same Latin word *videbitis*. Moreover, the fact that the first verb in the Greek is in the present tense and the second in the future would seem to support the view that it is during the *little while* that no sight of Jesus at all is possible, and that after it is finished further sight will be possible. This single *little while* would most naturally apply to the hours between the death of Jesus and the resurrection. Nor does the word *again* militate against this conclusion, for, as F. F. Field points out, it may have the same force here as it has in 1 John ii. 8, where it indicates an apparent contradiction of what has just been said. 'I write no new commandment unto you. . . . Again, a new commandment I write unto you.'[2]

It would seem then that the *little while* of which Jesus is speaking is considered under two aspects. First, it is the brief period during which the disciples have no vision at all of their Lord for He is dead and buried. But, secondly, it is the period during which the possibility of the disciples seeing Jesus again becomes greater with each moment that passes, for it is impossible for Him to be held in the pangs of death (see Acts ii. 24), and the third day, the day of resurrection, must dawn when He will be visible again. The words *because I go to the Father* are omitted in verse 16 in many important ancient MSS and should probably be regarded as a later insertion from verse 17, where the disciples would seem to be echoing

[1] *The Gospels and Epistles*, p. 132.
[2] See *Notes on the Translation of the New Testament* p. 103.

what Jesus had said in verse 5. They are not strictly relevant to the truth that after the resurrection the disciples would see Jesus again, and they are rightly omitted in RV and RSV.

The above interpretation is entirely in keeping with verses 20 and 21, where Jesus, elucidating the difficulty He knows to be in the minds of His disciples, seems to be comparing the *little while* with the transition from sorrow to joy that is characteristic of childbirth (21). The brief but distressing period that often precedes a joyous deliverance from suffering of any kind is frequently compared by the Hebrew prophets to the pangs of childbirth (see e.g. Mi. iv. 9, 10). In particular, they used such language with reference to the deliverances of Israel from earthly enemies and the new life which such deliverances made possible. The metaphor was therefore especially apposite to the greatest of all deliverances, when Jesus, having by His death destroyed death and made eternal life a reality for the redeemed, rose from the dead. The weeping and lamentation of the disciples during the temporary rejoicing of the world at its imagined triumph in the crucifixion will be turned, Jesus assures His friends, by the resurrection into a lasting and ever-deepening joy. Of that joy they can never be deprived; and it will banish their present distress, as surely as the joy of motherhood enables a woman to forget the pains of labour. *I will see you again, and your heart shall rejoice, and your joy no man taketh from you* (22).

The joy of the disciples after the resurrection will be the joy of a new life in which their relations with God will be more direct and more confident than they have been hitherto. They will be more confident because the period of anxious and doubtful questionings, of which several instances have been given in these chapters, will be over. No longer will the disciples ask anything of *Jesus*; but with fuller insight into the mind of their Lord they will be able to do something, that, owing to their limited understanding, they have not yet been able to do. They will be able to pray directly to the Father with the joyous certainty that God will answer their prayers in virtue of the victory won by Jesus on the cross. They will pray *in*

Christ's name pleading the merits of His sacrifice (23). It is no meaningless formality that Christians end their liturgical prayers with the words 'through Jesus Christ our Lord'.

In verses 25–33, which bring the last discourses to a close, the joyful confidence of the apostles after the resurrection, to which the New Testament as a whole bears abundant witness, is said to lie largely in the removal of what had appeared cryptic and enigmatic in the teaching of Jesus. 'Spiritual things are spiritually discerned'; and until the spiritual understanding of the apostles was more fully developed than it had been during the earthly life of Jesus, they were unable to interpret His teaching fully. Jesus was not a simple teacher in the sense that the meaning of His words was intelligible immediately to the casual hearer. There was, for example, as He Himself intimated, a 'mystery' about His parables (see Mk. iv. 11). These are not self-evident illustrations, but stories whose real significance often becomes apparent only in the light of the entire revelation of God given in the life, death, and resurrection of Jesus. He now tells His disciples that the hour is approaching when they will be able to receive more direct teaching about God than He has been able to give them. This will consist not of any fresh revelation, but of a fuller understanding of the revelation already given (25). Their approach to God in the future will be the approach of Christian prayer, a bold direct approach to the throne of grace, made in the certainty that God loves all who in loving faith and dutiful obedience have accepted Jesus as His Apostle who has now returned to His Father (28). The plain statement of this truth by Jesus in these verses is itself, as the disciples point out, an example of that direct teaching which avoids what is called in verse 25 *proverbs*. For the meaning of this last word see the note on x. 6, where it is translated in AV 'parable'. In the post-resurrection era the implication of revealed truth will become explicit through the agency of the Spirit; there will be no longer any need for it to be elicited by anxious questionings, as in the days when Jesus was present with His disciples. The apostolic testimony to Jesus, given to them by the Spirit after the resurrection and ultimately embodied in the documents of the New Testament, carries with it divine authority no less than the actual words spoken by Jesus on earth.

But the fullness of faith and joy is not yet the apostles' possession. They may *now* believe in some degree, but their faith is destined to be sorely tried almost at once. The 'little while', to be sure, has not yet begun, but the hour of darkness is already upon them; and during that hour their unity as a company of believers will be broken. For a brief space they will return to their old individual self-centred lives, units without cohesion. The sheep will be scattered abroad as though they had no shepherd, while the divine Shepherd lays down His life for them in loneliness (32). The loneliness, however, will not be absolute: outwardly it will be mitigated by the presence at the foot of the cross, for at least part of the passion, of His mother and the beloved disciple; and inwardly the Sufferer will be consoled by the knowledge that His Father is with Him, as He exhibits the glory of the divine love in the sacrifice of Himself. Only for a brief, though terrible, moment will that consciousness of the Father's love be withdrawn. Made sin on behalf of sinners He will experience the separation from God that is the essence of sin, and cry 'My God, why hast thou forsaken me?' But, as the words of Jesus recorded at the end of verse 32 make abundantly clear, throughout the remainder of the passion Jesus is sustained by the certainty that His Father is with Him; and it is into that Father's keeping that He finally commends His spirit (see Lk. xxiii. 46).

The last words of Jesus to His disciples in the upper room, recorded in verse 33, reflect what has been uppermost in His mind while He has been speaking to them. His friends, as He well knows, will have much tribulation to endure in the days that lie ahead, for they will be believers in the midst of an unbelieving world. But because of what He is about to do for them, they will also experience, as they remain united with Him, inward peace and courageous joy born of the certainty that He has won the victory over sin and death. *These things I have spoken unto you, that in me ye might have peace. In the world ye shall have tribulation: but be of good cheer; I have overcome the world.*

Additional Notes

xvi. 18. *What he saith.* A different word is used here in the Greek for *saith* from that used in the first part of the verse. Hence RSV, rightly, 'we do not know what he means'.

21. *A man* is the literal translation of *anthrōpos*. The word is used here generically in the sense of 'a human being'. RSV translates 'a child'.

23. *In that day* here and in verse 26 signifies the day of resurrection and afterwards.

Ye shall ask me. Me is in an emphatic position in the original, and the word *erōtaō*, here translated *ask*, is used in Hellenistic Greek of asking a favour as well as of asking a question. In the light of verse 24 it should probably be given that sense here. 'You will make no petition to *Me*. Your prayer will be addressed to the Father.'

In my name is probably rightly construed in AV with *ye shall ask the Father;* petition is offered pleading what Christ has done on the cross. The expression could, however, be attached, as the order of the words in the Greek might suggest, with *he will give it you.* It is taken in this latter way by RV and RSV, presumably with the sense 'for my sake'.

25. *These things* refer to all that Jesus has been saying about His forthcoming departure.

Proverbs is used here to cover the cryptic expression 'a little while' and the metaphor of childbirth used in verse 21.

Plainly translates *parrēsia* which combines the ideas of boldness of speech and unreserved speech.

28. *Again* here denotes a contrast with what has just been said, 'now on the other hand'.

30. This verse is connected in thought not only with verse 29 but also with verse 19. The disciples had been impressed by the power of Jesus to read their thoughts, and they regard such supernatural insight as a mark of His divine origin. He could satisfy their needs without their having to ask Him to do so.

31. The words *Do ye now believe?* can also be taken as a statement. This is preferable, as it brings out better the emphasis laid upon *now* in the original. 'You do *now* believe, but your belief will soon be shaken.'

h. The prayer of the great High Priest (xvii. 1–26)

Jesus has unfolded to His disciples the meaning of His approaching departure; and with this He concludes His ministry of teaching. His priestly ministry, however, is not yet ended; and He moves steadily toward its completion in the atmosphere of prayer. He turns His gaze from earth to heaven, from His disciples to His Father, and utters the prayer which can perhaps best be described as the prayer of the great High Priest. It is the only long, continuous prayer of Jesus recorded in the Gospels. In it He prays for Himself, for the welfare of His disciples after His departure, and for all who will become believers through their ministry.

For Himself Jesus makes two requests. He prays that in this hour which marks the climax of His earthly life and ministry He may be used by the Father for the full and final display of the divine love, as He offers His own life in sacrifice (1). And He also prays that His own humiliation in death may redound to His own glory (5). The hour of the passion is momentous both for Jesus and for all mankind. It is through the passion alone that Jesus can be exalted and His authority over all human beings fully exercised. It is from the cross that He is to reign and distribute His royal bounty. While to unbelievers the hour of the passion is an hour of judgment, to believers it brings the gift of eternal life, which consists in an ever-deepening experience of the only real God, an experience mediated through Jesus His Apostle (23). The entire earthly life of Jesus has been a setting-forth of the divine love. Herein lies its uniqueness. All that He has said and done, His teaching and His mighty works, has been prompted by the desire that men and women should enjoy that higher life, which is experienced in its fullness only when their sins are forgiven and they are reconciled to God. And when once the perfect sacrifice of Himself has been offered, which will effect that reconciliation, the gift of eternal life will be available for all believers. The purpose of His life will then have been fulfilled. It is therefore with confidence that Jesus prays that He may return to His Father's side and enjoy in His presence the glory of heaven which He was already enjoying when the world was created. In one respect His enjoyment of that glory will be greater than it was before He came down from heaven on His errand of redemption, for He will have finished the work His Father gave Him to do (4). He will have passed on to the disciples, who have been given Him by the Father, the fullness of divine truth; and by accepting that truth as *divine*, and by acknowledging that Jesus came from God and was sent by God, they will become the Church of God (8).

Jesus dies, leaving behind Him a new society standing out in marked contrast to the world. It is a society of believers, a people who belong to God, the property both of the Father and the Son. In this society, fashioned under the influence of His teaching and His example, the glory of Jesus will shine on through the ages, and the darkness will never destroy it. But the Church, though unworldly in origin, is nevertheless in the world and subject to the world's evil influence; and the protective power of Jesus' physical presence is soon to be withdrawn. He prays therefore that the holy Father, whose holiness separates Him from the world, will keep all who belong to Him holy and separate (11). He prays too that by their love one for another they may reflect the unity of will and purpose that exists between the Father and Himself. While Jesus has been with them, the revelation of the holy Father given to them by the sinless Son has saved them from the corrosive and disintegrating power of evil. However much they may have failed, their failure has never been complete. There has been only one exception, Judas Iscariot who in fulfilment of Scripture was bound to perish (12).

The society of the Church has been created by God for a specific purpose. Its *raison d'être* is to convey to the world the revelation imparted by Jesus, and to reflect the self-sacrificing love manifested by Jesus on the cross. The supreme joy of

Jesus lay in His willingness to make that sacrifice, and in the assurance that by so doing He would win the decisive victory against the prince of evil. And He now prays that His disciples may experience the same joy when they proclaim the gospel after His departure (13). He does not pray that they may escape from the world, for that would be to frustrate the divine purpose; nor that they may be immune from the world's hatred, for it is inevitable that that hatred should continue to be directed against both Jesus and His friends precisely because they cannot conform to the world's standards. The world, in so far as it lies under the evil one, and the society illuminated by divine truth, are eternally opposed. The one is from beneath, the other is from above. Jesus therefore prays the Father that the disciples may be so dedicated to their task, and so sanctified by the truth about God that He has taught them, that they may be able to fulfil their vocation as His apostles, as completely as He has fulfilled His vocation as the Apostle of God. The Father sent Jesus into the world to re-unite sinful man to Himself, and in so doing to reveal to them God's love for sinners; the apostles are sent by Jesus to proclaim the good news of this reconciliation, and to reflect the divine love in their personal conduct (18).

But no memory of Jesus' words apart from the abiding influence of His death will enable His disciples to discharge faithfully the duty that confronts them. They will only be dedicated and sanctified because Jesus dedicates Himself to a death which has cleansing power. Similarly, they will not be able to show love one towards another without the inspiration of the love of Jesus for them. So in verse 19, for the sake of His present disciples and all who will become believers in the future, Jesus consecrates His own sinless humanity to death, Himself the Priest and Himself the Victim in the perfect sacrifice which is to take away the sin of the world. Under the old dispensation the priests made themselves ceremonially clean before offering in sacrifice unconscious animal victims. Under the new dispensation, the sinless Priest offers His own immaculate life in a sacrifice which is personal, rational and spiritual. The divine *word* which is *truth*, by which Jesus prays that His disciples may be consecrated to their task (17), is to be found not only in the precepts they have learned from Him but in the all-sufficient sacrifice to which He dedicates Himself in the words 'And for their sake I consecrate myself, that they also may be consecrated in truth' (19, RSV); or, as Knox translates, 'And I dedicate myself for their sakes, that they too may be dedicated through the truth.'

Because in answer to Jesus' prayers the disciples will become dedicated and consecrated men, the fellowship of Christian believers will increase as the work of evangelism goes forward. Jesus accordingly prays, in conclusion, that the unity which He has already prayed may be a reality among His original disciples, may also characterize all who will become believers through their ministry (20, 21). This unity, like the love which produces it, is supernatural; it is fundamentally the same as the unity that exists between the Father and the Son. This is why the world, when it sees such unity among believers, will be led to recognize the divine mission of Jesus. But the perfection of this unity will only be reached so long as the believers keep in touch with their exalted Lord and contemplate the glory which has been His from eternity. He has always been the object of His Father's love; and the mutual love of Christian believers must have as its effective cause and its sustaining power their insight into the glory of their Master. As the eternal object of His Father's love He has a knowledge of the justice and holiness of God such as the world can never have. And it is the wonder of the Christian religion that that knowledge is given to all who accept Jesus as God's Apostle, and who are conscious of His presence as He continues to make known to them the mind and purposes of God (25, 26).

Additional Notes

xvii. 2. *Power over all flesh* means in this context 'authority to determine the ultimate destiny of men' (cf. Mt. xxviii. 18).

3. *That they might know.* In the Greek the verb is in the present subjunctive indicating that the 'knowledge' is a growing experience.

True translates the same word as that used in xv. 1, where see the note. There are many counterfeit gods (see 1 Cor. viii. 5), but only one genuine God.

4. *Finished.* Though not yet an accomplished fact the passion is 'completed' in the will and intention of Jesus.

5. *Now* is logical rather than temporal. Because Jesus has finished the work the Father gave Him to do, He can pray that He may enjoy once more the Father's glory.

With thine own self. The Greek idiom is better represented by 'in thy own presence' (RSV) or 'at thy side' (Knox).

6. *Thy name* in this context denotes all that is meant by the words 'God is love'.

7. *All things whatsoever thou hast given me;* i.e. the works He has performed in the Father's power and the teaching He has given under the Father's inspiration.

10. *I am glorified in them.* The Greek verb is in the perfect tense. Jesus' glory has already shone in the face of His disciples. They are already in a real though limited sense a reflection of Himself. They have caught the infection of His spirit, become interested in the things in which He is interested, learned to love what He loves and to hate what He hates. The perfect tense implies that this reflection of Jesus in His apostles will remain.

11, 12. For *those whom thou hast given me* in verse 11, and *those that thou gavest me* in verse 12, some MSS read 'which thou hast given me', 'which' referring in each case to *the name* which in the Greek text immediately precedes it. RV and RSV translate these better-attested alternatives in both verses 'keep them in thy name which thou hast given me', 'I kept them in thy name which thou hast given me'. Whichever reading is adopted *the name* here would seem to signify the power of the person who bears the name. Jesus, when He was on earth, displayed this divine power both in saving His disciples from physical death (e.g. by stilling the storm; see Mk. vi. 47–51), and in keeping them united. After His departure this preserving power will be exercised by the Father Himself.

One (11) here and in verse 21 is in the neuter in the Greek, and the sense is the same as in x. 30, where see note.

I at the beginning of verse 12 is emphatic in the original. This is well brought out by Knox 'As long as I was with them, it was for me to keep them'.

The son of perdition is a Hebrew way of saying 'one who is destined to be lost'; cf. 2 Thes. ii. 3.

The scripture would seem to be a reference to Ps. xli. 9, already quoted in xiii. 18.

13. *These things I speak.* The Greek verb *lalō* indicates that the prayer was spoken out loud.

15. *From the evil* can be either masculine or neuter. The same dilemma confronts the translator of the Lord's prayer (Mt. vi. 13). RV and RSV here translate 'from the evil one', probably correctly as Jesus seems to have regarded evil as a personal influence.

17, 19. In both these verses 'dedicate' or 'consecrate' is a better translation than *sanctify*. The word *hagiazō* means not only 'to make holy' but 'to dedicate what is already holy'. It is clear that the latter must be the sense in verse 19, and the verb would seem to have the same sense in verse 17.

19. *Through the truth.* There is no definite article in the original. Hence RV and RSV translate 'in truth', i.e. 'truly consecrated'. *Through the truth* meaning 'through the revelation Jesus has given them' seems to fit the context better.

25. Both the epithets attached to *Father* in this chapter, *righteous* in this verse and *holy* in verse 11, are full of meaning in the context. As H. B. Swete commented, 'God's holiness is the guarantee that He will keep His saints from the evil of the world; His justice forbids Him to abandon them.'[1]

VII. THE ARREST, THE TRIALS, AND THE CRUCIFIXION OF JESUS (xviii. 1–xix. 37)

a. The arrest of Jesus (xviii. 1–11)

In view of the central place occupied by the passion of Jesus in the preaching of the apostolic age it is probable that a

[1] *The Last Prayer and Discourse of our Lord* (Macmillan, 1914), p. 168.

connected story of it soon took shape in Christian tradition. All four evangelists give a similar sequence of events—the arrest made possible by Judas' treachery; a preliminary trial before the Jewish authorities; and a more decisive trial before Pilate the Roman procurator, as a result of which Barabbas is released and Jesus crucified. Yet each Gospel contains details not found in the others; and the special interests and objects of each evangelist can be seen in his particular selection of incidents and in his manner of describing them. John would appear to be most concerned to show that Jesus was active as well as passive throughout the whole of this last stage of His earthly life. However much an outside observer might have thought otherwise, the initiative remained with Him to the end. He welcomed the striking of this hour of destiny, for now the glory of His Father could most clearly be displayed.

Jesus had left the upper room with the express intention of going forth to meet the prince of evil and his human satellites (see comment on xiv. 30, 31), for He had already resisted the temptation to pray 'Father, save me from this hour', knowing that if that prayer had been granted, there would have been no complete glorification of His Father, and mankind would never have known the wonder of His redeeming love (see comment on xii. 27). So when He crosses the brook Cedron to a garden (1), which had been a favourite resort for Himself and His disciples, what is happening is that the second Adam is deliberately entering upon the final conflict with the prince of evil, reversing the situation in the garden of Eden where the serpent took the initiative in the assault upon the first Adam. When Judas, now completely in the grip of Satan (see xiii. 2), crosses the garden, leading a fully-armed band of assailants consisting of temple police and Roman soldiers (3), Jesus knowing all that is going to happen to Him and knowing that it is in accord with His Father's will, goes out to meet them and twice calls upon them to name the person they are looking for (4, 7). And when they twice reply *Jesus of Nazareth*, He says in words of majesty and divinity, *I am he.*

This scene is one of the most dramatic of the many dramatic scenes in this Gospel. On the one hand we see Judas and his 'army', representative of the world which is tainted by evil in its religion and its politics, and relies upon physical force to achieve its objects. On the other hand we are confronted with Jesus unarmed, unbefriended and apparently helpless in the face of overwhelming opposition, but having at His command invisible divine resources in virtue of His complete obedience to His heavenly Father. In consequence, His victory is assured in this last assault upon the citadel of evil. *As soon then as he had said unto them, I am he, they went backward, and fell to the ground* (6).

The desertion of Jesus at His arrest by the remaining apostles is not recorded by this evangelist, though we have already been informed that Jesus foretold that when the hour of the passion came, the disciples would be scattered and the unity of the flock temporarily broken (xvi. 32). But, because the death of Jesus was a voluntary act of the good Shepherd on behalf of His sheep, it was a vital part of His pastoral care to see that the sheep were protected during the dark hours of the passion, and that the little flock, even if scattered for the moment, should remain intact except for the inevitable loss of Judas. A prime concern of Jesus therefore, when He gives Himself up to His assassins, is that His disciples should retain their freedom. The great sacrifice is to be offered by Jesus alone, for He alone bears the divine name and can reveal the divine love. *If therefore ye seek me, let these go their way: that the saying might be fulfilled, which he spake, Of them which thou gavest me have I los none* (8, 9). Simon Peter makes an impulsive attempt to prevent the fulfilment of these words, and to substitute another method of attack upon the evil that confronts them than that chosen by his Master. He strikes a blow at Malchus, the high priest's servant. But Jesus stays Peter's hand before it perpetrates any further act of physical aggression; for evil can only be overcome if Jesus Himself drinks the cup of the wrath of God, and He is under a divine necessity to drink that cup alone and to drink it to the full.

Additional Notes

xviii. 1. For *the brook Cedron* (RSV, 'the Kidron valley') some MSS have 'the ravine of cedar trees' in accordance with the

LXX version of 2 Sa. xv. 23. The place called Gethsemane (Mt. xxvi. 36 and Mk. xiv. 32) is here described as *a garden.* The same word *kēpos* (lit. 'orchard') is used in xix. 41, where the commentary should be consulted for its significance.

2. The reference to the frequent visits of Jesus and His disciples to this secluded spot suggests that it was a favourite 'hide-out' for the apostolic band during the visits of Jesus to Jerusalem.

3. 'A band of soldiers' (RSV) is a better translation than *a band of men*, for the Greek word *speira* is a technical term for a detachment of infantry in the Roman army consisting of some 600 men. John alone of the evangelists uses this word, because the truth that underlies his narrative at this point would seem to be that it was the union of what on human standards might have been considered the 'best' elements in the political and religious life of the time that brought about the arrest of Jesus.

4. The pre-arranged signal for the arrest, the kiss, is omitted in this Gospel, the emphasis being upon the initiative of Jesus who gives Himself up after Judas has brought the search party to Jesus (see x. 18).

5. The Greek *ego eimi* rendered *I am he* might well suggest divinity to those familiar with the Greek Bible, for it is the rendering in the LXX for the sacred name of God (see Ex. iii. 14). The evangelist notices in verse 6 the numinous effect which its utterance had upon those who heard it.

8. *Me* by its position in the Greek is emphatic—'if it is Me you are wanting'.

9. *The saying* is a reference to the words of Jesus recorded in xvii. 12.

11. This Gospel assumes that the temptation to refuse the cup, mentioned in the other Gospels, had already been encountered and overcome.

b. The trial before the high priest (xviii. 12–27)

A much larger amount of space is given in this Gospel to the trial before Pilate than to the trial before the Jewish authorities.

As the text stands, the Jewish trial appears to be held before Annas, the father-in-law of Caiaphas the reigning high priest; and not until verse 24 is there any mention of the appearance of Jesus before Caiaphas. Moreover, into the scene of the trial is dovetailed the story of Peter's threefold denial. The very important old Syriac version of the Gospel, as represented by the manuscript discovered on Mt. Sinai in 1892, straightens the whole narrative out. It places verse 24 after verse 13, and thereby makes the trial take place before Caiaphas after a brief visit, perhaps out of courtesy or for consultation, to Annas; and it also groups the narrative so that the verses relating to the trial are kept separate from those describing Peter's denials. The actual order of the verses in this manuscript is 13, 24, 14, 15, 19–23, 16–18. But if this was the original order, it is difficult to see why it was ever altered to produce the more 'confused' arrangement with which we are familiar. Most scholars therefore maintain that the usual order of the text must be followed, although they also feel sure that the trial took place before Caiaphas as the earlier Gospels state, and that it is most unlikely that John would have made no reference to this. In verse 14 he draws attention to his statement in xi. 50 that Caiaphas, who took the initiative in desiring legal proceedings against Jesus, had insisted *that it was expedient that one man should die for the people.*

On the assumption that the traditional order is original verse 24 may perhaps be regarded as a 'deferred foot-note', to use R. A. Knox's expression; as though the author was saying in effect 'I ought to have noticed before that Annas had sent the prisoner to Caiaphas'. 'St. John', says Knox, 'who wrote his Gospel as a very old man, often gives names, times and places as a kind of afterthought.' Although this has been regarded by some as rather desperate exegesis, it would appear to have been the view of the makers of the King James' version, who translated verse 24 *Annas had sent him bound unto Caiaphas the high priest.* If, on the other hand, RV is right in insisting upon the strict meaning of the aorist tense of the verb and in translating 'Annas sent him (i.e. now for the first time) bound to Caiaphas', then, if we retain the traditional order, the Gospel is entirely silent as to what was said at the trial before Caiaphas, which as has already been noticed is improbable. Perhaps the solution of this difficult textual problem lies in adopting the reading of a somewhat late manuscript, which inserts verse 24 after the words *to Annas first* in verse 13. If this reading is accepted as original in spite of its late and slender attestation, we should have to suppose that a very early copyist accidentally omitted the words 'Annas therefore sent him bound to Caiaphas the high priest' when he was copying verse 13, and then, realizing his error, resorted to the common procedure of scribes when they found themselves in this predicament; he inserted the words at the first suitable place. Consequently they are found where they are (*viz* in verse 24) in nearly all our textual authorities.[1]

At the trial before the high priest, as at the arrest, Jesus is strictly master of the situation. When questioned about His disciples and His teaching, He says nothing about the character or good faith of His disciples, but points out that His teaching had been given *openly* in unambiguous language, and in public places such as the synagogues and the temple (20). There were many therefore who could be called upon to testify to the words they had heard Him speak, without the demand that He should bear unsupported witness to Himself in defiance of the Jewish law of evidence, which was the very thing that the Jews had previously accused Him of doing (see viii. 13). There has been nothing, Jesus insists, either in His teaching or in His actions of such a character as to justify the blow which He now receives at the hand of one of the high priest's assistants, who expresses horror that Jesus should speak to the high priest in such a cavalier fashion (23).

While this trial is going on, the reader is presented simultaneously, as though he were a spectator at a drama being performed on a double stage, with the denials of Simon Peter. John retells the story of the threefold denial culminating in the cock-crowing. The first question that leads Peter to disown his Master is put by the maid-servant on duty at the outer

[1] See C. C. Torrey, *The Four Gospels. A New Translation* (Hodder and Stoughton, second edition 1947), p. 329.

door, who admits Peter into the courtyard at the request of a disciple known to the high priest (16, 17); and the second is asked by several servants of the temple police who are warming themselves with Peter at the charcoal fire (25). Both these questions may be read, not as expecting the answer 'Yes', as the AV translation suggests, but as eliciting the answer 'No'. 'Surely you are not another of this man's disciples?' If so, Peter yields to the temptation suggested to him by the form in which the question is put, that he is not really a disciple at all. This is the manner in which temptation often comes to us. The third questioner is a relative of the wounded Malchus, who is very sure that Peter is the man he had seen in the garden at the time of that untoward incident. Peter denied again and just then a cock crew (26, 27).

Additional Notes

xviii. 13. *That same year* is not an indication that the evangelist wrongly believed the high priesthood to be a yearly office. Many earlier critics took it as such, and drew the inference that the author could not have been a Jew. In fact, the phrase carries with it the implication 'that notorious year', the *annus mirabilis*, when Christ redeemed mankind.

15. Some ancient MSS read 'the other' for *another*, thereby it would seem, identifying the unnamed disciple of this verse with 'the disciple whom Jesus loved'. The very fact, however, that the author does not use the latter description here would appear to indicate that the disciple 'known to the high priest' was a different person. Moreover, it is more likely that a Jerusalem rather than a Galilaean disciple, such as John the son of Zebedee, would have been sufficiently acquainted with the high priest for him to have been allowed such easy access to the latter's residence. It is one of the curious features of this evangelist that sometimes he seems to go out of his way for no particular reason to insert the names even of comparatively unimportant characters in the story (cf. 'the servant's name was Malchus' in verse 10), while at other times he seems deliberately to suppress the names of very important witnesses. It is unlikely that he would not have known the name of the man, upon the reliability of whose testimony he lays such stress in xix. 35; or the name of the disciple referred to in the present verse.

17. *This man's* in the Greek is contemptuous, more akin to 'this fellow's' or 'this person's'.

20. *Openly* translates *parrēsia*, which draws attention not only to the publicity of the teaching of Jesus but also to its outspokenness and its freedom from ambiguity. There was nothing esoteric about it, a truth which is also probably indicated in the expression *in secret.* Jesus had, of course, taught in many other places than the synagogues and the temple. Much of His teaching had been given to His disciples privately. As He Himself said, some of it had been taught them 'in darkness' (Mt. x. 27). Moreover, part at any rate of the purpose of teaching in parables would seem to have been the veiling of truth in the presence of the uninitiated. Nevertheless, as this evangelist is at pains to point out by the very setting in which he records the significant works of Jesus and the discourses which follow them, the essential nature of His Person and of His claims had been made abundantly clear on the occasions when the Jews were gathered together in the largest numbers, *viz* at the great festivals at Jerusalem. And nothing could have been plainer than his exposition of Isaiah lxi in the synagogue at Nazareth at the beginning of His ministry (see Lk. iv. 16–22).

c. The trial before Pilate (xviii. 28–xix. 16)

In the last watch of the night Jesus is brought from the high priest to Pilate. The Jews are unwilling, John records, to enter the procurator's residence, lest they should become ceremonially defiled before Passover. The irony of the situation is that they are anxious to avoid external defilement in order to observe a festival whose *real* significance was that, as well as reminding God's people of the ancient deliverance from Egypt, it pointed forward to the true Passover Lamb, whose sacrifice would bring to an end all distinctions between what was ceremonially clean and unclean, and effect an inward cleansing; and it was the death of that true Passover Lamb that the Jews at this moment are anxious to bring about.

There is no mention in this narrative of the exact nature of the accusation against Jesus made by the Jews to Pilate; but they protest that they would not have brought Him before a Roman tribunal unless He was guilty in their judgment of a criminal offence (30). They would gladly have put Him to death themselves, but, as verse 31 seems to imply, they were legally prohibited under the Roman occupation from inflicting the death penalty, and had to await the Roman procurator's decision. Moreover, it was essential for the accomplishment of the divine plan for man's salvation that Jesus should die, not by stoning, the penalty for blasphemy under the Jewish law, but, as He Himself had prophesied in words which the evangelist now recalls, by being 'lifted up from the earth', a manner of death which could be secured only by crucifixion (see xii. 32). The final exaltation of Jesus and His reign in glory would have been impossible apart from this preliminary exaltation.

The refusal of the Jews to enter Pilate's residence enables him to interview the accused in private. He denies emphatically that the charge that Jesus claimed to be the King of the Jews originated with himself. He is no Jew! And what could he possibly know about Jesus, an obscure Galilaean, except what he had been told by other members of the always difficult and often turbulent people to whom Jesus belonged (35)! As a practical administrator what he desires to discover is whether or not some specific crime has been committed. *What hast thou done?* he asks.

The reader is now presented with a dramatic scene, in which two types of kingship are contrasted; the kingship backed by the authority and might of imperial Rome represented by Pilate, a kingship *of this world* and upheld by this world's weapons, and the kingship of Jesus *not of this world*, in which the monarch is to reign by being lifted up on a cross (36). The narrative clearly presupposes that it had been intimated to Pilate that Jesus, by claiming kingship over Jewry, was in effect a political revolutionary and therefore a potential danger to Rome; but it lays the guilt for supposing Him to be such upon the Jews rather than upon Pilate. In reality, Jesus had come into the world for no political purpose whatever, but solely to *witness unto the truth*, the truth about God, to testify by word and deed to His justice and at the same time to demonstrate His love (37). It is therefore only those who are concerned with *ultimate* justice and not merely with the imperfect reflections of it seen in the exercise of human justice, and only those whose conception of power is not limited to physical force but who are sensitive to the strength that is inherent in love, who can understand the nature of the kingship of Jesus. This would seem to be the meaning of *Every one that is of the truth heareth my voice*. Pilate does not belong to such a company. He is satisfied with the imperfect and pragmatic judgments of earthly rulers, and he would equate belief in spiritual power with superstition. By asking *what is truth?* (38) he shows himself to be not *of the truth*.

The question *what hast thou done?* (35) has not been answered, and Pilate can obtain no definite information about any specific action of Jesus which might legitimately lead to His condemnation. But the procurator is used to finding a way out of his difficulties. Instead of acting against his personal conviction that Jesus is innocent, he reminds the Jews of the custom of releasing a prisoner at Passover and suggests that on this occasion that prisoner should be Jesus. But fanaticism prevails and with raucous shouts they demand the release of one who has been justly sentenced as a dangerous criminal—the bandit Barabbas; and Pilate for the moment is non-plussed (38–40).

He now tries to obtain direct evidence from Jesus by having Him flogged (xix. 1). At the same time he hopes that the Jews will be satisfied with this treatment of the prisoner and withdraw the demand for a death sentence. His soldiers also indulge in mockery. After placing a crown of thorns upon Jesus' head and arraying Him in royal purple, they keep coming up to Him, saluting Him as 'King of the Jews', and offering Him blows with their hands instead of the kiss of homage that loyal subjects would naturally give to their king (2, 3). Clothed in this ignominious apparel of royalty, Jesus is now brought by Pilate before the crowd, for his hope is that such a spectacle will elicit their pity. The famous words *Behold the man* (5) carry the implication 'Look, here is the poor fellow. Can you really regard such a pathetic figure as a rival king?' But the priests and the temple-police forestall any feelings of sympathy which the sight of Jesus in His present predicament might be expected to arouse, by vociferously clamouring for His crucifixion. Pilate would rather they should do their dirty work themselves than that he should be forced into a decision contrary to his conscience. His words *Take ye him, and crucify him: for I find no fault in him,* and also the Jews' rejoinder *We have a law, and by our law he ought to die, because he made himself the Son of God* (6, 7) are clear indications that the responsibility for the crucifixion lies with them rather than with Pilate. It is noticeable that for the moment the Jews have abandoned the charge of treason put forward to secure Pilate's attention to the case and fallen back on what to them was the primary charge of blasphemy.

The mention for the first time in Pilate's hearing of the expression *Son of God* (7) increases his fear—possibly a superstitious fear that, for all appearances to the contrary, he might be in the presence of a supernatural figure with all the sinister consequences that might involve, but more probably a fear that, in spite of the lack of evidence, here was one who really was claiming for himself the title to which the Roman emperor laid claim, *divi filius.* Thus in a curious manner what to the Jews was the primary charge of blasphemy becomes equated in the mind of the procurator with the secondary charge of treason. He therefore tries to discover more definite information about the origin of Jesus. His question is almost the most pertinent question that can be asked about Him, for to know where Jesus comes from is to know the most important thing about Him. But not even the reminder by Pilate that in the exercise of his political authority he possesses power over life and death can extract from Jesus the definite information that he desires (9, 10). Jesus, as has been made so evident in this Gospel, is 'from above'. His authority comes from His heavenly Father. Pilate's authority is also, in a sense, 'from above' for 'the powers that be are ordained of God' (Rom. xiii. 1). Pilate's sin in bringing about the crucifixion is therefore less, Jesus asserts, than that of the high priest, for Pilate, however wrongly he may be destined to use the power vested in him, is exercising a power legitimately entrusted to him, while the person who handed Jesus over to him is illegally using the secular power of Rome to obtain an unjust sentence against Jesus (11).

Pilate, somewhat relieved at the partial exoneration of himself implied in the words *he that delivered me unto thee hath the greater sin*, makes a last attempt to secure the release of Jesus. Fear however of appearing disloyal to the immediate source of his authority, the 'suspicious despot' Tiberius, in the end weighs down the scales of his conscience on the side of opportunism. To run any risk of not being thought *Caesar's friend* is intolerable (12). For him (in the words put into his mouth by John Masefield in his play *Good Friday*),

> 'there is but one religion, which is Rome,
> no easy one to practise far from home.'

But practise it Pilate will. So at the hour of 6 a.m. on the Friday in Passover week he takes his seat on the bench and passes the death sentence upon the prisoner. But before he finally hands Jesus over for crucifixion, he cannot refrain from enjoying his joke at the expense of the hated Jews. He presents Jesus to them again, but this time with the words *Behold your King!* (14). Nor does the raucous repetition of the shouts *Away with him, crucify him* prevent Pilate from rubbing in the salt of his irony with the question *Shall I crucify your King?* (15). This leads the chief priests to utter words, which are in fact words of blasphemy when they fall from the lips of worshippers of the God of Israel, *We have no king but Caesar.*

Additional Notes

xviii. 28. For *the hall of judgment* RSV has 'praetorium', a transliteration of the Greek. The word covers all the buildings which constituted the Roman governor's 'quarters'. The nearest modern equivalent is probably 'residence'.

Lest they should be defiled; i.e. by coming into a house from which leavened bread had not been removed (see Ex. xii. 18, 19).

Eat the passover. If this is a reference to the main Passover meal which took place on the first night of the festival, then the inference must be that that meal had not yet been eaten at the time when Jesus was brought before Pilate; therefore the Last Supper could not have been the Passover meal. Most modern scholars interpret the reference in this way, assuming either that John is here historically correct and the Synoptic Gospels mistaken, or that for theological reasons John has deliberately ante-dated by one day the meal in the upper room, so that Jesus the true Paschal Lamb is presented in his narrative as dying at the very time when the lambs were being slain in preparation for the Passover meal.

It may be, however, that by *the passover* in this verse the whole Passover festival, which lasted seven days, is meant; and that the expression *eat the passover* refers not to the main Passover meal which may have already taken place, but to the remaining meals that would be taken in the Passover season. In this case, there would be no contradiction between the evangelists (see further notes on xix. 14, 31).

30. In the original *thee* is emphatic. The Jews imply that Jesus had committed a crime in violation of Roman law, and that therefore He had to be *delivered*, i.e. brought for trial, before the procurator Pilate.

31, 32. Pilate refuses to regard the expression *malefactor* (lit. 'a doer of wrong') as synonymous with 'criminal' or offender against the Roman law, and challenges the representatives of the Sanhedrin, who pride themselves upon their moral rectitude, to decide the case in the light of their own law which they claim to be God-given and not man-made. His challenge is deliberately intended to irritate the Jews, for he knows that the penalty of stoning which their law allowed could not under the existing political status of Judaea be carried out. In verse 32 the evangelist notes that, even if the Jews had been permitted to stone Jesus, this would have been contrary to the divine will as expressed in Jesus' own prophecies about the manner of His death.

33. In the original *thou* is emphatic. Pilate says in effect 'Can you, poor creature that you are, really be a king?'

36. *Kingdom* in this verse refers not so much to the sphere in which the reign of Jesus is exercised as to the nature of the reign itself. RSV 'kingship' is therefore a better translation. His kingship is of such a character that it cannot be invalidated by His arrest at the hands of the Jews, or destroyed by His death.

My servants may be understood as 'My followers', i.e. My disciples; or possibly, but less probably, the reference might be to the 'legions of angels' that Jesus said His Father could send to His assistance if He so desired (Mt. xxvi. 53).

Would fight. The tense of the Greek is better rendered 'would now be fighting'. Arrest at the hands of the Jews would have indeed put an end to Jesus' hope of exercising kingship, if that kingship had been *of this world.* Precisely because it was not *of this world* it did not need the backing of physical force. The evangelist has already recorded a signal instance of the horror felt by Jesus lest anyone should regard Him as a 'worldly king'. When the restless and turbulent Galilaeans tried by force to make Him a king after He had lavished His royal bounty upon them by feeding five thousand men with five loaves, Jesus escaped, the evangelist records, to the hillside to be alone (see vi. 15).

37. Pilate's question *art thou a king then?* is asked, as the Greek particle introducing it suggests, in considerable surprise. 'So you are after all a king?' And in Jesus' reply *thou* is emphatic. *Pilate*, not Jesus, had used the word 'king' and he was not wrong to use it. Jesus had refrained from using it of Himself lest the nature of His kingship should be misunderstood. But He *was* a king, though not in the least the kind of king that could be justly accused of being a rival of the Roman emperor.

38. *Fault* is better rendered by RSV, 'crime'. It refers to an indictable offence (so also in xix. 4, 6).

39. The *custom* would give Pilate the chance of thwarting the wishes of the Sanhedrin and also of winning a reputation for clemency.

40. *Robber* suggests in modern English 'thief'. The Greek word *lēstēs* implies a desperate bandit or brigand. Mark tells us that Barabbas was a gangster who had committed murder in a recent disturbance (see Mk. xv. 7).

xix. 2. The *crown of thorns* has often been regarded, from the days of Clement of Alexandria onwards, as an instrument of torture, on the ground that it was woven in the form of a garland out of some plant bearing thorns on stems or branches sufficiently pliable for weaving. Recently H. St. J. Hart, in a very interesting and well-illustrated article,[1] has given cogent reasons for supposing that the crown was in fact a 'radiate' crown, constructed in the form of a diadem from which 'rays' of sharply pointed spikes extended upwards. Mr. Hart points out that evidence from coinage of the period shows that the wearing of such a crown was a sign of royalty and divinity. It may well have been then that Pilate's soldiers made a crown of this kind to mock the claims of Jesus to be a king and divine. Mr. Hart also suggests that such a crown could have been constructed from the species of palm-tree, found at Jerusalem, known as *phoenix dactylifera*, from whose stem separate inflexible thorns or spikes emerge, sometimes twelve inches long. That a crown made from this particular plant could have been described as 'a crown of thorns' is regarded as probable in the light of some passages from the Talmud quoted in the article. If this deduction is correct, the author concludes that 'when Pilate's soldiers had finished dressing up their prisoner, he wore a mock-royal robe of purple, he carried a mock-royal sceptre, and he was crowned with a mock-radiate crown'.

3. The late MSS followed by the makers of AV omitted the well-attested and essential words 'they kept coming up to him' at the beginning of this verse. The mockery of the 'homage' consisted in the fact that it was constantly repeated.

[1] H. St. J. Hart, 'The Crown of Thorns in Jn. xix. 2–5' (*Journal of Theological Studies*, 1952), pp. 66–75.

5. *The man* is contemptuous. Pilate is saying in effect 'Here he is—the poor fellow. Can you really think that such a caricature of a king is really a danger either to Israel or Rome?' Christians, re-reading these famous words, naturally see in 'the Man' in question humanity at its best, the suffering Servant in whom God delighted.

7. The *law* in question is the law of Lv. xxiv. 16.

8. As there has been no previous mention of Pilate's fear, it may be that the comparative *the more afraid* should be given a superlative force, such as it often has in New Testament Greek, and rendered 'exceedingly afraid'.

That saying refers to the expression *Son of God* rather than to the whole of verse 7.

10. *Me* is very emphatic in the Greek; it is the refusal of Jesus to speak to one who possesses such supreme human authority that amazes Pilate. RSV, 'You will not speak to me?' is better than the strictly literal AV.

11. *He that delivered me* could be a reference either to Judas or Caiaphas and the language of the evangelist seems to be deliberately vague.

12. The Greek *ek toutou* rendered *from thenceforth* can be interpreted either in a temporal sense 'from that moment', or inferentially, as in RSV, 'Upon this'. The latter is more probable. Pilate is flattered by what Jesus has said in verse 11 and in consequence tries still harder to release Him.

Cried out translates the reading which has the verb in the aorist tense. Probably the well-attested imperfect tense should be followed, giving the sense 'they kept shouting'. It was the persistence of the Jews in making a political issue of the case that was wearing Pilate out.

13. It is just possible that the verb translated 'sat down' should be taken in a transitive sense 'caused Jesus to sit down' (cf. 1 Cor. vi. 4). This might throw into greater relief the irony of 'Behold your King!' It is however unlikely that a Roman governor would not have himself sat in the seat of authority when passing judgment of such solemnity.

14. *Preparation of the passover.* The Greek *paraskeuē tou pascha* can mean 'preparation for the passover', which would naturally be interpreted as the day of preparation for the Passover festival which had not yet begun; in which case John would again be ante-dating the crucifixion and the Last Supper could not have been the Passover meal. On the other hand, the words could be translated 'the preparation day (for the sabbath, cf. Mk. xv. 42) belonging to the Passover festival', in other words 'Friday in Passover week'. Most modern scholars assume that the former rendering is more likely to be correct (see notes on xviii. 28 and xix. 31). But we may well hesitate to believe that the Gospels are in disagreement on such an important matter.

For *the sixth hour* a few MSS read 'the third hour' (9 a.m.) apparently to bring the text into harmony with Mk. xv. 25, though a few MSS in the latter passage by reading *the sixth hour* seem to be attempting to harmonize Mark with John! Westcott gives good reasons for supposing that this evangelist, instead of reckoning hours from 6 a.m. to 6 p.m., and 6 p.m. to 6 a.m., as was the Jewish custom, reckoned them from midnight to noon, and noon to midnight—a practice which we know from the *Martyrdom of Polycarp* was in use in Asia Minor at the time that document was written, and which is still followed in the West today. On this reckoning, it was 10 a.m. when Andrew and his fellow-disciple arrived at the place where Jesus was staying (i. 39); 6 p.m. when Jesus met the Samaritan woman at the well (iv. 6); 7 p.m. when the nobleman's son got better (iv. 52); and about 6 a.m. when Pilate passed sentence on Jesus (xix. 14). On this supposition the Johannine narrative of the crucifixion fits in very well with that of Mark, who, following the Jewish method of reckoning hours, states that it was 'the third hour' i.e. 9 a.m. when the crucifixion began.

d. The crucifixion (xix. 17–37)

The struggle between the two conceptions of kingship ends in an apparent triumph for the prince of this world and his human agents, the religious and political leaders of the day. Jesus goes out to the place of execution carrying the cross-beam for Himself, even as Isaac carried the wood on which his father Abraham had been told to offer him in sacrifice (Gn. xxii. 6). He hangs between two other condemned men, for the lot of the suffering Servant of God is with the transgressors (Is. liii. 12); and on the cross an inscription is fixed JESUS OF NAZARETH THE KING OF THE JEWS. John alone adds, perhaps in order to draw attention to the universal scope of the kingship which the crucified Jesus would exercise, *it was written in Hebrew, and Greek, and Latin* (20). The wording was not unnaturally offensive to the Jews and the chief priests tried to persuade Pilate to alter it. But the Roman procurator had vacillated and temporized long enough. The last word was going to be with him and not with the Jews. What he had written, he had written; and his words, like the words of Jesus, were destined never to pass away!

In John's narrative a group of four women stand beside the cross; the mother of Jesus, His mother's sister, Mary the wife of Cleophas, and Mary of Magdala. The reader is thus confronted with another of the dramatic contrasts, in which this Gospel abounds, between faith and unbelief, for these four faithful women are seen over against the quaternion of soldiers in charge of the crucifixion. Christ divides mankind in His death, as He had done in His life, and as He has done ever since. The soldiers, though ignorant of the significance of what is happening, nevertheless unconsciously fulfil the words of prophecy by dividing the clothes of Jesus, their legitimate perquisites, into four parts and by 'tossing up' for the possession of His tunic (see Ps. xxii. 18). This garment is described as *without seam, woven from the top throughout* (23). It is as the great High Priest offering the perfect sacrifice that Jesus is dying; and it is stated in the Jewish law that the robe of the priest's ephod shall be of woven work and so constructed that it be not rent (Ex. xxviii. 31, 32).

Part of the work of Jesus the great High Priest is to create a new fellowship of the redeemed, and to unite human beings one with another by virtue of their common loyalty to Himself. So while He hangs on the cross He bids His mother and the beloved disciple find in their attachment to Himself the basis of a new spiritual relationship to one another (26, 27). Beneath the cross Christian fellowship is born, a fellowship wholly different from all purely human fellowship based on natural kinship, mutual sympathy, or a common outlook upon human affairs. The great and distinctive characteristic of this new fellowship is that all who enjoy it are drawn to one another by the consciousness that they are all brothers for whom Christ died.

The active ministry of Jesus to others is now over. There is, however, one act of service which He receives from others before His own sacrifice for them is complete. He has come from God, and to God He is about to return. It may be, in part at least, the intensity of His desire to go back to the Father which is in His mind when He cries *I thirst.* On this supposition, it would seem that the passage of Scripture which the evangelist was recalling when he wrote *Jesus knowing that all things were now accomplished, that the scripture might be fulfilled, saith, I thirst* (28), was not, as is usually supposed, 'They gave me also gall for my meat; and in my thirst they gave me vinegar to drink' (Ps. lxix. 21), but 'My soul thirsteth for God, for the living God: when shall I come and appear before God?' (Ps. xlii. 2). It has been argued that the reference to the fulfilment of Scripture would have come more naturally after verse 29 if the former passage had been in the evangelist's mind. Be this as it may, the cry is taken by the soldiers literally, and rightly so, for it was in the main prompted by acute physical need; there was moreover one word of stupendous import which Jesus wanted to utter with special clearness, and only if His thirst was assuaged, could it so be spoken. The soldiers are moved to raise to His lips a sponge full of sour wine; and after accepting it, this final word, so expressive of the glory and the triumph of His finished work, resounds over Calvary's hill. *It is finished* (30). The soldier's wine has been drunk; but what is more important, the earthly life of the sufferer has reached its only possible conclusion; the work that He had come into the world to do has been accomplished; the one, perfect, all-availing sacrifice has been offered. Jesus bows His head in a last act of submission to the Father's will, and surrenders His spirit to Him who had sent Him into the world to achieve so great a salvation.

The occurrence of the death of Jesus earlier than the authorities had expected made it unnecessary for the soldiers to hasten the end by breaking His legs so that the body might be removed and buried before sunset, when the new day began, which was not only a sabbath but the Passover sabbath. There was thus no violation of the Jewish law that the body of a condemned man must not hang all night upon a tree (Dt. xxi. 23). The evangelist is also careful to note that another law, relating to sacrifice, was also fulfilled. This stated that no bone of the sacrificial lamb should be broken (Ex. xii. 46). The sacrifice of the true Passover Lamb is thus shown to have been complete both in the perfection of its own inner self-offering and in its external details.

The evangelist is also concerned to show throughout his account of the crucifixion what were the results of Jesus' sacrifice, for at many points in his previous narrative these results have been predicted. To this end he inserts a tradition, which he states he has received on the most reliable authority of an eyewitness, who remains unnamed, that when a soldier stabbed the side of Jesus' dead body with a lance there was an immediate flow of *blood and water* (34, 35). This is not a miraculous phenomenon, for it has often been regarded as perfectly natural on medical grounds. The most recent medical discussion known to the present author is to be found in a paper *How our Lord died* read to the Third International Congress of Catholic doctors at Lisbon in June 1947 by John Lyle Cameron, M.D., F.R.C.S. After pointing out that the unexpectedly early death of Jesus is a clear indication that a fatal complication had suddenly developed, he asserts that the insatiable thirst and the post-mortem treatment of the body described in John xix. 34 substantiate the conclusion that this complication could only have been acute dilatation of the stomach. He then adds:

'The soldier was a Roman: he would be well trained, proficient, and would know his duty. He would know which part of the body to pierce in order that he might obtain a speedily fatal result or ensure that the victim was undeniably dead. He would thrust through the left side of the chest a little below the centre. Here he would penetrate the heart and the great blood vessels at their origin, and also the lung on the side. The soldier, standing below our crucified Lord as He hung on the cross, would thrust upwards under the left ribs. The broad, clean cutting, two-edged spearhead would enter the left side of the upper abdomen, would open the greatly distended stomach, would pierce the diaphragm, would cut, wide open, the heart and great blood vessels, arteries and veins now fully distended with blood, a considerable proportion of all the blood in the body, and would lacerate the lung. The wound would be large enough to permit the open hand to be thrust into it. Blood from the greatly engorged veins, pulmonary vessel and dilated right side of the heart, together with water from the acutely dilated stomach, would flow forth in abundance. The whole event as described by St. John must, indeed, have happened, for no writer could have presented in such coherent detail so recognizable an event, unless he or someone had actually witnessed its occurrence.'

There can, however, be no doubt that the evangelist found deep spiritual significance in what had happened. The order, *blood and water*, is important. The shed blood signifies that salvation has been procured, for without the shedding of blood there is no remission (Heb. ix. 22); and the water that flowed with it is symbolic of the new spiritual life made possible only by the sacrifice of Jesus. Water in this Gospel is a symbol of the baptism of repentance practised by John; but it is also a symbol of the power available for all who are created anew in Christ. Jesus promised the woman of Samaria that whoever drank of the water He gave him would never thirst, but that the water would become an inner spring welling up to eternal life (see iv. 14). And in the last days of the festival of Tabernacles He spoke words interpreted by the evangelist as predicting the gift of life-giving water, which would be available only after the glorification of Jesus in death (see vii. 38, 39). It is significant therefore that when this glorification is accomplished there flows at once from the side of the Crucified what can be symbolically regarded as redeeming blood and invigorating water. In the language of theology both justification and sanctification are direct results of the crucifixion of Jesus.

In the stabbing of the side of Jesus some words of the prophet Zechariah also found partial fulfilment. The prophet is describing the grief which Israel would feel for its offences against God on the day when He would seek to destroy all the nations that came against Jerusalem, and would pour upon the inhabitants of Jerusalem the spirit of grace and supplications (see Zc. xii. 9, 10). When Jesus died on the cross this 'spirit of grace' was poured out in full. The Jews looked upon *him whom they pierced* (the part of the prophecy quoted by John in verse 37), but their look was not prompted by the godly sorrow that leads to repentance (see 2 Cor. vii. 10). It was left for the new Israel, converted Jews and converted Gentiles, to turn in penitence to the pierced side of Jesus and receive from Him the gift of forgiveness and eternal life.

Additional Notes

xix. 17. The last half of verse 16 in AV has rightly been taken by later editors as the first part of verse 17 and marking the beginning of a new paragraph. *They took* is literally 'they received from' (i.e. from Pilate). The subject is unexpressed and the meaning is perhaps best expressed in English in a passive form. 'Jesus was now taken in custody.' The words *and led him away* in verse 16 of AV are omitted in most ancient MSS and are not represented in RSV.

Why the place of crucifixion was known as *the place of a skull* is very uncertain. Origen says it was the traditional burial place of Adam. Others have surmised without any definite evidence that many skulls were buried there; but in that case the plural 'skulls' would have been a more fitting description. Others, again without evidence, have conjectured that the hill was skull-shaped.

19. *Title* came into the AV from the Vulgate *titulus*. Its use in the present verse is somewhat archaic, and some such word as 'inscription' should be substituted for it. *Put it* is causal in sense. Pilate ordered it to be put on the cross.

23. The words *and also his coat* are as difficult in AV as they are in the Greek. If they are original, the only sense they could have must be expressed in the paraphrase, 'They also took his tunic but treated it differently'. RSV on the evidence of the original scribe of Codex Sinaiticus, the old Latin MSS and other ancient authorities omit the words altogether, and the case for the omission is further strengthened by their apparent absence from the recently discovered Bodmer papyrus, now at Geneva, which is dated *circa* 200 and is the oldest continuous text known to us of the Gospel of John.

24. The AV verse division is again not very happy at this point; it is better to regard the last sentence of verse 24 as the opening sentence of verse 25 (so RSV). This arrangement helps to bring into clearer relief the obviously contrasted groups of people standing near the cross.

25. Mark and Matthew mention by name three of a group of women who were 'looking on afar off'. They both mention Mary Magdalene, and omit the mother of Jesus. The woman called by John *his mother's sister* seems to be the woman named 'Salome' by Mark and the 'mother of Zebedee's children' by Matthew; while *Mary the wife of Cleophas* would appear to be identical with 'Mary the mother of James and Joses' in the Synoptic narratives. Such an identification cannot, however, be regarded as certain. The women are mentioned at a later point in the passion story in Matthew and Mark than in John, and they may have moved away from the cross after the death of Jesus and then gazed upon it from afar. The mother of Jesus had probably by this time been removed by the beloved disciple from the scene of the crucifixion (see Mk. xv. 40 and Mt. xxvii. 56).

26. For the significance, or lack of significance, of the expression *Woman* see note on ii. 4.

27. *From that hour* may be interpreted, and perhaps should be interpreted, as 'from that moment', i.e. immediately; in which case we must assume that the beloved disciple spared the mother of Jesus the agony of seeing the actual death of her son, and must also conclude that the beloved disciple was not the eyewitness of the incident recorded in verse 35. On the other hand the expression 'the hour' is so often used in this Gospel to designate the crucifixion as a whole, that it may be that the evangelist simply means 'after the crucifixion'.

His own home. The Greek *eis ta idia* does not necessarily imply 'to his own house'; and if the beloved disciple was John the son of Zebedee it is improbable that he had a house at Jerusalem. The expression implies that Mary now passed into the keeping of the beloved disciple and his relations and friends. (Cf. the use of the same words in i. 11.)

29. *Vinegar*, *oxos*, is better rendered 'sour wine' It is, of course, not to be confused with the drugged wine, the 'wine mingled with myrrh' of Mk. xv. 23 which Jesus refused, but was the wine taken to the cross by the soldiers for their own refreshment during what normally was a long time of waiting.

Hyssop was a bunch of thin strips of wood tied together and used ceremonially as a sprinkler (see Heb. x. 19). It is very strange that such an article should have been available for use by Roman soldiers at the place of crucifixion. Matthew and Mark both say that the sponge was placed on a 'reed' or stick. It is also very difficult to think of any symbolical purpose that could have been served by the insertion of this word by the evangelist at this point. Under these circumstances we are probably justified in adopting the reading of a late MS in which the scribe originally wrote *husso* not *hussopo* (the former meaning 'javelin') and in assuming that a very early scribal error gave rise to the variant 'hyssop'. On the other hand, Professor G. D. Kilpatrick has recently pointed out in *The Bible Translator* (July 1958) that the word *hyssos* translates the Latin *pilum* which was a weapon used by legionary troops but not by other troops in the Roman army, and no legionary troops were stationed in Jerusalem before AD 66, the troops under Pontius Pilate being auxiliaries.

30. It is a reasonable assumption that the words *It is finished*, spoken just before Jesus died, formed the content of the utterance, described by Mark in the words 'Jesus cried with a loud voice, and gave up the ghost' (Mk. xv. 37).

Gave up the ghost translates *paredōken to pneuma*, which is capable of more than one interpretation. If *to pneuma* is taken to signify 'breath' or the principle of life, then the meaning is 'He breathed His last'. If *paredōken* is given the sense of handing over, which it often has, then the evangelist is saying that Jesus handed over His spirit (the immortal part of Him) to Him who gave it. This would seem to be the interpretation of RSV, He 'gave up his spirit'. The third suggested exegesis which takes *to pneuma* as a reference to the Holy Spirit would necessitate the translation 'He handed over (presumably to His followers) the divine Spirit', who, as the Nicene creed states, proceeds from the Father and the Son. This interpretation is, however, not the most natural and is less in keeping with the other Gospels. Mark and Luke use the word *exepneusen*, exactly translated in RSV as 'he breathed his last', and Matthew the expression *aphēken to pneuma*, translated in RSV 'yielded up his spirit'. Probably this is also the right interpretation of the Johannine wording.

31. By *the preparation* the day of preparation for the Passover festival may be meant, in which case Jesus is represented by John as dying on the afternoon before the beginning of the festival on the ensuing evening. The word, however, could also mean the preparation day for the sabbath, i.e. the Friday in Passover week, in which case the Passover festival would have begun on the night before (see notes on xviii. 28 and xix. 14).

35. We have no means of identifying this important witness. It would seem unlikely to have been 'the beloved disciple', otherwise he would surely have been mentioned as such; it is moreover possible, as has been noted, that he was no longer present at the cross. On the other hand, the one who vouches for the truthfulness of the witness might be the beloved disciple who has supplied the evangelist with this information; but again we wonder why he was not mentioned as such instead of by the ambiguous, *ekeinos*, *he*. Strictly speaking the only people who could know for certain that the witness was telling the truth were the witness himself and God. It is just possible that by *ekeinos* (lit. that man) God is meant, and some scholars draw attention to the use of this word for Christ in 1 John iii. 5; more probably it is here used to refer back to the witness himself.

That ye might believe should be translated 'so that ye also may believe' (i.e. with the confidence that can be placed on an eyewitness report).

VIII. THE BURIAL AND RESURRECTION OF JESUS (xix. 38–xx. 31)

a. The burial (xix. 38–42)

In the preaching of the early Christian Church the death, burial and resurrection of Jesus were regarded as closely linked events, all of which happened 'according to the scriptures' and together formed the gospel of salvation (see 1 Cor. xv. 1–4). Our evangelist has already laid emphasis upon the benefits which resulted from the passion of Jesus, particularly in the dramatic symbolism of the piercing of the side of the Crucified and of the emergence of blood and water. In the same way, his account of the burial and resurrection would appear to have been influenced by the desire to show that the events he describes are of unique significance because of the spiritual truth they reveal. Here in the final incidents of the earthly ministry of Jesus clear expression is given to teaching already recorded in earlier parts of the Gospel; and in consequence, the faith of the disciples becomes full Christian faith, and their sense of apostleship is revived.

The evangelist brings together the death, burial and resurrection even more closely than the other Gospels, by emphasizing that the tomb in which the body of Jesus was buried was near the place of execution, and that the garden which contained both the cross and the sepulchre was the scene of the first appearance of Jesus after He was raised from the dead.

In the place where he was crucified there was a garden (41). The fall of the first Adam took place in a garden; and it was in a garden that the second Adam redeemed mankind from the consequences of Adam's transgression. The burial is carried out by Nicodemus and Joseph of Arimathaea. Both men would seem previously to have been 'secret' disciples of Jesus; but they are now courageous enough to come out into the open and perform this last labour of love. Nicodemus had first come to Jesus, the evangelist reminds his readers, *by night*, i.e. in secret; and Joseph, who had hitherto been kept back from fully committed discipleship by *fear of the Jews*, now boldly confronts the procurator with a request for the body of Jesus. Matthew states that Joseph was a rich man, and Mark describes him as a man of honour who was longing for God finally to establish His reign upon earth. Both Mark and Luke, moreover, give the further important information that Joseph was a member of the Sanhedrin; and Luke tells us that he had not consented to the policy and practice of that august body when it stooped to deeds of shame in bribing a disciple of Jesus to betray his Master; in sending armed forces to arrest Him as though He were a desperate bandit; in leaving Him to the mercy of the high priest's henchmen while they tried to find falsewitnesses at His so-called trial; and in playing upon the passions of the crowd and inciting them to demand His execution when Pilate had already found Him innocent. But now all fear of what men might do to him had vanished from Joseph's mind; and after obtaining Pilate's consent he went alone to the cross and with his own hands removed the body to prepare it for the grave.

The two men dutifully embalm the corpse in accordance with Jewish custom, avoiding the possibility of mutilation and binding it with strips of linen interspersed with the myrrh and aloes brought by Nicodemus. So great is the amount of spices used, that the words of Psalm xlv. 8, though not quoted, seem to find a literal fulfilment, 'All thy garments smell of myrrh, and aloes'; and the death of Jesus, which is the very centre of the Christian gospel, is shown to have in itself what Paul, speaking metaphorically, described as one of its characteristics 'an odour of a sweet smell' (Eph. v. 2, RV). The body is then laid in a new tomb free from all corrupting influences; God's Holy One is not destined to see corruption, and He must rise from the dead with His human body unimpaired except for the scars of His passion.

Additional Notes

38. All the four evangelists describe Joseph as *Joseph of Arimathaea.* It would seem that from earliest days he had been distinguished in this manner from other Josephs connected in one way or another with the Christian movement. As the word translated *secretly* is, in the original, a perfect participle passive, the sense might be that Joseph had not always been a 'secret' disciple but had recently gone into hiding, perhaps after the arrest of Jesus, *for fear of the Jews,* and had now come boldly out of his seclusion. It would seem, however, more probable that the evangelist means his readers to infer that both Joseph and Nicodemus remained uncommitted disciples till after the crucifixion.

40. The other three Gospels state that the body was wrapped in a single shroud, while John's language implies that the limbs were bound together with separate strips of cloth. The body of Lazarus would appear to have been prepared for burial in the same way (see xi. 44).

41. The fact that the tomb was hewn out of rock is made explicit in Lk. xxiii. 53, and is implicit in Jn. xx. 1 in the mention of the stone that lay across the entrance.

42. *The Jews' preparation day* means the eve of the Jewish sabbath. The references to Jewish customs both in this verse and in verse 40 are only two of a large number of references which suggest that the Gospel was written for readers unfamiliar with Jewish customs.

b. The resurrection appearances (xx. 1–29)

In John's record of the passion and burial of Jesus, as a recent writer has said, 'life is present in death';[1] and it is, very signifi-

[1] A. M. Ramsey, *The Resurrection of Christ,* p. 82.

cantly, in the actual grave clothes, still lying in their original folds, untouched by human hands yet no longer containing the crucified body, that the beloved disciple finds the evidence he needs for full Christian faith, which is faith in Jesus crucified-and-risen (8). This evidence came to him as a new revelation, for as the evangelist notes in verse 9, the disciples had not yet understood that the resurrection was foretold in Scripture, in such passages presumably as that quoted by Peter on the day of Pentecost, 'Thou wilt not leave my soul in Hades, neither wilt thou give thy Holy One to see corruption' (Ps. xvi. 10; Acts ii. 27, RV).

To the sorrowing Mary of Magdala, who finds no consolation for her tears in the vision of the angels within the empty tomb, and who repeats her sad refrain *They have taken away my Lord, and I know not where they have laid him* (13), the same assurance of faith is obtained only by personal contact with the risen Lord. The figure at first mistaken by her in the hazy early morning light for the gardener is recognized as the risen Shepherd of the sheep when He addresses this individual member of His flock by name. *Jesus saith unto her, Mary* (16). Never was there a one-word utterance more charged with emotion than this. The life that the good Shepherd has laid down for the sheep has been laid down for each separate sheep; and His resurrection life is now available for every single believer—but under conditions different from those to which Mary has hitherto been accustomed. When she tries to cling to her Master and keep Him at her side, she is accordingly told that she must cease touching Him, for the satisfaction of her desire would frustrate the ultimate purpose of the crucifixion and resurrection. Jesus suffered and rose again, in order that He might ascend to His Father, and in virtue of His finished work on Calvary intercede for all who would draw nigh unto God through Him. There is no record in this Gospel of the physical ascent of Christ into heaven. But the cross is often spoken of as His supreme glorification, and His death is viewed as the means of His return to His Father. His being lifted up on the cross is in fact regarded as the beginning of the ascension. Jesus is therefore to be thought of as in the process of ascending to His Father when Mary meets Him. She must not therefore try to prevent Him from completing this ascent and from entering fully into His rightful inheritance. She must return to the rest of the little flock with the news that Jesus is now crowning the triumph of His earthly mission by returning to Him, whose will He has so unceasingly obeyed—His Father and their Father.

But the Son of God does not return to His Father exactly as He had come forth from the Father. Having taken upon Himself human nature He goes back with that human nature, still bearing the wounds inflicted upon Him when He was 'bruised for our iniquity'. As 'life is present in His death', so 'the note of death is still to be heard in the midst of life'.[1] Accordingly, on the first Sunday evening, when the risen Jesus appears to the ten disciples huddled together behind locked doors for fear of the Jews, not only does He bestow upon them the peace bequeathed to them in the upper room (19; cf. xiv. 27), the peace of reconciliation to God made possible by His passion, the peace of the justified sinner, but He shows them His pierced hands and side. The sight of His risen body still bearing the marks of His sacrifice transforms their temporary grief into permanent joy (20). The 'little while' is over. Christian joy has been born, the joy of the redeemed, which Jesus had promised would be theirs after the travail pangs had passed (see xvi. 20–22).

With the advent of this peace and joy the disciples' sense of apostleship, dormant since the passion began, can now be re-awakened. So Jesus commissions them, in words already used in His intercessory prayer (xvii. 18), to an apostleship similar to His own. He also breathes upon them and imparts to them the Holy Spirit, through whom the sanctifying power of His risen life is conveyed—the Holy Spirit whom He had prayed His Father to send them, and whose coming He had implied would only be possible when He returned to the Father by way of the passion and resurrection (see xiv. 16, xvi. 7). Paul gave expression to the same truth when he said, 'The first man Adam was made a living soul; the last Adam was made a

[1] A. M. Ramsey, *op. cit.*, p. 82.

quickening spirit' (1 Cor. xv. 45). The possession of that Spirit enables the apostles to bestow, or withhold, not arbitrarily but as the Spirit might direct, the fruits of the redemption which the second Adam had won, as they set forth upon their mission of reconciliation. The gospel, which in the power of the Spirit they will be able to proclaim, will inevitably lead to the forgiveness of some who hear it and to the hardening of hearts in the case of others. *He breathed on them, and saith unto them, Receive ye the Holy Ghost: whose soever sins ye remit, they are remitted unto them; and whose soever sins ye retain, they are retained* (22, 23).

The evidence of *sight* had been sufficient to enable the beloved disciple, Mary of Magdala, and ten of the apostles to know that their Lord was risen indeed, and so to reach the fullness of Christian faith. But Thomas, who had not been with the others on the evening of the day of resurrection, demands the evidence of *touch* as well as of sight. To this disciple, therefore, who has already been presented in this Gospel as loyal and courageous if pessimistic (see xi. 16, xiv. 5), a special offer is made of the evidence he desires in another appearance of the risen Christ a week later, an appearance designed solely for this purpose. But the evidence of sight proves to be sufficient for Thomas also, causing him to cry *My Lord and my God* without accepting the invitation to handle his Master's risen body (28). The time will nevertheless come, and come very soon, when the evidence neither of sight nor of touch will be possible, for Jesus will have completed His return to the Father beyond the range of the physical senses. Yet He will still be visible to the eyes of faith. It is therefore with reference to all who will become believers, as the result of the preaching of the gospel by the original witnesses of Him after His resurrection and by their successors, that Jesus utters the benediction *Blessed are thev that have not seen, and yet have believed* (29). 'This last and greatest of the Beatitudes', wrote Westcott, 'is the persistent treasure of the later Church.'

Additional Notes

xx. 1. It might be supposed from this verse that Mary of Magdala came to the tomb alone, for no mention is made, as in the other Gospels, of the other Galilaean women who accompanied her. The fact, however, that Mary uses the first person plural in verse 2, *We know not*, shows that this supposition would be wrong. Mention is made only of Mary, we may suppose, partly because she was the spokesman of the group and partly because the evangelist intends to give, in greater and more personal detail than the other Gospels, an account of the Lord's appearance to her. She who owed so much to her Master during His earthly life (see Mk. xvi. 9) needed most of all to be reassured at the earliest possible moment that death had not put an end to the benefits she could receive from Him.

5. *Stooping down, and looking in* translates both here and in verse 11 the word *parakupto*, which seems in the New Testament to have the sense of 'peering into', because there is something important which the viewer desires to see, even though it may be difficult for him to see it and grasp its significance all at once (cf. its use in Jas. i. 25 and 1 Pet. i. 12). The word *lying* is in an emphatic position in the original. The beloved disciple standing outside the tomb noticed that the clothes had not been removed though the body, he surmised, had been.

7. Peter entering the tomb is able to see additional evidence not visible to the beloved disciple. The napkin which had been placed over the head was *wrapped together* (RSV, more accurately, 'rolled up') *in a place by itself*, i.e. apart from the other wrappings, perhaps on the raised ledge where the head had been laid.

8. *Then* is not the inferential 'so then', as it is in verse 10, but temporal. It was at that moment that the beloved disciple, encouraged by the example of Peter, entered the tomb for the first time; and on the evidence of what he now saw, without having had any encounter with the risen Lord, he believed that the Lord's body had not been removed by human hands, but raised by divine intervention. He is thus in a real sense the forerunner of those counted 'blessed' in verse 29, the innumerable company who 'have not seen, and yet have believed'.

15. *Thou* is emphatic in the Greek. Mary is convinced that someone has removed the body; and it seems to her most probable that *the gardener* has done so, for he was the only person likely to visit the garden at such an early hour. In her anxiety and bewilderment she assumes that she is speaking to the gardener and that he knows to whom she is referring when she speaks of *him*.

16. In the deepest experiences of life, particularly in the reunion of those who have meant much to one another, words are wont to be few. The familiar terms of address *Mary* and *Master* are significantly recorded in their Aramaic forms to which both parties had long been accustomed. By contrast in verses 1 and 11 'Mary' is given in its Greek form.

17. In the English versions it might be supposed that Mary never touched the risen Jesus and was forbidden to do so; and if the variant reading found in some ancient authorities, which inserts after the word *Master* 'and she ran forward to touch Him', is accepted, this would seem to be the only possible interpretation. But why should Jesus be so determined to prevent Mary from doing what later He invites Thomas to do? Moreover in the Greek the verb *touch* is a present imperative; and when used as a prohibition this should normally give the meaning 'Stop touching me' or 'Do not touch me any more'. The right translation would therefore seem to be, 'Do not cling to Me' (RSV 'Do not hold me'). Conditions have now changed, and the relationship between Master and disciple must now assume a somewhat different character. The verb translated *I am not yet ascended* is in the perfect tense, and implies, 'I have not yet completed my ascent'. *My brethren* does not refer to those who were Christ's brothers by natural relationship, but to the new family of the redeemed made possible by Himself becoming man (cf. Rom. viii. 29; Heb. ii. 11). *I ascend* should be taken as a continuous present 'I am in the process of ascending'. The Father of Jesus is also the Father of Christ's brethren; but Jesus does not speak of Him as 'Our Father', for the reasons why His disciples can address God as their Father are different from those which enable Jesus so to do. Hence *mv Father* and *your Father*. The difference was well stated by Nestorius, 'God is Father to Me on the one hand by nature, to you by grace; but God to Me on the one hand by grace and to you by nature.' In other words, we can only call God 'our God' as His creatures, while Jesus Himself belongs to the Godhead. Jesus as the second Person of the Blessed Trinity is the *eternal* Son of the Father; Christians only *become* sons of God by adoption and grace (see i. 12).

19–23. The repetition of the salutation *Peace be unto you* in verses 19 and 21 is surely not without significance. In verse 19 it seems little more than the ordinary Semitic greeting. Before its occurrence in verse 21 Jesus has showed His disciples *his hands and his side*; and their gladness, noted by the evangelist, appears to be due not solely to the relief that Jesus is no longer dead, but to the knowledge that they now have as their *Lord* One who has allowed His hands to be pierced for them in a sacrificial death, and from whose pierced side there had flowed the water and the blood symbolic of redemption and sanctification. The peace of verse 21 is the peace of the pardoned sinner, the peace which Jesus called 'my peace' (see xiv. 27), for He alone could bestow it, and He could only bestow it after His passion. As the recipients of this peace and infused by the Spirit of their Lord, the disciples can now become the apostles of Jesus, as He had been the Apostle of His Father, and exercise like Him a ministry of reconciliation.

24. Although Thomas has already been twice mentioned in the Gospel, the evangelist not only repeats that he was nicknamed *Didymus*, i.e. the twin, but also states that he was *one of the twelve*. For even though he is unable to accept at its face value the good news they convey to him, his doubts do not lead him into disloyalty.

25. In place of the second reference to the *print* or mark (*tupon*) of the nails some ancient MSS read 'the place' (*topon*). This variation should probably be adopted. Thomas wants not only to see the scar made by the nails in the hands, but also to put his finger into the place where the nails had been. *Thrust* is too strong a translation, as the word it translates (*ballō*) was often used at this time with a weaker significance;

hence RV 'put'. There is no mention in this Gospel, or in Matthew and Luke, of the piercing of the feet. That the feet of Jesus may have been nailed to the cross, rather than fastened with a rope which was the common practice, is an inference from Lk. xxiv. 39.

26. Thomas is found in the company of the others a week later, although neither he nor they had any reason to expect another appearance of their Lord. A concessive meaning should be given to the words *the doors being shut*. Although the doors were locked, Jesus entered.

27. That this visit of the risen Christ was made especially for the benefit of Thomas is shown by the fact that immediately after the salutation *Peace be unto you* offered to all who were present, the Lord at once (*then* translating *eita* 'next') addresses Thomas. The injunction *be not faithless* implies that there can be no permanent faith in Jesus except faith in Him as the risen Lord who still bears the scars of His atoning death. Thomas was therefore faced with the alternative either of Christian faith or unbelief.

29. The statement of Jesus to Thomas in the first half of this verse can also be taken as a question. Hence RSV 'Have you believed because you have seen me?' There is, however, little difference in the sense, for the question obviously expects an affirmative answer.

c. The purpose of the evangelist (xx. 30, 31)

If, as is probable, chapter xxi was added later after chapters i–xx, verses 30 and 31 of chapter xx constituted the original conclusion of the Gospel. They certainly would appear to have been written as such (see Introduction). The *many other signs* should, therefore, be taken as a general reference to the deeds of Jesus during His earthly life, a brief selection of which has been given in the previous chapters. The expression however may also include other appearances of the *risen* Jesus which this evangelist has left unrecorded. Christian faith, to strengthen which was the primary purpose for which the Gospel is stated to have been written, rests on the conviction that

Jesus is the Christ, the Son of God; and though He is presented as such throughout this Gospel, He was nevertheless, as Paul asserts, 'declared to be the Son of God with power . . . by the resurrection from the dead' (Rom. i. 4). It is moreover faith in Jesus as crucified-and-risen that is the source of *life*, that higher or eternal life which is the possession of the Christian. In fellowship with his risen Master the disciple shares His Master's life.

Additional Notes

30. *Truly* is a mistranslation of the Greek particles of transition (*men oun*) which are better rendered 'therefore' in RV, and 'now' in RSV.

31. The verb translated *believe* is found in some MSS in the present tense, and in others in the aorist. If the distinction is to be pressed, the former, read by most editors, would give the sense 'that you may continue to believe' and the latter 'that you may come to believe'.

Through his name does not mean 'through the naming of His name', but through the power of the Person who bears the name. In the Bible the 'name' of God is not merely the name by which He is designated, but all that He is in Himself.

IX. THE EPILOGUE (xxi. 1–23)

The primary purpose for which this section was added may well have been to correct an error which had arisen owing to a misquotation of what Jesus had said about the survival of the beloved disciple till the Lord should return in glory, for it is with the quotation of Jesus' actual words on this subject, spoken at the time when Peter was recommissioned as a shepherd of Christ's flock, that the narrative somewhat abruptly ends. Rumour had it that the Lord had prophesied that the beloved disciple would be alive when He came again, and the evangelist is anxious to make it perfectly clear that Jesus had only spoken hypothetically about such a possibility. *Jesus said not . . . He shall not die; but, If I will that he tarry till I come* (23). But, in other ways, this section makes a most fitting appendage to the Gospel. Few passages in the New Testament have a more numinous quality, or are so haunting in their beauty; and there can be few readers who remain insensitive to the awe and mystery which pervade it.

Some of the disciples have gone out fishing with Simon Peter, but after a night's toil their labour has proved unavailing. The coming of dawn finds them tired, baffled and hungry. Nor is their frustration relieved when they have to answer 'No' to a voice calling to them from the shore and asking them whether they have made a catch. There is, however, a note of authority in the voice, and they respond readily to it when it bids them cast the nets once again, and promises them success. The result is the netting of a shoal of fish (when they came to count them later the number proved to be a hundred and fifty-three), but without the net being strained to breaking-point. The experience must have reminded the disciples of a similar incident many months before, though on that occasion the net was broken and the boat began to sink (see Lk. v. 1–11); and they naturally strain their eyes to see who the person on the shore may be. As they peer through the grey morning mist, the beloved disciple is the first to identify Him, and we can almost hear him catch his breath as he whispers to his comrades *It is the Lord* (7). How natural that the recognition should be made by this sensitive brooding disciple, who had so readily deduced from the evidence of the grave-clothes that Jesus was raised from among the dead! He who had leaned on his Master's breast at supper has the quickest and surest perception of Him as the risen Lord.

But it is Peter, the disciple who on the earlier occasion had fallen at Jesus' knees saying, 'Depart from me; for I am a sinful man, O Lord', who is now most eager to come as quickly as possible to the Saviour, as he snatches his jacket and plunges into the water. For Peter is still a sinful man; the stains of recent disloyalty are upon his conscience, and the penetrating gaze of his Master is still fresh in his memory (see Lk. xxii. 61). More than his six colleagues present with him in the boat he needs to be personally assured of the forgiveness made possible by Jesus' death and resurrection, for without that forgiveness he will be unable (and he knows it) to be what Jesus had said that one day He would make him, 'a fisher of men'. Moreover, as the task laid upon Peter as the leader of the Christian Church in the first anxious days of its history may well prove to be more exacting than that laid upon the other apostles, he will need even greater love for his Lord than they; and it is those who are forgiven much who love much (see Lk. vii. 47). He had once boasted that his own devotion to his Master was greater than anyone else's. 'Although all shall be offended,' he had said, 'yet will not I' (Mk. xiv. 29). But three times that love had been tested and found wanting in the courtyard of denial. Jesus must now be convinced that never again will Simon so treacherously disown Him. Accordingly, after the disciples have accepted His invitation to break their fast with Him in a fellowship meal, and have thereby become aware that, however changed He may be, He is still the same Jesus in whose company they had so often eaten in the past, three times He asks the question *Simon, son of Jonas, lovest thou me?* Simon, humbled by failure and deeply penitent, three times declares his love, and three times receives the charge to feed Christ's flock, old and young alike, lambs as well as sheep. For Christian love must express itself in service even for the least of Christ's brethren, but without love for Christ that service can never be rendered. Such love alone enables the disciple to keep Christ's commandments and to remain loyal to Him, even though, as will be the case with Peter, he may discover as life goes on, that love does not make life easy, but that duties become more exacting and personal freedom more restricted with advancing years; and even though his discipleship may lead him, as it led Simon Peter, to imprisonment and death.

In the case of Peter, 'following' Jesus would mean a life of continuous care for Christ's sheep, culminating in a martyrdom which would redound to God's glory. He had been told in the upper room that he could not at once follow Jesus by laying down his life for Him, but that one day he would (see xiii. 36, 37). It is to a discipleship issuing in this kind of 'following' that Jesus now calls him; such at least is the evangelist's interpretation of the words *thou shalt stretch forth thy hands, and another shall gird thee, and carry thee whither thou wouldest not* (18).

For the beloved disciple, on the other hand, 'following' Jesus will mean something different. His service will be less dramatic and not so obviously heroic. He will play, as the earlier chapters of Acts make clear, a less primary part than Peter in welding the early company of believers into the universal Church of Christ. His unique contribution will come later. After he has settled in the pagan, cosmopolitan city of Ephesus, he will recall men from drifting on the uncharted seas of vague religious experience and abstract speculation to the sure and certain anchorage of God's self-revelation in the historical figure of the Word-made-flesh. As a man of thought rather than action, able to see beneath the surface and penetrate to the heart of things, his vocation will be to testify to the truth as it is to be seen in the man Christ Jesus, and to combat the many anti-Christs who will be seen before the Lord returns in glory. Against all who would deny the reality of the incarnation of the Son of God, he will bear witness to what he himself has seen, heard and handled with reference to the Word of life, passing it on to others in language as simple as it is profound. Peter and John have different vocations; but neither is to question why the other's vocation should be different from his own. *What is that to thee?* (22) is Jesus' rebuke to Peter when he shows himself idly curious about the future of his friend; and the last word of Jesus to Peter is similar to His first, *follow thou me* (see Mk. i. 17).

Additional Notes

xxi. 1. *After these things* is the evangelist's usual expression for denoting that what he is about to relate took place not immediately, but at some unspecified time, after the last recorded incident. The various resurrection appearances cannot be listed in any strict chronological sequence; and although the evangelist describes this appearance at the lake-side as *the third* (verse 14), this probably means the third of the appearances that he himself has recorded.

4. *Was now come* is a translation of the reading which has the verb in the aorist tense (*genomenēs*). Other ancient MSS have the verb in the present tense (*ginomenēs*) so RSV, probably rightly, 'Just as day was breaking'.

5. The word translated *children* (*paidia*), though diminutive in form, does not here have a diminutive sense, and is used in addressing young men. Jesus does not elsewhere use this term of His disciples; R. A. Knox translates 'friends'.

Meat translates *prosphagion*, which means something to eat with bread to make the latter more palatable; in this context 'fish' (so RSV). The word translated *have* was used colloquially, particularly with reference to fishing and hunting, in the sense of 'getting possession of'. So the question here could be translated 'Have you made a catch?' The form of the question in the original expects the negative answer which it receives.

6. *The right side of the ship;* i.e., in modern parlance, 'the starboard'.

7. *Naked* means, in our idiom, 'stripped to the waist'.

8. *A little ship* is inaccurate, for there is a definite article in the Greek; and though a diminutive noun is used it does not necessarily have a diminutive sense. Almost certainly it is the same ship as that mentioned earlier in the narrative. So RSV 'the boat'. *As it were two hundred cubits* should be understood as 'about a hundred yards'.

12. Modern readers may well think it strange that the AV should use the word *dine* with reference to an early morning meal. The English word, however, is derived from the late Latin *disjejunare* which means to break a fast at any time of the day (cf. the French *déjeuner*, used of an early meal).

15. By three times addressing Peter as *Simon, son of Jonas* Jesus would seem to be deliberately avoiding the name which He Himself had said would one day be his (see i. 42). Not yet had Peter proved himself worthy to be designated 'the man of rock'.

More than these may mean *either* 'more than these others do', in which case Jesus would be recalling to Peter's mind the boastful assertion he had made before the passion (see Mk. xiv. 29), *or* 'more than you love anything else'. Perhaps both meanings are implied. It is significant that Peter in his reply avoids the comparison contained in the Lord's question.

15, 16, 17. AV, probably rightly, makes no attempt in these verses to give a different translation of the two words used in the original for *love* and *feed*. Some commentators, however, particularly Westcott, Plummer and Temple, have attempted to find considerable significance in the change of words used for *love*. In verses 15 and 16, in the first and second questions put by Jesus to Peter, the word *agapaō* is used, which is said to denote a higher form of love than the word *phileō* used by Peter in each of his three replies. The fact that when Jesus asks the question the third time in verse 17 He uses the word *phileo* is regarded by these scholars as the reason why Peter was grieved. Jesus seemed to be doubting whether Peter felt even the lesser form of love for Him. It is, however, very doubtful whether this subtle distinction of meaning can be maintained, as, in this Gospel at any rate, the verbs would appear to be synonymous. Both are used to denote the Father's love for the Son, and to describe the love of Jesus for Lazarus and for 'the beloved disciple'. The Vulgate attempted to retain a distinction by using *diligo* and *amo* respectively; but AV, RV, and RSV use 'love' throughout.

The use of synonyms is a prominent feature of style in this Gospel, not least in these three verses, where two words are used for *knowest* in verse 17, and where there would appear to be no significance in the substitution, in verse 16, of *poimaine* (RV and RSV 'tend') for *boske*, *feed*, in verses 15 and 17. Here the Vulgate makes no attempt to distinguish the words, but translates both by *pasce*.

Similarly, it is too subtle to see much significance in the change from *lambs* in verse 15 to *sheep* in verses 16 and 17. It is true that in these last two verses the MSS vary between *probatia* 'little sheep' and *probata* 'sheep', and it might be, as

Bernard suggests, that 'the charge to Peter first entrusts to his care, "lambs", then "the young sheep", and lastly "the whole flock".' But even so these three expressions are but different ways of designating the one flock of Christ. There is no indication, as Roman Catholic exegetes maintain, of a distinction between ordinary secular believers ('lambs'), and other pastors ('sheep'), all of whom are under the sovereignty of Peter. Temple distinguishes between the comparatively easy task of 'feeding the lambs', the young of the flock who are ready to accept the sustenance offered them; the more experienced work of 'tending the sheep', i.e. of exercising a general supervision of the flock; and the most difficult task of all 'feeding the sheep', i.e. supplying the needs of the more mature members of the flock who 'often have no knowledge of what their own needs are, or, still worse, suppose that they know when in fact they do not'. This would seem altogether too ingenious.

17. The repetition of the question a third time naturally causes Peter grief, for it could not fail to remind him of his threefold denial.

X. THE CONCLUSION (xxi. 24, 25)

24. Few verses have given rise to more voluminous discussion than this; and because the allusions contained in it are so obscure we cannot be sure that we know what the meaning is. The problem centres very largely upon two questions. What is meant by *these things*? And who are the *we*? It may be that the three following 'solutions' present the least difficulties:

i. The author of the whole Gospel is here saying in effect to his readers, though in a curiously indirect manner: 'I have described myself in this Gospel as "the disciple whom Jesus loved". I bear constant witness in my teaching to the truths which I have embodied in this book; and I and the other leaders of the church where I am writing know that my testimony is true.' On the whole this may be said to be the traditional interpretation.

ii. The elders of the church, probably at Ephesus, are here identifying the author of the Gospel with 'the disciple whom Jesus loved' and giving a kind of *testamur* that his witness is reliable. On this interpretation, the verse constitutes the earliest external evidence for the authorship of the Gospel. This view is held probably by the majority of modern scholars, though they differ as to whether the elders' statement about the authorship is right or wrong.

iii. The author of the Gospel, having added chapter xxi some little time after chapter xx, is telling his readers that 'the disciple whom Jesus loved', a person other than himself, bears witness in his teaching to the important statements contained in chapter xxi and has moreover put them in writing, perhaps in a letter to the evangelist, the contents of which the latter has embodied in this closing section of his Gospel. On this view, verse 24 is not a piece of external evidence for the authorship, but a statement by the author himself stressing the reliability of the material to be found in the preceding verses.

The weak point of i as against ii and iii is that it is difficult to see why the evangelist should use this indirect method of describing his identity, and follow it almost at once by a reference to himself in the first person singular. The weak point of ii as against i and iii is that it excludes the evangelist from the company referred to by the undefined *we*, in contradistinction to the natural interpretation of the pronoun in i. 14. With no subject expressed, *we* would seem naturally to mean 'I and others'. On the whole, iii would appear to be the least free of difficulties. For it is reasonable to assume that as *This* (Gk. *houtos*; Latin *hic*) must refer to the disciple just mentioned, so *these things* (the neuter plural of the same Greek pronoun) should refer not to all the things that have been previously mentioned, i.e. chapters i–xx as well as chapter xxi, but to the incidents last described, i.e. chapter xxi. The problem is naturally bound up with other questions such as, Did the author of i–xx himself add xxi immediately after he had written i–xx, or was the last chapter added later, either by himself or someone else? And is it less likely that the author would have described himself as 'the disciple whom Jesus loved' than that another should have so designated him? On these matters critics remain sharply divided (see Introduction). Whatever interpretation we may adopt, it would seem that the present tense *which testifieth* (RSV 'who is bearing witness') indicates that the beloved disciple was still alive when verse 24 was written; and that *wrote these things* implies that he had himself written down some at least of the information contained in the Gospel, for it is scarcely legitimate to translate, as Bernard does, 'caused these things to be written.'

25. The difficulty of this verse lies in the use of the first person in the expression *I suppose.* It can obviously be more naturally referred to the author if either the interpretation i or iii of verse 24 is adopted; for if ii is followed the change from *we* to *I* is much more harsh. But, on either of these views, it is somewhat strange that the author should once only, and that in the very last sentence of his book, use the first person singular with reference to himself; and the nature of the statement in this verse does not seem quite to befit him.

As there is one scrap of evidence that the Gospel may have circulated for a time without this verse, it may be that it was added by the person who first copied and bound the four Gospels together in codex or book form. When he had come to the end of his task, he may well have reflected that neither the Gospel of John nor all the four Gospels together contain more than a fragmentary selection of the doings and sayings of Jesus, and have been moved to give playful expression to his observations in the somewhat grandiose statement of this verse.

The scrap of evidence which perhaps makes this suggestion of the present commentator not wholly untenable, comes from the famous fourth-century Codex Sinaiticus. Since the arrival of this MS in the British Museum it has been subjected to ultra violet ray treatment.[1] This has revealed beyond dispute that the scribe of the MS originally omitted this verse and brought his writing to an end after verse 24. Later he erased

[1] See H. J. M. Milne and T. C. Skeat, *Scribes and Correctors of the Codex Sinaiticus*, p. 12.

the concluding ornamental colophon, added verse 25, and inserted a fresh colophon after it. It may therefore be that the MS he was originally copying was without this verse, and that he subsequently inserted it from another authority, for it is unlikely that the original omission would have been accidental.